CAR AND DRIVER
YEARBOOK 1992

CAR AND DRIVER

YEARBOOK 1992

 GROLIER ENTERPRISES, INC.

Danbury, Connecticut

Published by Grolier Enterprises, Inc.

The publisher wishes to thank CAR AND DRIVER Editor William Jeanes and his staff for the creation of the articles upon which this yearbook is based, as well as for creation of new texts and photos. Special thanks go to CAR AND DRIVER's Phil Berg, the project editor.

Book design: Nancy Norton, Norton & Company Design
Composition: Dix Type Inc.
Cover photo: David Dewhurst

Grolier Enterprises staff:

  President: Dante Cirilli
  Vice President & Publisher: Rosanna Hansen
    Editorial Director: Neil Soderstrom
    Editorial Assistant: Cindy Stierle
  Vice President Annual/Yearbook Division:
    John Weggeman
    Product Manager: Sara Stringfellow
  Vice President Manufacturing: Joseph J. Corlett
    Senior Production Manager: Susan Gallucci
    Assistant Production Manager: Diane Hassan

Grolier Enterprises, Inc., offers a varied selection of both adult and children's book racks. For details on ordering, please write:

  Premium Department
  Grolier Enterprises, Inc.
  Sherman Turnpike
  Danbury, CT 06816

ISSN: 1050–9682
ISBN: 0–7172–8259–7

Manufactured in the United States of America

10   9   8   7   6   5   4   3   2   1

CONTENTS

(Continued)

PREFACE

By William Jeanes

Among the stories in this yearbook are many road tests. After all, car testing makes up the bulk of our work at *Car and Driver.* So this year, we thought you'd be interested in the story "How We Test Cars," beginning on page 86.

But obtaining cars to test is often a complex matter. Like all other car magazines, we borrow test cars from the carmakers. We care about our relationship to the car industry, and judging from the letters we receive from you, it's a relationship you'd like to know more about.

Though you'll find no advertising in this yearbook, some letter writers express amazement that our magazine accepts ads from carmakers. The advertising is there because we write about cars and because you read us to learn about cars. There is no better, more efficient place for an automaker to hawk its wares. About half of this nation's new-car buyers seek information—for as long as a year—from car magazines. Does the weight of advertising influence our editorial content? Not for a minute. And for a simple reason: the quickest road to hell on earth is trod by favoring one of the three dozen automakers with which we deal at the expense of the others.

Without advertising, we'd probably cost $10 a copy. Almost no magazine in the world makes money on its subscription and newsstand sales. You might also like to know that our advertising staff is in another city and that they don't read what we write before you do.

Other letters ask why we don't buy our test cars from dealers, as *Consumer Reports* does. The answer here is also simple: were we to wait until a car went on sale, we'd be late informing you—the car enthusiast—about it, meaning that we would lag behind other information sources by as much as six months. This failure to get you the information that you seek on a timely basis would, beyond doubt, sink us. So we use new cars from the press fleets that exist for this purpose, as does every purely automotive magazine in the world.

Your letters demonstrate a growing awareness of what the *Wall Street Journal* called "the cozy ride." This issue, one that cries out for examination, involves automakers who hire automotive writers, often the same ones who critique cars for you, to moonlight for pay.

Let's begin with a few facts. A car, for the average American, represents the second-largest purchase that person will ever make. This leads to an inescapable conclusion: car magazines have a responsibility to their readers that goes far beyond entertaining them. When our magazine assumes the responsibility of advising you —and, through you, your friends—on how best to spend your money, we assume a number of obligations.

First, we must know what we're doing. That's why we do our own testing at *Car and Driver* and why we employ four automotive writers with engineering degrees. A large part of all our judgments is subjective, as it should be, but what's important to you is that we're not easily fooled.

Second, we must seek to tell the truth. Cars today have reached an amazing level of quality and capability. When some of us—and many of you—started driving, shortly after the church had stopped the ritual burning of heretics, no trip of more than 200 miles seemed possible without the ignition points sticking, the fuel system developing vapor lock, the cooling system overheating, or a tire going flat. If you drove sports cars, you left home not with an American Express card but with a box of parts and tools to be used as needed, knowing that they would be. But however good cars have become, it's possible for us to compare them and tell you —based on reason, knowledge, and experience—that one is better than another. Alert readers will have noticed that few comparison tests in magazines other than this one will tell you who won. We do. And we tell you why.

Third, we must maintain a respectable distance from the industry we cover. This in no way implies distancing ourselves from friends in the industry or, God forbid, from the enjoyment of cars. (Indeed, the one bias that we have here is *wanting* to like every car we test. That's not because we're out to please everyone, but because we love cars.) This third requirement, maintaining distance from the industry, has—rightly—come under increasing scrutiny from the outside.

In March 1990, the *Wall Street Journal* wrote of car magazines, including this one, that had persons on their staffs who accepted money for services performed for car companies. Most of the services were harmless enough, but it's a practice that—made public—would doubtless distress a reader of car magazines. No wonder. It distresses us that U.S. senators and congresspersons accept fees and contributions from industries that they regulate. Ethics are ethics. Or aren't.

A relationship between an auto writer and a car company or its advertising agency is, in most cases, one of four kinds: payment for certified testing, payment for appearances in sales training films used by car companies to train dealer personnel, payment for speeches, and payment for writing press kits or other sales promotional material. It must be said that these relationships came about rarely from evil intent. They developed because car-magazine staffs were excellent sources of automotive knowledge. In any case, a lot of us here thought it was wrong. Some of us *knew* it was wrong. And no matter how harmless it may have been, we thought you would think it was wrong, too. So we stopped it about two years ago. Does this make us better than other car magazines? We, naturally, think we were already better, but in this instance we did no more than wake up and smell the coffee. And change our policy on conflicts of interest.

Our policy is simple: no one who writes about new products for *Car and Driver* can derive personal gain *of any kind,* directly or indirectly, from an automaker. We do not accept gifts from automakers. We don't create "magazines" that have only one advertiser and cover only products made by that advertiser. Our writers do not appear in TV commercials that sell cars. We can't even buy cars at a discount. And so on.

A lot of folks have had their say about this issue; we thought you should know where we stand.

DAVID DEWHURST

SECRET JAPANESE PLAN

By Patrick Bedard

Defective is not the only word that comes to mind when trying to describe our system of auto insurance—*gyp, swindle,* and *plunder* are right there on top of the pile too—but let's go with defective for the moment because we can deal with that. These days, everybody knows the fix for defective stuff. All it takes is a dose of Japanese competition.

Remember when Detroit was building shoddy cars? No more. Japanese efficiency and devotion to customer satisfaction forced Detroit to clean up its act. The same thing would happen in insurance. Once the Japanese started writing policies, our current clan of insolent insurance biggies would have to match Japanese efficiency or they'd be out, reduced to polishing the urinals down at McDonald's.

The Japanese do their homework. So do I. And I've discovered a document they'd surely rely on in their quest for insurance efficiency. It's an engineer's report titled *Driver Speed Behavior on U.S. Streets and Highways.* It was prepared for the 60th annual meeting of the Institute of Transportation Engineers by Samuel C. Tignor, Ph.D., who happens to be chief of the Traffic Safety Research Division of the Federal Highway Administration, and Davey Warren, an engineer in the same organization. The FHA, by the way, is a gen-uine government office within the Department of Transportation, so these guys have —genuflect, everybody!—credentials.

Their report is based primarily on two traffic surveys so extensive they could only be done by the government.

You may already know that, as a rule of thumb, traffic engineers recommend setting speed limits at the 85th percentile of free-flowing traffic. In other words, let drivers go whatever speed they feel safe. Select the speed exceeded by only the fastest fifteen percent of all traffic, and use that as the speed limit.

"Properly established speed limits," Tignor and Warren say, "foster voluntary compliance and separate the occasional high-risk driver from the vast majority of drivers. On the other hand, speed limits which are set artificially low tend to be ignored and misallocate resources, apprehending and prosecuting motorists driving at safe speeds."

In their surveys, the authors found poor compliance with speed limits, noting that "less than ten percent of the sites had more than fifty-percent obedience with the posted speed."

It's well known that ordinary drivers have no interest in scaring themselves, so they choose a speed they feel is safe. How do they decide? The most influential factors, the authors say, are the number of entry points to the road and the amount of commercial activity along it.

So now we come to the jackpot question. Is speed really the killer? On this point I think you should hear the engineers speaking in their own words. "The accident involvement rates on streets and highways in urban areas were *highest* for the slowest five percent of traffic, lowest for traffic in the 30-to-95-percentile range, and increased for the fastest five percent of traffic [emphasis added]."

They go on to say: "Many current speed limits coincide with 30-percentile speed which is near the lower bound of safe travel speed. Speed limits should be set in the 70-to-90-percentile range or roughly 5 to 10 mph above the average speed to correctly reflect maximum safe speed. Speed limits are set in multiples of 5 mph; the 70-to-90-percentile range will almost always include a 5-mph multiple. Allowing a 5-mph tolerance, enforcement would then be targeted at drivers who are clearly at risk."

Right here is where the Insurance Institute for Highway Safety usually bleats, "Yeah, but then everybody drives 5 to 10 mph over the limit." Does that happen? The engineers say no. "Raising the speed limit by various amounts up to 15 mph has little or no effect on speeds over a broad range of road types and speed levels." And lowering the limit doesn't slow motorists either, they report.

Although the authors are continuing their study, they say "the findings to date suggest that, on the average, current speed limits are set too low to be accepted as reasonable by the vast majority of drivers. Only about one in ten speed zones has better than 50-percent compliance. *The posted speeds make technical violators out of motorists driving at reasonable and safe speeds* [emphasis added].

"Our studies show that most speed zones are posted 8 to 12 mph below the prevailing travel speed and 15 mph or more below the maximum safe speed. Increasing speed limits to more realistic levels will not result in higher speeds but would increase voluntary compliance and target enforcement at the occasional violator and high-risk driver."

With their quick reflexes for cost cutting, the Japanese would use this information to underprice every auto insurer in the business. The first thing the efficiency-minded Japanese would do is fire every salaried suit working on "Speed Kills" propaganda. I think we're talking millions there. Then they'd stop payment on all the support checks to the Insurance Institute for Highway Safety, the Advocates for Highway and Auto Safety, and all the other puppet "Centers for (name any safety cliché here)" that churn out bogus carnage-on-the-highway statistics. They'd stop funding GUARD (Group United Against Radar Detectors), which, among other daffy activities, harangues magazines (this one included) for accepting radar-detector advertising. And of course they'd dismiss all the lobbyists clogging the corridors of Congress waiting for the chance to grease some detector-banning paragraph into a totally unrelated bill.

Oh, yes, no more political contributions either. The insurance industry is so fond of saying that the only reason to own a radar detector is to speed. Need I point out that the only reason to slip money to a congressman is to induce him to do something the electorate opposes?

If the insurance industry stopped funding the anti-speed campaign, there would be not a single voice against reasonable speed limits. Certainly the citizens want them: they vote with their feet every day.

Once the limits were sensible, then violation records would reliably identify the risky drivers. Let them pay for their sins. The rest of us would enjoy fair dealings with efficiency-minded businessmen. The Japanese would have a lock on another industry. And, ho ho, the guys who gave away our insurance trade would be swabbing urinals where they belong.

HOW THAT FORD BECAME A FOREIGNER

By Rich Ceppos

Bill Osos is mad. Mad at the Indianapolis Motor Speedway. Mad at Chrysler Corporation. Mad because the Dodge Stealth was at one time named the pace car for the 1991 Indy 500.

Osos, the director of the United Auto Workers' Region 3 (Indiana and Kentucky), says, "I think it's morally wrong to use a 100-percent Japanese-built car right here in the heart of Indiana. It's a slap in the face of the American auto worker."

Osos's frustration is understandable. The Brickyard is the home of the quintessential all-American automotive ritual, and the Stealth's arrival there is symbolic of our nation's slide from manufacturing preeminence, yet another sign of our eroding industrial base. It's enough to make any red-blooded American mad.

Next time, maybe the Speedway ought to consider selecting a domestic car to pace the race—say, a Honda Accord.

Don't laugh. The way things are going in the car business, it could happen. You see, the question of where cars are made and where their parts come from has become so complex that you can't tell the imports from the domestics without an EPA scorecard.

There are currently eight Japanese manufacturers building cars in the U.S. and Canada, either directly or in joint ventures. Honda has two car plants in Ohio, turning out Accords and Civics, and another Civic plant in Canada. Toyota builds Camrys in Kentucky. Nissan assembles Sentras in Tennessee. Mazda makes MX6s, 626s, and Ford Probes in Michigan. Toyota and GM have a joint-venture plant in California that manufactures Geo Prizms and Toyota Corollas. Suzuki and GM turn out Geo Metros in Canada. Subaru and Isuzu are building Subaru Legacys in Indiana. Chrysler and Mitsubishi bolt together Plymouth Lasers, Eagle Talons, Mitsubishi Eclipses, and versions of the Colt sedan in Illinois. And those are just the passenger cars—many of these companies also build light trucks here.

So which cars are imports and which are domestics? It's anything but obvious. "Several years ago," says Tom Ball, the EPA's chief of certification, "we were set to publish our annual top-ten fuel-economy list and realized that it was difficult to distinguish the imports from the domestics. People see a Chevrolet in the import category and don't understand. They don't understand domestic content."

According to the Energy Policy Conservation Act of 1975, the content of a car is defined as the dollar value of the parts, paint, and assembly labor that goes into manufacturing it. For a car to be considered domestic, 75 percent of its content has to originate in the U.S.

Congress passed the domestic-content regulations to protect American jobs. Back in the mid-1970s, the U.S. carmakers weren't sure they could meet the federally mandated Corporate Average Fuel Economy bogey, and they faced big-time fines if they failed. The simple solution was to import lots of economy cars from Japan and put American names on them.

But that meant fewer cars would be built here, a thought that chilled congressional hearts. So the pols refused to permit this mixing of imports with domestics for averaging purposes. The goal was to encourage American companies to build economy cars at home.

And that's why Chevrolet can count the Canadian-made Geo Metro, an exact copy of the Suzuki Swift, as a domestic product. (The feds decided that Canadian-built cars are "domestics.") The Metro contains 75-percent domestic content.

It's almost the same story with the Honda Accord. The 360,000 Accords that are being built annually in Ohio contain 75-percent domestic content. Even their engines are cast at Honda's Ohio foundry. But the EPA lists the Accord as an import because one-third of all Accords sold here are built in Japan—which pulls down the line's average.

If you're hoping to buy American as a patriotic gesture, good luck. Even the EPA can't sift out the imports from the homegrowns on a car-by-car basis. If you could discover the domestic content of each car sold in the U.S.—and you'd need inside information to do it—you would find some surprising anomalies: import models hidden within domestic car lines, and vice-versa.

Based on the Mazda Protegé, the Mercury Tracer, for example, is built in Mexico but has enough U.S. parts in it (including an American-made engine) to qualify as a domestic car line. But the LTS model, with its Mazda-built engine, probably would be categorized as an import if taken by itself, Ford admits. Are you buying American if you put your money down on a Tracer LTS? Would Bill Osos object if an LTS paced the Indy 500?

As with almost any regulation, the do-mestic-content laws have spawned some unexpected consequences. Take the bizarre case of the 1992 Ford Crown Victoria. This new wide-body will, incredibly, be registered as an import with the EPA, even though it's built here and is powered by an American-made V-8.

The Crown Vic's parts were carefully chosen to qualify it as an import—albeit by a cat's whisker—allowing Ford to average its fuel economy with the company's high-economy imports, the Ford Festiva and the Mercury Capri. This will enable Ford to sell more of the profitable big cars.

"That's one of the unintended results of the law," laughs Ron Boltz, Chrysler vice president of product strategy and regulatory affairs. "It wasn't foreseen."

Which brings us back to the symbolism of Bill Osos's complaint about the Stealth. No one could have foreseen the transplantation of Japanese carmakers to the States—most set up operations to circumvent the voluntary-restraint agreements limiting imports, rather than because of any fuel-economy concerns. Nonetheless, they are here. And they are building automobiles with the help of a lot of American workers while using a fair number of U.S. parts—all of which sure beats the alternative.

Bill Donaldson, the Speedway's vice president of marketing, advises facing reality. "How is the Indianapolis Motor Speedway ever going to police the sourcing of parts?" he asks. "For us, the question was not *if* this was ever going to come up—but *when.*"

DUFFY'S DILEMMA

By Brock Yates

Not long ago, I saw the ominous black snout of a New York State Police Ford Mustang search-and-destroy coupe poke into the parking lot of the Cannonball Run Pub. My defense mechanisms immediately went on red alert. It is raw instinct, I suppose, based on years of equating highway patrolmen with sharks, seeing them as capricious, unpredictable, and utterly amoral. At least when it comes to filling monthly ticket quotas, I acknowledge this as an irrational reaction based on pure prejudice. The fact is, over the years I've enjoyed the friendship of any number of state cops who are thoroughly good guys and who try to treat the motoring public with far more compassion than I might muster in a similar situation. (More on that in a moment).

So it was that I watched warily as the intruder in downtown Wyoming, New York, parked right where, as a pal of mine says, "The stoplight would be if there was one." The cop, whom we'll call Duffy, had come to talk about his prized Corvette that he drives on weekends and to comment on his Mustang, a marque that's found favor with a number of highway patrols across the nation.

"It's a blast to drive," Duffy proclaimed, expressing confidence that he could run down anything this side of a Lamborghini Diablo if necessary. However, the Mus-

tang has its Achilles' heel in the shift linkage of its five-speed. "We've replaced four linkages in this thing already," he said. "Some of the guys just don't drive it very well. And we're due for a new clutch pretty quick."

Still, Duffy had a nice deal. There he was, armed with this potent little black blivet, the king of the road. A man beyond the laws he was empowered to enforce and able to run his Mustang on the public highways at any speed he chooses, at any time he chooses. ("Official" policy says that cops always drive at the legal limit unless in pursuit or in an emergency situation. Sure.)

Duffy's job is to enforce the traffic laws of New York state, where he faces an unstoppable tidal wave of those the safety nuts call "professional speeders" and I identify as normal citizens who feel perfectly safe in modern automobiles operating at 10 to 20 mph beyond the posted limits. According to a recent survey, 90 percent of the drivers traveling on the 55-mph-posted New York Thruway run 65 or more. To the south, in double-nickel-choked Pennsylvania, the 85th-percentile speed (the speed maintained by 85 percent of the drivers) on its Interstates is 68 mph, despite a radical increase in speed-limit enforcement. Reality shows that Duffy and his associates, for all their gadgetry and powerhouse machines, cannot stem the commission of what the public considers to be a rational act.

It's my belief, therefore, that speed enforcement today has been reduced to a form of 20th-century motorsport. It has no social function, in that accident reduction has never, ever been correlated with aggressive ticketing programs, and aside from generating revenue and permitting some posturing by the poltroons who rule us, such weapons as radar patrols, VASCAR strike forces, and spies in the sky function as little more than nuisances that must be avoided like other road hazards. Cops are valiant in accident and crime situations, but in the elemental act of chasing speeders they are as frivolous and silly as spinner hubcaps.

Still, as Duffy roared away from my town, I could not help but envy him. What must it be like to have carte blanche on the highways? I tried to put myself in his position. Suppose I was on the other side in this game? How would I behave? I reached no conclusion until Labor Day weekend, while I was on my way to Lime Rock, Connecticut, moving east in heavy holiday traffic. I had hooked up with a stream of vehicles running the New York Thruway at about 80 mph, which seemed to be the velocity of the day. On a flat, open stretch I sighted a trooper in the westbound lane. Everyone slowed as he swept past, then sped up again as he drifted out of sight.

Just as the cruiser had become no more than a black dot in my rear-view mirror, I saw him jump the median and come after us. The thrill of the hunt! Now running a modest 65 mph, the de facto speed limit in New York, I watched in fascination as the cop ate up the distance in pursuit. He blasted by me at perhaps 120 mph, a lion charging into a herd of panic-stricken impala. Moments later, he carved out a red Dodge Daytona from Michigan and hauled over the baffled college kid behind the wheel. The kill had been made.

The whole incident meant nothing, but I had to admire the cop for his work. He executed the move like a true professional. And I admitted to myself that had I been in the trooper's boots, I would have done exactly the same thing. The lure of the hunt would have been too much. I would have behaved like the worst hunter-killer on the road. Who would I nail? Probably the same prey as he: people in flashy red sports coupes, preppies in Porsches, yuppies in BMWs, fat cats in Caddys, and smart asses in clapped-out muscle cars. I would also, of course, land those dorks who sit in the fast lane and block faster traffic. And I would stay on the lookout for weavers and wobblers who might be drunks or dopers. But overall, to be honest, I would operate like other highway patrolmen. Surely I'd rationalize my efforts as promoting safety, but in the end I'd know in my heart of hearts that I was a predator operating in a macadam killing field packed with hapless prey.

This would be a massive power trip. Just imagine driving a powerful automobile down a stretch of road and knowing that every other driver on the road, when he sees you, will cower behind the wheel, ease off the throttle, and nervously eye the speedometer. Imagine that rush in being able to pick a juicy victim out of the pack, chase him down in your high-powered cruiser, and yank him over for any reason you choose—a cracked taillight lens, a bent license plate, a soft tire, a pretty lady in the passenger seat. Imagine all that power and horsepower and then consider how much prudence and discipline you've seen most highway patrolmen display.

Sure it's a game. But generally it's a game that most professionals on the other side, like Duffy, play fairly. Being painfully truthful, that's probably more than I'd be able to say about myself if I were wearing their colors.

TORQUE OF THE TOWN

By Csaba Csere

I once received a letter from a Porsche 944S2 owner asking about the optimal shift points for achieving the best acceleration. His notion was that they were in the 4500-to-5000-rpm range. Given that his car's 3.0-liter engine develops 208 hp at 5800 rpm and 207 pound-feet of torque at 4100 rpm, he didn't display much understanding of the relationship between power, torque, and acceleration. He shouldn't feel bad. Neither do some senior managers I've encountered running powertrain departments in Detroit.

It's a difficult relationship to master, because torque is physically tangible, whereas power is a more ephemeral calculated value. To understand power, one must start with the basic definitions of force and work.

Force is a push or a pull exerted by one object on another. If you push on your car, you are exerting a force on it. However, you are not necessarily doing any work, because by definition work demands motion. Work equals force times distance. No matter how great the volume of sweat pouring off your brow as you push on the rear bumper, if the car doesn't move, even if you just left the parking brake on, no work is recognized (sweaty force × 0 = 0). On the other hand, if a steady 100-pound force will move your car and you push it 50 feet,

you have performed 5000 foot-pounds of work (100 lb × 50 ft).

So far we haven't said anything about time, but if you push your car 50 feet in twenty seconds, that's a lot easier than doing so in five seconds, even though the work performed is 5000 ft-lb in each case. This difference leads us to the concept of power, which is the *rate* at which work is performed. Moving the car in 20 seconds requires a power level of 250 ft-lb/sec (5000/20), while doing so in 5 seconds requires 1000 ft-lb/sec (5000/5).

Power also equals force times speed. In the first case, your speed of 2.5 ft/sec (50 ft/20 sec) multiplied by 100 lb of force equals 250 ft-lb/sec. At 10 ft/sec (50/5), we get 1000 ft-lb/sec. Whether calculated from work/time or force × speed, one horsepower is defined as 550 ft-lb/sec.

An engine produces rotary rather than linear motion, but the concepts are the same. Torque is simply the rotational equivalent of force. If you apply one pound of force to the end of a one-foot-long wrench, you are exerting one pound-foot of torque on the object you are trying to twist. To differentiate between the units for torque and work, we express torque in pound-feet (lb-ft) and work in foot-pounds (ft-lb). As you might expect, the common unit of rotary speed is revolutions per minute (rpm).

Multiply torque and rpm (the rotary equivalents of force and speed) and divide by a constant (to accommodate the switch from linear to rotational units and the conversion from ft-lb/sec to hp) and you have power (hp = torque × rpm/5252). By reversing this basic power equation, we can see that while the 944S2 engine develops its peak of 207 lb-ft of torque at 4100 rpm, it only offers 188 lb-ft at its power peak (torque = hp × 5252/rpm). However, before we start short-shifting the engine to run it near the torque peak, we need to consider the effects of gearing.

Gearing provides a way to trade off the two factors that create power: torque and rpm. To see how, we can calculate the S2's available power and torque at 55 mph in second, third, and fourth gears.

gear	engine rpm	power (hp)	torque (lb·ft)
2	6050	203	176
3	4100	162	207
4	3050	106	183

At this speed, the engine offers the most torque in third gear and the least torque in second gear. However, the task of accelerating the car is performed at the rear axle, where torque equals engine torque times the transmission ratio times the final-drive ratio, as shown below.

gear	final-drive ratio × transmission ratio	×	engine torque	=	rear-axle torque
2	3.88 × 2.06	×	176	=	1407
3	3.88 × 1.40	×	207	=	1124
4	3.88 × 1.03	×	183	=	731

The figures confirm what most of us already know—cars almost invariably accelerate harder in the lowest available gear. That's where the greatest horsepower is available. And because power is proportional to torque and speed, at any given speed you get the most torque at the rear wheels in the gear that lets the engine produce the greatest power. Therefore, for best acceleration, one should shift so as to maximize the engine's power output.

This means never shifting lower than the engine's power peak. The exact point can be determined if you have the engine's power curve and the various transmission and final-drive ratios. The object is not to shift until there is more power available in the next higher gear. From first to second, for example, shifting at the 5800-rpm power peak would drop the revs to about 3400 rpm—where the engine can deliver no more than 116 hp. Even with the power falling past the power peak, there's no percentage in going from a 208-hp point on the engine's power curve to one 92 hp lower. In fact, even at its 6500-rpm redline, the Porsche four-cylinder is developing about 175 hp, which is more than the 140 hp available after the shift into second drops the engine to 3825 rpm.

Shifting at the redline is also the best you can do in second gear. But third and fourth gear are a bit closer, and a redline shift will only drop the engine to about 4800 rpm, where 185 hp is available. That suggests that a slightly earlier shift would better use the available power. In fact, by shifting at 6400 rpm you can transfer the engine from the 184-hp-and-falling point on its power curve to 4725 rpm, where the curve shows 184 hp and rising. From fourth to fifth, which are even more closely spaced, the ideal shift point is at 6350 rpm.

With a low-revving engine like the Corvette's pushrod L98 V-8, the optimal shift points can fall well below the redline in every gear. But whether your engine is a low-revving tractor engine or an 8000-rpm screamer, you'll get the best performance by shifting at the exact point where the grass is greener on the other side of the power curve.

NEW CARS AND

HOOJAE LEE

TEN BEST CARS OF 1991

GARY RICHARDSON ILLUSTRATION

By William Jeanes

Of all things that we do at *Car and Driver,* this annual selection heads the agenda. There are times when we think the selection receives more attention than it deserves, and there are times when we think it's not taken seriously enough. At still other times, we're convinced that it must be worth doing if for no other reason than it's so much trouble.

But we persevere. Flinging ourselves once more into that dreadful breach populated by outraged auto executives, frightened public-relations persons, and readers who alternate between demanding that we confess to being hapless tools of the auto industry's advertising departments and commending us for our honesty, though they might not share our opinions.

This year's crop of nominees, which are listed on page 27, represent fine work from a lot of companies. Over and over during our week-long drive-off, some one of us was forever uttering the comment, "I can't believe all these cars are so good." Well, we're pleased to tell you that, yes, they are good.

You may be interested in our rules.

First, all cars—including minivans—with a base price of no more than $35,000 are eligible. That figure is roughly two and one-half times the price of the average car as delivered, and we have long contended that any car costing more than $35,000 had better be of the absolute best quality.

Second, each winner must receive a simple majority of the votes cast. That meant that it took six votes of ten to make this year's list. (Of the 36 cars nominated, 22 got at least one vote. Two of the selections were unanimous.)

Third, no nameplate can place more than two cars on the Ten Best list.

Finally, any car nominated must be for sale by January of 1991.

Beyond that, subjectivity comes into play. Our first criterion, of course, is excellence. The second might be stated as a question: "Would we buy and be seen in this car?" Third is how well the car does the job for which it was intended.

You will find no wimp-out "Import" or "Domestic" designations on our list. We look at cars the same way 80 percent of new-car buyers do: we look for the best one. As noted, you will find no more than two cars from any one manufacturing division on the list and no car appears that did not get a majority of the votes cast.

Our report appears on upcoming pages.

19

TEN BEST FOR UNDER $35,000

By William Jeanes

Welcome to the ninth annual Ten Best issue of *Car and Driver,* our traditional kickoff of the coming year. The toughest responsibility we have to our readers, picking the Ten Best Cars, has been made more difficult, once again, by the increasing number of quality cars being produced worldwide. Not that it gets any easier to tell which is which. What has gotten easier to do is to tell you that cars are better than ever.

As we stand one year short of a decade of Ten Best issues, we're worried that we may also be standing at the high-water mark where enthusiast cars are concerned. We face continued uncertainty in the Middle East and, given the historic instability of that tortured part of the planet, may do so forever. This situation has heightened the nation's awareness of potential oil shortages. Before that fact registered, a vigorous attempt was mounted in Congress to raise the Corporate Average Fuel Economy standard to 40 miles per gallon by the first year of next century. More government mandates loom, as the safety zealots add weight to cars for "safety" and other arms of government take away weight for "economy." No arm of government has the courage to raise gasoline taxes significantly, which would both help reduce the size of cars and conserve oil reserves. The appellation "congressional leaders" has become the most recent Washington oxymoron.

But remember that Thomas Jefferson once despaired of his country's survival in the face of its failure to produce any good domestic wine, a deficiency since remedied. So we will doubtless get through these times just as we have persevered through earlier troubles. And to help you along the way, we've got our usual fun-filled and fact-laden Ten Best lineup.

We assure you that there could have been a Top 40 instead of a Ten Best, and

DAVID PORATH

Vehicle type: front-engine, front- or 4-wheel-drive, 2 + 2-passenger, 3-door coupe
Base price: $13,954–17,529
Engine: turbocharged and intercooled DOHC 16-valve 2.0-liter 4-in-line
Power (SAE net) . . . . 190–195 bhp
Transmissions . . . . 5-speed, 4-speed auto
Wheelbase . . . . 97.2 in
Length . . . . 170.5–172.4 in
Curb weight . . . . 2850–3150 lb
EPA fuel economy, city driving . . . . 20–22 mpg

MOST PHOTOS BY DICK KELLEY

EAGLE TALON TSi

FORD TAURUS SHO

Vehicle type: front-engine, front-wheel-drive, 5-, 6-, or 8-passenger, 4-door sedan or 5-door wagon
Base price: $13,352–22,071
Engines: 2.5-liter 4-in-line, 3.0-liter V-6, DOHC 24-valve 3.0-liter V-6, 3.8-liter V-6
Power (SAE net) . . . . 105–220 bhp
Transmissions . . . . 5-speed, 4-speed auto
Wheelbase . . . . 106.0 in
Length . . . . 188.4–193.2 in
Curb weight . . . . 2950–3400 lb
EPA fuel economy, city driving . . . . 18–21 mpg

that no one would have been embarrassed by the list. So read, enjoy, and count yourself fortunate to live in what ranks as the best country in the world for auto enthusiasts.

DIAMOND-STAR TURBOS

We stand in awe at the blend of excellence, value, and performance these cars deliver. Our award this year covers the five Diamond-Star turbos, which are built in Normal, Illinois, at the manufacturing facility owned jointly by Chrysler and Mitsubishi. The winners are the front-drive Eagle Talon TSi, Mitsubishi Eclipse GS Turbo, and Plymouth Laser RS Turbo, plus the all-wheel-drive Talon TSi AWD and Eclipse GSX.

The value-to-performance ratio remains high on these cars. The 1991 base prices range from $17,529 for the all-wheel-drive models down to $13,954 for the front-drive Diamond-Stars. Each of the cars can reach 60 mph in less than seven seconds and is capable of 135 mph.

Inside and outside, the Diamond-Stars are handsome, stylish cars. They were unanimous winners.

FORD TAURUS/MERCURY SABLE

Despite the concern for fuel economy, we're not sure that you ought to buy a four-cylinder Taurus even though our Ten Best award goes to the entire Ford Taurus/Mercury Sable line. Reason? The Taurus four-cylinders just won't overwhelm you with energy.

The Taurus, for the first time in its six years on our list, began to show some weakness at the polls, due largely to its having become too, well, familiar. Though a freshening is in order, and quickly, the Taurus/Sable line still provides the best range of family sedans geared to the mind of the practical folk and the heart of the enthusiast. Even the wagons are fun.

Of all the Taurus/Sable selections, though, the stem-winding Taurus SHO with the Yamaha engine still gets our nod. The Taurus appears on *C/D*'s Ten Best Cars list for the fourth time.

HONDA ACCORD

We griped about the new Accord (the third all-new car in the nine years the Honda Accord has won a Ten Best slot) because we didn't think its styling was as advanced as the rest of the car. We still feel that way, but the rest of the car's so all-fired good that we're willing to overlook the trailing-edge styling and make the Honda Accord the only automobile to appear on all nine of our Ten Best lists.

We've got company when it comes to high regard for this compact yet comfortable family car. The Accord was the country's best-selling car for the 1990 model year, with 416,957 units sold. Honda Accords—80 percent of them—are built by U.S. auto workers at Honda's Marysville, Ohio, plant.

Just as we went to press, the Honda man called the office and said the company was sending over an Accord wagon. Watch your in-box.

HONDA CIVIC

The Honda Civic line, which includes a four-door sedan, a three-door hatchback, and a sort of funny-looking wagon, continues to amaze us and the buying public. The Civic made the nation's best-seller list, racking up sales of 255,159 for the 1990 model year, good for seventh place.

The Civic continues to rate superior

HONDA ACCORD

Vehicle type: front-engine, front-wheel-drive, 5-passenger, 2- or 4-door sedan
Base price: $12,345–19,545
Engine: SOHC 16-valve 2.2-liter 4-in-line
Power (SAE net) . . . . 125–140 bhp
Transmissions . . . . 5-speed, 4-speed auto
Wheelbase . . . . 107.1 in
Length . . . . 184.8 in
Curb weight . . . . 2750–3000 lb
EPA fuel economy, city driving . . . . 22–24 mpg

HONDA CIVIC

Vehicle type: front-engine, front- or 4-wheel-drive, 5-passenger, 3- or 4-door sedan or 5-door wagon
Base price: $6895–13,140
Engines: SOHC 16-valve 1.5-liter 4-in-line, SOHC 16-valve 1.6-liter 4-in-line
Power (SAE net) . . . . 70–108 bhp
Transmissions . . . . 4-speed, 5-speed, 6-speed or 4-speed auto
Wheelbase . . . . 98.4 in
Length . . . . 157.1–168.8 in
Curb weight . . . . 2150–2650 lb
EPA fuel economy, city driving . . . . 24–33 mpg

marks in the categories most important to us: driving pleasure, quality, and value. We continue to be astonished that Honda can make what is essentially a subcompact economy car feel like so much more. All versions of the Civic except the wagon are now built in North America.

The Civic, due for major changes this year, is all the more distinguished for the competition it faces. In a tough, tough market segment that includes such giants as Nissan and Toyota, the Civic maintains a small edge.

MAZDA MX-5 MIATA

Nostalgia is selling bigger than camo jogging suits these days. No wonder then that Mazda's Miata, king of the retro rockets, garnered a unanimous vote from our smitten panel and returns for the second consecutive year.

It isn't really a rocket, of course, and that's a big part of its charm. "What it is," said one observer, "is a 1964 British sports car that doesn't leak oil in your driveway." True enough.

MAZDA MX-5 MIATA

Vehicle type: front-engine, rear-wheel-drive, 2-passenger, 2-door convertible
Base price: $14,200
Engine: DOHC 16-valve 1.6-liter 4-in-line
Power (SAE net) . . . . 105–116 bhp
Transmissions . . . . 5-speed, 4-speed auto
Wheelbase . . . . 89.2 in
Length . . . . 155.4 in
Curb weight . . . . 2200–2250 lb
EPA fuel economy, city driving . . . . 24–25 mpg

We would have thought that the appeal of a return to *al fresco* driving as it was meant to be would have paled during the past year, but it didn't. We put 35,000 miles on one of these jewels, suffering the windburn, the high noise level, and the envy of every last soul that saw us.

We remain convinced that everyone on the continent—any continent—ought to have one of these zippy, good-handling, swift-looking funsters in the garage.

MAZDA MPV V6 3.0i

Mazda MPV V6 3.0i

As you'll see a few paragraphs further along, two minivans made the 1991 Ten Best Cars list. A third minivan, Chrysler's Caravan/Voyager, fell victim to the price-tag wars, but is a fine vehicle.

The rear-drive Mazda MPV with the V-6 engine and the automatic transmission again makes the Ten Best cut, after the MPV scored a surprise victory last year. We had all liked the vehicle, but we didn't know how much until we drove it back-to-back with the other nominees. Whether compared with cars or with other minivans, the MPV came off well. It was easy to use, pleasant to look at, and a joy to drive down the road.

We find the MPV useful in everything we do other than setting out to impress the high-rollers of the world. It is, after all, a prosaic-enough vehicle. But what a personality. If ever a vehicle exuded that elusive quality called drivability, it's the Mazda MPV V6 automatic.

Mercury Tracer LTS

This Tracer appears as other models, and in a quite similar form as the Mazda Protegé, but the Tracer LTS gave us more of what we like in a small sedan. There's excellent fit and finish, enough room, a reasonable price, and a twin-cam four-cylinder engine that takes Tracer driving

Vehicle type: front-engine, rear-wheel-drive, 7-passenger, 4-door van
Base price: $16,865
Engine: SOHC 18-valve 3.0-liter V-6
Power (SAE net) . . . . .150 bhp @ 5000 rpm
Transmission . . . . 4-speed auto
Wheelbase . . . . 110.4 in
Length . . . . 175.8 in
Curb weight . . . . 3650–3800 lb
EPA fuel economy, city driving . . . . 17 mpg

MERCURY TRACER LTS

NISSAN SENTRA SE-R

Vehicle type: front-engine, front-wheel-drive, 5-passenger,
2-door sedan
Base price: $10,970
Engine: DOHC 16-valve 2.0-liter 4-in-line
Power (SAE net) .... 140 bhp @ 6400 rpm
Transmission 5-speed
Wheelbase .... 95.7 in
Length .... 170.3 in
Curb weight .... 2500 lb
EPA fuel economy, city driving .... 24 mpg

Vehicle type: front-engine, front-wheel-drive, 5-passenger,
4-door sedan
Base price: $11,636
Engine: DOHC 16-valve 1.8-liter 4-in-line
Power (SAE net) .... 127 bhp @ 6500 rpm
Transmissions .... 5-speed, 4-speed auto
Wheelbase .... 98.4. in
Length .... 170.9 in
Curb weight .... 2550 lb
EPA fuel economy, city driving .... 23–26 mpg

out of the humdrum and into the high-grin world.

Built at Ford's plant in Hermosillo, Mexico, the Tracer joins the Honda Civic in providing strong evidence that workers on this continent have no difficulty building high-quality small cars, even if large companies have difficulty making profits on such items.

Tracer drivers will profit nicely, however, from the pleasures delivered by this quick, crisp sports sedan.

During 1991, the showrooms at Lincoln-Mercury dealers will be among the rare places where you'll find two Ten Best winners on sale.

NISSAN SENTRA SE-R

When we drove Nissan's terrific new Sentra SE-R for the first time last year, we noted that we'd always maintained that there's no good reason that small cars can't be as good as big cars. We then went on to cite the SE-R as the best evidence we'd seen to date that something we'd wanted for years—BMW 2002 punch at a Datsun price—had at last become a reality. The names have changed, of course, but you get the point.

The entire driveline, from an engine that stands out (in a big crowd) with smooth delivery of power to a shifter that finds gears as if by divine guidance, sends the driver who truly loves the act of driving close to affordable nirvana than he may yet have come.

The Sentra SE-R in our test pack cost

less than $13,000 delivered. If you don't think that's value for money, we urge you to treat yourself to an SE-R drive. We guarantee you'll come away a believer.

NISSAN 300ZX TURBO

Our staff felt the normally aspirated 300ZX didn't have enough zip for the money. But with a blower—the price increase is not substantial—the car won handily. So we picked the 300ZX Turbo model to accept a Ten Best trophy all alone.

Not surprisingly, smoothly delivered speed has its way with us. We just can't seem to resist its allure. And the 300ZX has the best combination of smoothness, speed, and all-around civility of any car below our $35,000 cutoff.

How could anyone resist a package that looks this good and performs this well: 0 to 60 in 5.9 seconds and a solid 155-mph top speed?

The Nissan 300 ZX offers its owner 300 horsepower and the excitement that goes with it. To say nothing of pride of ownership.

TOYOTA PREVIA

If you aren't charmed by the Previa's styling, how can you resist the down-on-its-side engine? For once, when someone says that you've never seen anything like this before, you can believe it.

The Previa is easily the most distinctive vehicle in the fast-selling Toyota line (more than a million vehicles in model-year 1990). Its exterior is spacey-looking, and its interior is amazingly spacious. Toyota's designers have achieved that sought-after impossibility the hypesters call smaller on the outside, bigger on the inside.

The engine, as you may know by now, is a four-cylinder that lies on its side, unseen by prying eyes. Look under the hood and you'll find the air-conditioner compressor, the alternator, and some other bits, but no engine.

The Previa, under way, has an excellent carlike feel, and the dash design is as pleasingly modern as we've seen.

NISSAN 300ZX TURBO

Vehicle type: front-engine, rear-wheel-drive, 2-passenger, 3-door coupe
Base price: $33,500–34,300
Engine: twin-turbocharged and intercooled DOHC 24-valve 3.0-liter V-6
Power (SAE net) . . . . 280–300 bhp
Transmissions . . . . 5-speed, 4-speed auto
Wheelbase . . . . 96.5 in
Length . . . . 169.5 in
Curb weight . . . . 3450–3500 lb
EPA fuel economy, city driving . . . . 18 mpg

TOYOTA PREVIA

Vehicle type: mid-engine, rear- or 4-wheel-drive, 5- or 7-passenger, 4-door van
Base price: $14,398–21,908
Engine: DOHC 16-valve 2.4-liter 4-in-line
Power (SAE net) .... 138 bhp @ 5000 rpm
Transmissions .... 5-speed, 4-speed auto
Wheelbase .... 112.8 in
Length .... 187.0 in
Curb weight........................ 3750–4050 lb
EPA fuel economy, city driving .... 18–19 mpg

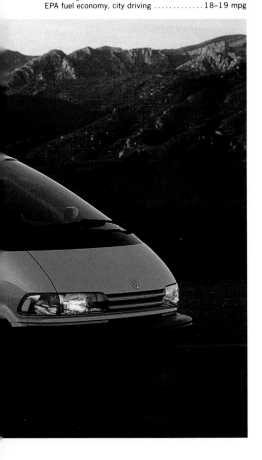

FULL SLATE OF TEN BEST NOMINEES

BMW M3
BMW 318is
Buick Park Avenue Ultra
Diamond-Star Turbos
Dodge Caravan/
    Plymouth Voyager
Dodge Spirit R/T
Dodge Stealth ES
Ford Probe LX
Ford Taurus/
    Mercury Sable
Ford Thunderbird SC
Geo Metro LSi Convertible
Honda Accord
Honda Civic
Infiniti G20
Isuzu Impulse RS
Lincoln Town Car
Mazda MPV V6 3.0i
Mazda MX-5 Miata
Mazda Protegé LX

Mercury Capri
Mercury Capri XR2
Mercury Tracer LTS
Mitsubishi 3000GT VR-4
Mitsubishi Galant VR-4
Nissan 240SX
Nissan 300ZX
Nissan 300ZX Turbo
Nissan Maxima SE
Nissan NX2000
Nissan Sentra SE-R
Oldsmobile Ninety-Eight
    Touring Sedan
Pontiac Bonneville SE
Saab 9000 Turbo
Saturn
Subaru Legacy Sport Sedan
Toyota MR2
Toyota MR2 Turbo
Toyota Previa
Volkswagen Passat GL

TEN BEST PERFORMERS, 1990 *

Acceleration, 0 to 60 mph .... Chevrolet Corvette ZR-1, 4.6 sec
Quarter-mile .... Chevrolet Corvette ZR-1, 12.9 sec @ 111 mph
Top-gear acceleration** .... BMW 750iL, 7.4 sec
Top speed.................... Chevrolet Corvette ZR-1, 176 mph
Braking, 70 to 0 mph .... Acura NSX, 157 feet
Roadholding................. Chevrolet Corvette Z51 FX3, 0.91 g
Interior sound level @ 70 mph ..... Mercedes-Benz 560SEL, 66 dBA
Road horsepower @ 50 mph................. Ford Escort GT, 11 hp
EPA city fuel economy .... Suzuki Swift GT, 29 mpg
C/D observed fuel economy................ Honda CRX Si, 32 mpg
                                Suzuki Swift GT, 32 mpg

  * includes only U.S.-specification production cars tested by C/D in 1990
  ** sum of 30-to-50-mph and 50-to-70-mph acceleration times

TEN WORST PERFORMERS, 1990 *

Acceleration, 0 to 60 mph .... Toyota 4Runner 4WD SR5 V6, 15.7 sec
Quarter-mile .... Isuzu Trooper LS, 20.8 sec @ 66 mph
Top-gear acceleration** .... Dodge Colt GT, 31.2 sec
Top speed........................ Jeep Wrangler Sahara, 81 mph
Braking, 70 to 0 mph .... Isuzu Trooper LS, 235 feet
Roadholding.............Toyota 4Runner 4WD SR5 V6, 0.63 g
Interior sound level @ 70 mph............. Geo Storm GSi, 87 dBA
Road horsepower @ 50 mph.......... Jeep Wrangler Sahara, 23 hp
EPA city fuel economy .... Bentley Turbo R, 10 mpg
C/D observed fuel economy............... Porsche 928GT, 13 mpg

  * includes only U.S.-specification production cars tested by C/D in 1990
  ** sum of 30-to-50-mph and 50-to-70-mph acceleration times

OTHER NOMINEES

By Phil Berg

To prepare for our January issue each year, we editors gather in a conference room to nominate our favorite cars. Heated discussions and arguments ensue. At the end of this meeting, we have a list, which totaled 39 cars for the 1991 model year. Then we round up one model of each car and corral nominees at a secluded test site. We spend a week testing these cars. When we're finished, we vote. The ten that get the most votes become our Ten Best. The remaining 29, for the 1991 model year, are presented here alphabetically. Some came close to making the Ten Best list. Some didn't.

GARY RICHARDSON ILLUSTRATION

BMW M3

When BMW's near-racer M3 was introduced in late 1987, it was a 192-hp rocket. It also had an exotic price of $34,800. For 1991, the price had barely changed at $34,950, but for half that you can buy a Diamond-Star turbo that offers as much performance. Competitive two-doors have improved in this hotly contested market segment. Refinement is now of a high level. The M3 is fast and smooth, but it has not kept pace in value.

BMW 318is

This small BMW boasts a price within reach of most serious car fans, but its $22,000 base price is still high above many quicker sedans. True, the 318is is smooth and has a perfectly matched five-speed transmission. It is rewarding to drive in its own right, but its performance is not on par with V-6 Nissan Maximas and Diamond-Star coupes.

BUICK PARK AVENUE ULTRA

Most of us refer to this car as an American Jaguar. Its lines are pretty, and it is comfortable to ride in. It is also a capable highway cruiser. Pushed to its limits, however, this Buick is not a high-performance car. We question the use of rear drum brakes on such an uplevel sedan, and a few couldn't make friends with the instrument panel.

DODGE CARAVAN/ PLYMOUTH VOYAGER

The Dodge version of these minis is the most popular minivan ever and, as such, is available in a bewildering variety of models and trim packages. Most buyers opt for a base Caravan outfitted with a V-6 engine, which sells for roughly $14,500. Equipped like the Toyota Previa and Mazda MPV that won places on our Ten Best list, the Dodge costs only a little more. In this hotly contested market segment, you'll be comparing these minivans mostly on subjective merits.

DODGE SPIRIT R/T

A wonderful, free-revving twin-cam engine was added to the rather lackluster Spirit sedan for the 1991 model year. This engine gives real spirit to performance. The car accelerates from 0 to 60 mph in 5.8 seconds, which is just a tick quicker than a Nissan 300ZX Turbo. That's impressive for a four-door sedan that gets nearly 20 mpg. Still, the Spirit R/T has not shed its economy-sedan conduct, and its chassis falls short on roads with demanding corners and lumpy asphalt.

DODGE STEALTH ES

For less than $20,000 you can buy a slick-looking Dodge Stealth with a 222-hp motor. It is not as fast as the 300-hp Stealth R/T Turbo, and it doesn't have four-wheel-drive. But a price within reach and a zoomy-looking body make this lower-line model nearly irresistible. There are some points of refinement that we might argue with, such as the notchy shifter and a rear seat that is made for pets only. For a sporty coupe this size, style has clearly won out over function.

FORD PROBE LX

A V-6 engine became available in Ford's sporty Probe coupe for the first time in 1991. It's the same 3.0-liter engine that you'll find in a Taurus, but you can couple it to a five-speed manual transmission in the Probe. Not many of the dozen sport coupes you can buy offer a V-6, though a Probe so-equipped is actually slower than a Probe GT with a turbo-charged four-cylinder. This car, then, is intended more for commuters than hardcore car fans.

FORD THUNDERBIRD SC

The Thunderbird is one of the most popular cars in the sporty/luxurious two-door market, and the 210-hp supercharged SC model is one of the best performers. The SC is rewarding to drive fast, though we prefer the automatic simply because the five-speed's clutch and shifter are not as refined as they could be. Four adults will fit easily inside this big cruiser, which some of us think is a bit too big.

GEO METRO LSi CONVERTIBLE

This car looks cute and has an irresistible base price of only about $10,000. But 20 minutes on the freeway is enough to persuade that the Metro convertible is more enjoyable on slower city streets. Powered by a 1.3-liter three-cylinder—the smallest engine in our collection of nominees—the Metro is light and nimble. And in five-speed manual transmission form, it returns 41 mpg (EPA, city).

INFINITI G20

For a four-cylinder sedan, the $18,000 G20 is one of the most refined and well made that we've driven. At that price, however, you can buy a Toyota Camry, Ford Taurus, or Nissan Maxima with a V-6 engine. The Infiniti is powered by a quick, 140-hp 2.0-liter four cylinder that would feel more at home in a sports coupe. No six cylinder is available. The G20's chassis handles all manner of road surfaces with competence.

ISUZU IMPULSE RS

If you like modern hardware but are on a tight budget, Isuzu's Impulse RS is your best buy. It comes with a turbocharged four-cylinder engine that makes 160 hp, and it accelerates briskly. Power is dispatched to all four wheels, just as in the slick Mitsubishi Eclipse GSX/Eagle Talon sport coupes. But the Impulse is nearly $2000 less expensive. It's slightly noisier and a bit slower but just as fun.

LINCOLN TOWN CAR

The all-new V-8 engine that debuted in Lincoln's Town Car in 1991 is a winning design. It uses overhead cams, and runs smoothly, efficiently, and makes 210 hp with a dual exhaust option. With this engine, this luxury car is rated at 17 mpg (EPA city). We rate it as one of the best ways to carry six people plus more luggage than they will all need for a week. But, you may need a tugboat to dock the Town Car in some parking spots.

MAZDA PROTEGÉ LX

This LX is the uplevel model in Mazda's Protegé small sedan line. It comes with a zingy 125-hp twin-cam engine. This quick little car is also as smooth on the highway as some larger sedans. This car comes from Japan, but similar versions are built in Michigan as the Ford Escort and in Mexico as the Mercury Tracer. The two-door Escort GT and four-door Tracer LTS share the fast motor with the Protegé LX.

MERCURY CAPRI

With base price under $13,000, this model of Mercury's convertible, new for 1991, is the least expensive sporty soft-top you could get. It is slightly cheaper than Dodge's new sedan-based Shadow convertible, and significantly less expensive than Mazda's Miata roadster. Some of us think the Capri is homely looking, others find the Capri a much more useful size than the two-seat Miata. The base Capri is powered by a 100-hp 1.6-liter, which gives it adequate acceleration. The Capri also makes less racket than the Miata.

MERCURY CAPRI XR2

The uplevel version of the Capri is powered by a 132-hp turbocharged 1.6-liter four cylinder, and it'll cruise comfortably at 120 mph if you ask it to. It jumps to 60 mph much faster than Mazda's Miata roadster, too, but is priced about $1500 higher. Freeway cruising is the XR2's strong suit. It rides at brisk, steady speeds more comfortably than the Miata. However, the front-drive XR2 can't match the Miata's moves on a twisty road.

MITSUBISHI 3000GT VR-4

Because it offers so much, we labeled this car the "Swiss Army Knife of Sports Coupes." This 300-hp, 150-mph coupe also looks aggressive. Powered by a 3.0-liter V-6 with twin turbochargers, it accelerates its 3800-pound bulk with verve. Its suspension is driver-adjustable. The rear wing moves up automatically at quick speeds. The 3000GT JR-4 uses full-time four-wheel-drive and anti-lock brakes. There's not much more we can think of adding to a car, except some refinement in the steering and in the shifter.

MITSUBISHI GALANT VR-4

This four-wheel-drive sedan does everything: It has windshield wipers that automatically speed up and slow down with the car's speed. It has shock absorbers that automatically change firmness, depending upon the road conditions. And it has anti-lock brakes. But we like it for more than its gadgetry. Its turbocharged 2.0-liter twin-cam four cylinder makes 195 hp and revs quickly and smoothly. This is a fun and balanced car to drive.

NISSAN 240SX

A boost from 140 hp to 155 hp renewed our interest in this well-balanced, slick sports coupe. The nose also looks cleaner. The 240SX is a rear-drive sports coupe, which makes it a rarity in the field of Mitsubishi Eclipses, Honda Preludes, and Ford Probes—all front-drivers. The Nissan's handling is therefore very predictable, and the car is rewarding to drive on twisty roads. Its other controls—including the shifter, the brakes, and the steering—are crisp and sure.

NISSAN 300ZX

The turbocharged, 300-hp version of Nissan's fast GT coupe made it on our Ten Best list, but we felt this entry-level model didn't offer enough performance for its near-$28,000 base price. It is powered by a 222-hp 3.0-liter V-6, which is 78 hp shy of the 300ZX Turbo. The base 300ZX goes from 0 to 60 mph in 6.7 seconds, which is slower than Toyota's less-expensive Supra Turbo. When you pay for a car that looks as exotic as the Nissan, you expect performance just as exciting.

NISSAN MAXIMA SE

This is one of our favorite do-everything sedans, and it has placed very close to the Ten Best list in our voting each year. It's powered by a 3.0-liter V-6, and we like it coupled to the five-speed manual transmission. This combination is smooth and powerful and inspires sport driving. The Maxima is roomier than many other Japanese sedans, since it was designed exclusively for the U.S. market. You'll notice the extra width inside.

NISSAN NX2000

New for 1991, Nissan introduced a replacement for its entry-level Pulsar sport coupe, calling it the NX. The NX2000 is the quickest version of this new car, powered by the same 2.0-liter, twin-cam engine that you'll find in the Infiniti G20 and Nissan Sentra SE-R. The NX2000 is faster than Honda's CRX Si, Volkswagen's Corrado, and Geo's Storm GSi. But you get more than speed from this small coupe. It is balanced, easy to drive, and well built.

OLDSMOBILE NINETY-EIGHT TOURING SEDAN

This large luxury sedan is built on the same platform as Buick's Park Avenue, but Oldsmobile has aimed its Ninety-Eight Touring Sedan at sportier drivers. Its suspension is firmer than the Buick's. Some of its ride qualities may be a bit too firm, we feel. Still, for a car that can carry six people with ease and comfort, it offers surprisingly crisp steering and a great deal of road-holding ability.

PONTIAC BONNEVILLE SE

This sedan is one level down the price scale from Pontiac's top-line Bonneville SSE. But we like the SE model better. With antilock brakes, it still costs about $4000 less than the $26,000 SSE. The SE looks neat and trim, and doesn't share the wide side skirts and large spoilers of the SSE. Both models have the same 3.8-liter V-6, and their acceleration is acceptable, though slower than a similarly priced Mazda 929 or Toyota Cressida.

SAAB 9000 TURBO

This car drew raves for its powerful turbocharged 2.3-liter four-cylinder, which is substantially faster than a V-8-powered Lexus LS400. The 200-hp Saab engine is smooth, too, and exhibits very little of the boost lag problem that most turbocharged cars suffer from. Sounds good so far, but there's more: The Saab is larger inside than the Lexus, and it costs less. Its ride, however, is very firm, and some of our test drivers became frustrated trying to operate some dash controls.

SATURN

We tested a four-door sedan with the optional 123-hp 1.9-liter motor. Its performance was good, but we object to the racket the powertrain makes when you rev the engine. We really liked the interior design of this sedan; it is comfortable and will hold four adults with room to spare. The driving position is uncommonly large for a small car. The Saturn's body is plastic, and our test car looked well made.

SUBARU LEGACY SPORT SEDAN

The Legacy is Subaru's entry into the competitive mid-size market. Until this turbocharged Sport Sedan model came to the U.S. in late 1990, it was as mainstream as any five-passenger sedan. The Sport Sedan has some nice qualities: Its turbocharged 2.2-liter motor is refined and moves the car faster than a similarly powerful Maxima SE V-6. The Subaru's suspension also soaks up bad roads with grace. Overall, however, the styling and the driving impressions we get are uninspiring.

TOYOTA MR2

This mid-engine two-seater was introduced early in 1990, replacing a much smaller car of the same name. The new, bigger MR2 is powered by the same engines you'll find in Toyota's Celica coupes, which are more powerful than previous MR2 models. A 130-hp 2.2-liter four cylinder is standard. This engine is gutsy, if not spectacular. The new MR2 handles curvy roads well, if not as crisply as the previous, smaller version.

TOYOTA MR2 TURBO

This version of the new MR2 is powered by the 200-hp 2.0-liter engine from Toyota's Celica All-Trac. So motivated, the MR2 Turbo will get to 60 mph in the six-second range, about the same as the Diamond-Star turbo coupes. This mid-engined Toyota looks more like a junior Ferrari than any other sport coupe. Its base price begins about $20,000.

VOLKSWAGEN PASSAT GL

This is a tightly built machine, both taut and responsive. But in the areas of noise isolation and comfort, it falls behind plusher sedans. Still, the VW is very roomy, especially in its rear seat area. It's powered by a twin-cam 2.0-liter that makes a healthy 134 hp and delivers good power, but it's also a bit buzzy at highway speeds. Passats start at $15,000.

THE EROTICARS

By Patrick Bedard

If they draw crowds when they stop and draw cops when they move, if they're priced like real estate and powered like orbital launchers, if they seem too wild to roam the same streets with the Avon lady and the meter man, then they must be Eroticars. Or else the latest rock band.

Obviously, this is a car magazine so we're talking cars. But the cars we're talking about in this review are way out at the edge of the definition, way out there where one more tweak will put them over the line into Learjets.

Think of them as Learjets for the ground.

In Europe, where the famous labels first became famous, Ferrari, Lotus, and Porsche have always meant speed. That's the point: cars that get you there fast. As in the Learjet, such purposefulness is sexy. Pull the skin tight over muscles hard enough to break 160 mph and there you have it, the Eroticar.

Traditionally, Europe was the only source of Eroticars. The names still tingle the senses—Ferrari, Maserati, Lamborghini, Aston Martin. But others are crashing the party. Upstart Honda is introducing the NSX, to be sold as an Acura in the U.S. Chevrolet has stepped up with its Corvette ZR-1. Do they belong on the list?

Who has the list, anyway?

In fact, the list is hopelessly out of date. The time has come to check credentials again, round up all the players and see where they *really* stand.

The NSX and the ZR-1 have to prove themselves against the big guys. Anything packing Ferrari credentials has a standing invitation, and it just happens that Ferrari is replacing its popular 328 series with an all-new pair of aero-slotted models, the 348tb coupe and the 348ts targa-type Spyder. We obtained a Spyder for this test.

The new Lamborghini Diablo is not quite ready yet. Aston Martin is between models as well, and Maserati no longer builds two-seaters in this Eroticar class. Lotus stands ready with its wedge-shaped and fiercely turbocharged Esprit Turbo SE, however.

We test the fast ones (clockwise from top): Lotus Esprit Turbo SE, Porsche 911 Carrera 4, Ferrari 348ts, Chevrolet Corvette ZR-1, and Acura NSX.

PHOTOGRAPHY BY DAVID DEWHURST

36

And then there's Porsche. Back in the days when the polysyllabic Italians were dazzling the world with vibrant engines and sultry bodywork, Porsche was turning out quirky and affordable sports cars. Now Porsches are increasingly pricey, increasingly sophisticated, and increasingly rare. The four-wheel-drive Carrera 4 looks like a 911 on the outside, but it promises far more.

The logical Porsche for this Learjet class is the Carrera 4 coupe. Such a car was on its way to the festivities when, in the hands of a transportation company, it fetched up against an immovable object. The only substitute available on such short notice was the Carrera 4 Cabriolet you see here.

Probably you think a face-off of five Eroticars is fun, and—heh, heh—you're right. But it's also one of the toughest jobs we've stepped up to in years. Our stan-dards demand that we push these automobiles to their limits, just as we would any econobox—never mind that the risks and the required run-off room are ever so much greater at jet speed. But we look at it this way: the legends of the future proceed from the performance marks set today. And we refuse to be a part of baloney legends. So the cars were driven to the max. Ambient temperatures edged above 100 degrees some of the time, into the zone where our weather corrections may not fully compensate for the adversity. That may be why some of the power-related numbers are slower than we've achieved with similar models in the past. But because this entire group was tested under the same conditions, you can be sure their relative capabilities shine through.

Enough for preliminaries. Now it's time for our judgments.

Plenty of great roads for us and a great location for photog David Dewhurst, top.

The legends of the future proceed from the performance marks set today. Since we refuse to be part of baloney legends, we test legends and challengers on equal terms.

Lotus Esprit Turbo SE
5th place

This Giugiaro-designed Lotus dates to the Paris show of 1975, back when sports cars were supposed to be a little uncomfortable, one more way of reminding that they weren't for everyone. Once you squeeze in through the narrow door, you find yourself in a capsule that's tight around the shoulders, narrow in the hips, and pinchy on the feet. The cramped cockpit seems an anachronism now, albeit an anachronism lined in the British manner with burled elm and wonderfully fragrant leather. Expect your first few miles of settle-in time to be accompanied by plenty of elbow banging and windshield-wiper flicking.

Then, amazingly, you get used to the space, the claustrophobia fades, and you find room to work.

Such traditional sports cars also featured recalcitrant engines, a sure way of shrugging off drivers lacking in ardor. The Lotus's 2174cc four is a stumbling wimp when the boost is down. A normal launch starts with a blip to 2500 rpm or better, and ends with the final trading of clutch slip for forward motion. No blip, no motion.

This initial coaxing in no way prepares you for the change in mood when the boost rises. The engine has a water-to-air intercooler and an electronic management system that invites, when temperatures permit, a hefty overboost below 3000 rpm. This boost beyond the normal limit of 12.4 psi does for the mousy four-cylinder what a dose of adrenaline does for your heart. Hang on. Few sensations in automobiling can match the thrill of the Lotus with its pressure rising.

The intimacy of the cockpit gives you no choice but to notice Lotus details. The impression is somewhere between hand-crafted and homemade. The round instruments look like off-the-shelf items inserted into a board. They're relatively small—there isn't much space—and the speedometer face, with mph and kph markings, is extremely busy. When the door is open, the heli-arced hinges look to be straight from the fab shop, without an intermediate stop at the paint booth. It must be said, too, that the cockpit seems all the more intimate because you can't see out. The rear corners are blocked, the view directly back is bisected by the wing, curbs are hidden by the high belt-line, and the driver's windshield pillar obscures left turns that would surely be fun if you could see them.

And yet, somehow, when the boost comes up and the scenery begins to blur, every staffer agrees that this Lotus has charm. You steer with your finger tips, urge the car on with your toe. Speed comes easily. This car goes like it looks.

FERRARI 348TS
4TH PLACE

This may be an all-new model, but it's still Ferrari as all hell—vivid in character, uncompromising in attitude. The body looks like a bright-red heat exchanger, flaunting enough slots and vents and scoops and grilles to cool the entire Italian Air Force. The exterior shape is narrow in front, flaring to enclose wide rubber in back. Huge seventeen-inch-diameter wheels dominate the profile.

Inside, amazingly, you'll find a terrific amount of room. The cockpit is wide and unconfining. Visibility, even to the rear corners, is quite good. The Spyder's lift-off roof is a snap to remove and reasonably quick to store aboard. Body structure, for an open car, is excellent.

The "t" stands for *transversale,* referring to the transverse five-speed mounted behind the longitudinal, 3405cc V-8. The traditional balkiness of Ferrari shifters has been carefully preserved in this car. We find it inexcusable.

Ferraris, being Ferraris, always generate a list of inexcusable details. The 348, in fact, is better than most, but there *is* a list, starting with seatbelts made in such a way that only fat guys can avoid slack in the lap strap.

This car has a tilt steering column, but when the wheel is lowered for an easy reach, the wheel rim cuts through the speedometer and the tach. That's better than an unreachable wheel, as on past models, but still inexcusable.

Finally, there is the inexcusable handling. This car feels as if it had four-wheel steering—with the rears steering in the wrong direction. Above 70 mph on twisting, undulating blacktops, the rear gets antsy. It wants to step out as you pick up the arcs of curves. Above 100 mph on such a road—particularly in a cross-wind—the car is difficult to hold in one lane. The instability is such that the top-speed run, a test our technical department has missed only once in our last 1025 car reviews, was a maybe thing for several days. Then the wind died and we did top speed. Our driver's words when he returned: "This is a terrible car to drive fast."

It also must be said that, even though the Ferrari topped the ranking on the skidpad at 0.90 g, it's so untidy at its limit that we'd never push anywhere near that hard on the road.

This is an exciting car, a little more exciting than we can stand at times.

Highs: *Snorty V-8, easy-off roof, generous cockpit space.*
Lows: *Balky shifter, queasy handling.*
The verdict: *A hey-look-at-me extrovert that just stops being fun at speed.*

The Ferrari sports elegant details, such as this door handle.

CHEVROLET CORVETTE ZR-1
3RD PLACE

This machine illustrates the incessant battle between the great and the goofy at Chevrolet. The 32-valve V-8 is nothing short of heroic, an engine to be reckoned with *anywhere*. And all the time you're driving it, you have to look at a glowing warning on the dash's message panel that says "Full Engine Power." Oh, you could kill the warning by switching off half the injectors (just turn the power key back to "Normal"), but who's going to pay nearly $20,000 extra for the ZR-1 option and then wean it?

The Corvette bursts with confused details: an instrument panel of contrived gauges in low-contrast orange on gray, adjustable-everything seats with so many buttons that you can never quite find comfort, a fancy black ratchet for removing the bolts holding on the roof when the roof really shouldn't be a bolt-on in the first place. This car is a rolling embarrassment to America until you stand on the gas.

And then... Get out of the way, Linguine Breath, Yankee Doodle coming through! Make no mistake: horsepower covers for a lot of sins.

Actually, the ZR-1's engine is not all wonderfulness. It starts hesitantly, a surprise in this day of electronic controls, and it broadcasts rude resonances at the low revs that are common when cruising in sixth gear.

At the same time, the car around the engine is not all bad. The air conditioner works great; both the Tour and the Sport positions on the electric shocks produced a reasonable ride on any road we found; and the seventeen-inch Goodyear Eagle ZRs stick to the pavement like epoxy. You can pull some g's in this car. You have to get used to hair-trigger steering response on the turn in, but once you've made friends with that you can use a high percent of the tires' capability.

This is a car that produces great numbers on the test track, and yet, when the day is done and the beer mugs are making rings on the bar, we always find ourselves saying, "If only..." If only it didn't rattle and creak so much. If only the instrument panel weren't so gauche. If only Chevrolet would get *serious*.

The Corvette is a love-hate kind of car, and the ZR-1 just makes it more so.

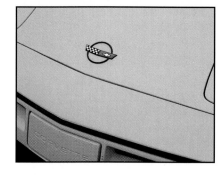

Highs: *Major-league horsepower, respect from those who know what ZR-1 means.*
Lows: *Overstyled instrument panel, gimmicky personality, junky construction.*
The verdict: *An all-star jock that runs like the wind but can't carry on a decent conversation.*

PORSCHE 911 CARRERA 4
2ND PLACE

At first, you'd swear that nothing had changed. You still sit chair high and dining-room upright. You look at the world through a picture windshield. Two front fenders loom large in the view, and the black wipers still park high on the glass. The dash holds five round dials right up where you can get a good look at them. Your legs angle inboard to clear the front-wheel hump, and the pedals swing awkwardly from their pivots on the floor. Yep, this is a 911 all right.

But the first push of the lever into low gear tells a different story. This is an entirely new car dressed to look like a 911.

Compared with the others, the 911's dress is dowdy, a molded–Jell-O shape going on three decades old. This is understated flash, a Coach bag rather than an Aigner, and maybe it would be boring were it not for the machinery below. The machinery has a winning way. The engine is unfussy, strong down low in the revs. The four-wheel-drive part is invisible in the dry. All the driver knows is that the Carrera 4 doesn't drive like a 911. You can lift from the power in the middle of a hard turn. Nothing untoward happens. The car just slows. Dip into the power and it doesn't flinch. Such stability is beyond imagining in a 911, and yet there it is.

There's more. The shifter, before always a vague long-distance connection to the gearbox back in the tail, now feels like a local call. It's clear and direct. And the steering has lost its kickback when traversing the rough stuff. Now it just steers, slowly at first as you turn off center, then intuitively and reliably as you increase the angle. The chassis feels honest and forthcoming in this car.

What the old body shape lacks in zoominess it more than makes up for in convenience. Entry is easy, you can see out in every direction, there's room behind the seats for your gym bag. The folding top minimizes the sound of rushing air too. The engine seems to smooth up and quiet down at highway speeds. Cruising is relatively painless for a sports car. We think the seats deserve special mention for their combination of firmness for good support, yet plushness too.

The best thing about the Carrera 4, though, is the way it drives. Imagine a 911 that knows how to act.

Highs: *Bountiful torque, intuitive response to your every input.*
Lows: *Not much pizazz for 80 grand.*
The verdict: *An agreeable new car dressed as a 911.*

A movable rear wing is just one clue that the Carrera 4 is no ordinary 911.

C/D Test Results

| | | acceleration, sec* | | | | | | | | | | |
		0–30 mph	0–60 mph	0–100 mph	0–130 mph	1/4-mile	top gear, 30–50 mph	top gear, 50–70 mph	top speed, mph	braking, 70–0 mph, ft	roadholding, 300-ft skidpad, g	maneuverability, 1000-ft slalom, mph
ACURA NSX		1.8	5.2	13.3	24.9	13.8 @ 102 mph	8.3	8.0	163	157	0.86	69.0
CHEVROLET CORVETTE ZR-1		2.0	4.9	11.3	19.8	13.4 @ 109 mph	14.6	14.2	171	159	0.88	65.5
FERRARI 348ts		2.0	6.0	15.3	28.9	14.5 @ 99 mph	8.8	8.3	166	187	0.90	63.5
LOTUS ESPRIT TURBO SE		1.6	4.8	12.7	25.3	13.5 @ 103 mph	14.8	9.5	157	186	0.79	65.0
PORSCHE 911 CARRERA 4 CABRIOLET		1.9	5.3	14.3	28.5	14.3 @ 100 mph	8.8	9.2	161	169	0.81	67.0

* Because our standard weather corrections could not fully compensate for the 100-degree temperature and 2300-foot altitude of our West Coast test site, the acceleration times published here may be slightly slower than normal.

Vital Statistics

| | | price, base/ as tested | engine | SAE net power/torque | transmission/ gear ratios:1/ maximum test speed, mph/ axle ratio:1 | dimensions, in | | | |
						wheel-base	length	width	height
ACURA NSX		$58,000 (estimated)/ $58,300 (estimated)	DOHC 24-valve V-6, 182 cu in (2977cc), aluminum block and heads, Honda electronic engine-control system with port fuel injection	270 bhp @ 7100 rpm/ 210 lb-ft @ 5300 rpm	5-speed/ 3.07, 1.72, 1.23, 0.97, 0.77/ 46, 82, 115, 146, 163/ 4.06	99.6	173.4	71.3	46.1
CHEVROLET CORVETTE ZR-1		$58,995/ $59,795	DOHC 32-valve V-8, 349 cu in (5727cc), aluminum block and heads, GM electronic engine-control system with port fuel injection	375 bhp @ 5800 rpm/ 370 lb-ft @ 5600 rpm	6-speed/ 2.68, 1.80, 1.31, 1.00, 0.75, 0.50/ 56, 83, 114, 150, 171, 149/ 3.45	96.2	176.5	74.0	46.7
FERRARI 348ts		$101,050/ $103,400	DOHC 32-valve V-8, 208 cu in (3405cc), aluminum block and heads, 2 Bosch Motronic electronic engine-control systems with port fuel injection	296 bhp @ 7000 rpm/ 224 lb-ft @ 4000 rpm	5-speed/ 3.21, 2.11, 1.46, 1.09, 0.86/ 45, 69, 99, 133, 166/ 3.56	96.5	166.5	74.6	46.1
LOTUS ESPRIT TURBO SE		$81,950/ $83,095	turbocharged and inter-cooled DOHC 16-valve 4-in-line, aluminum block and head, 133 cu in (2174cc), Lotus-GM electronic engine-control system with port fuel injection	264 bhp @ 6500 rpm/ 261 lb-ft @ 3900 rpm	5-speed/ 3.36, 2.05, 1.38, 1.03, 0.82/ 41, 67, 100, 134, 157/ 3.89	97.8	170.2	73.2	45.7
PORSCHE 911 CARRERA 4 CABRIOLET		$77,800/ $80,257	SOHC flat 6, aluminum block and heads, 220 cu in (3600cc), Bosch Motronic electronic engine-control system with port fuel injection	247 bhp @ 6100 rpm/ 228 lb-ft @ 4800 rpm	5-speed/ 3.50, 2.12, 1.44, 1.09, 0.87/ 40, 67, 98, 129, 161/ 3.44	89.4	168.3	65.0	52.0

Engines left to right:
Lotus, Ferrari, Corvette,
Porsche, Acura.

	interior sound level, dBA			fuel economy, mpg		
Mile	**full throttle**	**70–mph cruising**	**70–mph coasting**	**EPA city**	**EPA highway**	**C/D 650-mile trip**
9	89	78	78	19 (projected)	24 (projected)	19
3	87	78	78	16	25	16
1	93	83	83	13	19	17
2	88	79	79	17	27	18
7	89	80	79	15	22	20

curb weight, lb	weight distribution, % F/R	fuel tank, gal	interior volume, cu ft			suspension		brakes, F/R	tires
			front	**rear**	**luggage**	**front**	**rear**		
3020	41.7/58.3	18.5	49	N/A	5	ind, unequal-length control arms, coil springs, anti-roll bar	ind, unequal-length control arms and a toe-control link, coil springs, anti-roll bar	vented disc/ vented disc; anti-lock control	Yokohama A-022; F: 205/50ZR-15, R: 225/50ZR-16
3520	52.8/47.2	20.0	49	N/A	18	ind, unequal-length control arms, transverse plastic leaf spring, 3-position cockpit-adjustable electronically controlled shock absorbers, anti-roll bar	ind; fixed-length half-shaft, 2 lateral links, and 2 trailing links per side side; transverse plastic leaf spring; 3-position cockpit-adjustable electronically controlled shock absorbers; anti-roll bar	vented disc/ vented disc; anti-lock control	Goodyear Eagle ZR; F: P275/40ZR-17, R: P315/35ZR-17
3300	39.4/60.6	25.1	47	N/A	7	ind, unequal-length control arms, coil springs, anti-roll bar	ind, unequal-length control arms, coil springs, anti-roll bar	vented disc/ vented disc; anti-lock control	Bridgestone RE71; F: 215/50ZR-17, R: 255/45ZR-17
2980	41.6/58.4	18.5	47	N/A	8	ind, unequal-length control arms, coil springs, anti-roll bar	ind, 1 trailing arm and 2 lateral links per side, coil springs	vented disc/ disc	Goodyear Eagle ZR; F: 215/50ZR-15, R: 245/50ZR-16
3280	42.7/57.3	20.3	43	13	4	ind, strut located by a control arm, coil springs, anti-roll bar	ind, semi-trailing arm, coil springs, anti-roll bar	vented disc/ vented disc; anti-lock control	Bridgestone RE71; F: 205/55ZR-16, R: 225/50ZR-16

Acura NSX
1st Place

If you made up a list of mandatories for your Eroticar, then drove an NSX, you'd swear that Honda had snuck a peak at your list.

You'd specify a brilliant engine, one with big power and nice noises and a redline as high as a phone number. The NSX's V-6 is exactly that. It's terrifically flexible around town at 1500 rpm, and it just gets stronger and stronger all the way to eight grand. The music it makes as it climbs would be a hit on CD.

Your list would include Olympic-class handling. The NSX has that too: good grip —but more important, usable grip. The chassis is free of bad habits, and the steering transmits clean information to the driver. We've always found the Honda Prelude to be a special car in the sense that its limits are not particularly high but a driver can comfortably use virtually all the car has to offer. The same is true of the NSX. This car is very quick on its feet, quicker than all except possibly the Corvette ZR-1, which has an advantage in power.

Unless you're a masochist, your list would call for a cockpit that fits like a Barcalounger. Again, the NSX delivers. This car has plenty of elbow room, the controls are placed where they belong, and the seat—amazingly—fits all sizes. Staffers on this test ranged from moderately tall skinny guys to man-mountain types, and, to the man, they liked the seats. The NSX's buckets are the only street seats we can think of that offer a measure of shoulder restraint during cornering, and we found that to be particularly useful.

Your list would call for excitement, too, that indefinable symphony of details that sets your pulse on fast forward when you drive. Again the NSX delivers. It starts with the view. The sky and the road seem so close you could reach right out and touch them. The steering column tilts and telescopes for a driving position that fits *you*. The controls work so smoothly. The gauges are so easy to read. This car makes a hard-wire connection between you and the joy of driving.

What more could you ask?

The NSX will make a profound change in the market for Eroticars. Because, apart from the near-$60,000 price, there is no hardship to driving this car. Getting in and out is easy. The ride is fine. There are no bad noises. The climate control works flawlessly. You can have an automatic transmission and power steering if you want. The rich guys in Bev Hills will be buying NSXs for their floozies.

Lucky floozies.

Honda revitalized the motorcycle market in the sixties and reshaped the small-car market in the seventies. Now it's going to teach the world how to build Learjets for the ground.

Highs: Love at first drive.
Lows: Having to leave the cockpit.
The verdict: The first Herocar with impeccable manners.

The winning NSX has it all: stunning looks, a comfortable and inviting cockpit, a rev-forever engine that's perfectly happy motoring around town, and confidence-inspiring handling.

		engine	trans-mission	brakes	handling	ergo-nomics	comfort	ride	refinement	cachet	fun to drive	OVERALL RATING
Editors' Ratings	**ACURA NSX**	9	9	9	9	9	9	9	10	8	10	**93**
	CHEVROLET CORVETTE ZR-1	8	8	8	9	8	8	9	7	7	8	**81**
	FERRARI 348ts	8	4	8	5	6	7	7	7	9	7	**69**
	LOTUS ESPRIT TURBO SE	7	7	8	8	5	5	7	6	8	7	**66**
	PORSCHE 911 CARRERA 4 CABRIOLET	8	9	9	9	8	8	7	9	8	9	**87**

Five editors rated the vehicles in each of eleven categories; the scores presented are averages. A 1-to-10 scale (10 being best) was used for all categories except the Overall Rating, where a 1-to-100 scale was used. The Overall Rating for each vehicle was assigned independently; it is not a summation of the vehicle's points in the other categories.

PHOTOGRAPHY BY KEN HANNA

BUICK PARK AVENUE ULTRA

By Brock Yates

Among the nation's thought police, it is well understood that praising an American automobile is akin to serving Velveeta squares at a wine-and-cheese party. Status slaves know that Detroit iron stands at the first turnoff on the road to social ruin.

Never mind that any number of second-rate imports enjoy knee-jerk celebration in the same circles. Several unreliable British crocks, a few aging Swedish beauties, and a number of overpriced German panzers confer instant credibility.

One root of this pandering has been Detroit's dereliction of duty over the past few decades. The American automakers' slump in product planning and quality control has become the stuff of legend and need not be repeated here. Thankfully, that dismal slippage is now being corrected. Lo and behold, several of the cars appearing from the dingy realms of the Motor City may force the trendies to choke on their brie.

May we offer the Buick Park Avenue Ultra as an example of this Motown transformation? Of course, until recently a Buick—*any* Buick—was considered to be at the very least jejune, at the very worst, terminally gauche. But in case you have been vacationing on Ellesmere Island or have been a guest of the Islamic jihad for the past few years, let us bring you up to date: the Buick Division of General Motors is on a roll. Its product lineup

and general level of quality have made great advances under the leadership of general manager Ed Mertz and his engineering-oriented staff.

Formerly known as the Electra, the new Park Avenue series sports a profile openly derivative of Jaguar's XJ6 and a lavish interior in the American idiom. Unfettered by reality, Detroit stylists can often go berserk in the gadget department, and in this sense the Park Avenue did not escape unscathed. Surely the installation of dual lighted vanity mirrors in the rear-seat compartment of the Ultra model borders on wretched excess, as do its passenger-side climate controls, mounted on the right-side door panel. This is a convenience item, but when one considers the other components that might have been incorporated into the car (rear-wheel disc brakes come immediately to mind), the passenger-side climate controls seem to represent not only added complexity and cost but also a faint taint of parvenuism.

Not so the seats, which are leather-covered and quite comfortable for all occupants save devotees of pure buckets. (The base-model Park Avenue gets cloth upholstery.) Our test car's front seats were fully adjustable and provided excellent support on long hauls. Unlike some entrants in the luxury class—including the Lexus LS400 and the Infiniti Q45—the Park Avenue Ultra gives its front-seat passengers the same range of adjustments as it gives the driver. This ought always be the case in cars of this ilk, and, to its credit, Buick has paid proper attention to this sometimes-ignored issue. Mercifully, Buick has also ended its fascination with video-game instrument panels. Upscale Buicks now have neat, unpretentious analog dials.

An even greater adjunct to the Park Avenue Ultra's appeal is the bargain-priced ($17) optional Gran Touring suspension,

which offers a slightly tighter, 3.06:1 final drive; stiffer spring and shock rates; and Goodyear Eagle 215/65R-15 GT+4s mounted on tasteful cast-aluminum wheels.

Motivational energy comes from the latest version of Buick's 3.8-liter V-6 with port fuel injection and a counterrotating balance shaft. When this torquey 170-hp powerplant is coupled with GM's new electronically controlled 4T60-E Hydra-matic four-speed automatic, the result is a drivetrain that provides world-class smoothness, responsiveness, and economy (18 mpg in the city and 27 mpg on the highway, according to the EPA).

As our $29,369 test car ascertained, the Park Avenue Ultra is now a serious over-the-road passenger car. Its slippery shape (0.31 Cd) offers impressive economy and silent running at lusty Interstate speeds. A recent 300-mile trip at a steady 80 mph resulted in 26 mpg and two thoroughly comfortable passengers.

By comparison, an identical journey made a few days earlier in a Lexus LS400 left both riders agreeing that the Buick rivaled the Japanese wondercar in terms of silence, high-velocity tracking, and general road manners. Of course, the 170-hp Park Avenue can't match the performance of the 250-hp Lexus or other high-powered luxury cruisers. The Buick is strong off the line, and 60 mph comes up in a respectable span of 9.7 seconds; but the surge to 100 mph takes a lengthy 24 seconds more, and top speed is a mere 106 mph. Braking is also unimpressive, with stops from 70 mph requiring 207 feet.

Still, the car would be perfectly at home—on the Interstate or the autobahn —at 80–100 mph with four passengers aboard. Partially offsetting the general aura of quality and tautness is the Park Avenue's overwrought styling, with its glutinous blob of chrome brightwork on the lower beltline representing a throw-

back to the worst days of Detroit gim-crackery. Buick design chief William Porter calls this treatment a reaction to "Euro-somebody" and "Japanese stir-fry" styling. We call it cornball overkill.

Presuming that one resists the temptation to torch the extra glitz off the door panels, the Park Avenue Ultra is a heartening expression of the venerable American spirit of "can do." Yes, the machine could use rear-wheel disc brakes. Yes, a console-mounted shift lever with a manual control button for third-to-fourth gear changes would be a pleasant addition. Yes, the suspension can get a bit wormy on lumpy surfaces, and torque steer becomes an ugly reality when the Park Avenue is pressed hard in tight corners.

Those deficiencies notwithstanding, one dares to speculate that nine out of ten Pavlovian loyalists to the European luxury-car credo, if blindfolded and put into this Buick, would be convinced they were aboard one of the best of breed from BMW, Mercedes-Benz, or Jaguar. Whether those loyalists like it or not, the Buick Park Avenue Ultra is that good.

Highs: *First-cabin comfort and excellent drivetrain.*
Lows: *Gobs of Motown retro-glitz, no four-wheel disc brakes.*
The verdict:
Outstanding comeback in a luxury sedan.

BUICK PARK AVENUE ULTRA

Vehicle type: front-engine, front-wheel-drive, 5-passenger, 4-door sedan

Price as tested: $29,369

Options on test car: base Buick Park Avenue Ultra, $27,420; Delco GM-Bose music system, $723; premium option package (includes power antenna, instrumentation package, illuminated entry, low-oil indicator, reminder package), $529; California emissions, $100; Gran Touring package, $17, freight, $580

Standard accessories: power steering, windows, seats, and locks, A/C, cruise control, tilt steering, rear defroster

Sound system: Delco GM-Bose AM/FM-stereo radio/cassette, 4 speakers

ENGINE
Type . . . . V-6, iron block and heads
Bore x stroke . . . . 3.80 x 3.40 in, 96.5 x 86.4mm
Displacement . . . . 231 cu in, 3791cc
Compression ratio 8.5:1
Engine-control system . . . . GM with port fuel injection
Emissions controls . . . . 3-way catalytic converter, feedback fuel-air-ratio control
Valve gear . . . . pushrods, hydraulic lifters
Power (SAE net) . . . . 170 bhp @ 4800 rpm
Torque (SAE net) . . . . 220 lb-ft @ 3200 rpm

DRIVETRAIN
Transmission . . . . 4-speed automatic with lockup torque converter
Final-drive ratio 3.06:1

Gear	Ratio	Mph/1000 rpm	Max. test speed
I	2.92	8.4	44 mph (5300 rpm)
II	1.57	15.6	82 mph (5300 rpm)
III	1.00	24.4	106 mph (4350 rpm)
IV	0.70	34.9	106 mph (3050 rpm)

DIMENSIONS AND CAPACITIES
Wheelbase . . . . 110.8 in
Track, F/R . . . . 60.5/60.2 in
Length . . . . 205.2 in
Width . . . . 74.9 in

Height . . . . 55.7 in
Ground clearance . . . . 5.6 in
Curb weight . . . . 3626 lb
Weight distribution, F/R 62.6/37.4%
Fuel capacity . . . . 18.0 gal
Oil capacity . . . . 5.0 qt
Water capacity . . . . 11.7 qt

CHASSIS/BODY
Type . . . . unit construction with a rubber-isolated powertrain cradle
Body material . . . . welded steel stampings

SAE volume, front seat . . . . 56 cu ft
rear seat . . . . 54 cu ft
luggage space . . . . 20 cu ft
Front seats . . . . bucket
Seat adjustments . . . . fore and aft, seatback angle, front height, rear height
General comfort . . . . poor fair **good** excellent
Fore-and-aft support . . . . poor fair **good** excellent
Lateral support . . . . poor **fair** good excellent

SUSPENSION
F: . . . . ind, strut located by a control arm, coil springs, anti-roll bar
R: . . . . ind, strut located by a control arm and a lateral link, coil springs, automatic-leveling shock absorbers, anti-roll bar

STEERING
Type . . . . rack-and-pinion, power-assisted
Turns lock-to-lock 3.1
Turning circle curb-to-curb . . . . 39.4 ft

BRAKES
F: . . . . 10.9 x 1.3-in vented disc
R: . . . . 8.9 x 1.8-in cast-iron drum
Power assist . . . . vacuum with anti-lock control

WHEELS AND TIRES
Wheel size . . . . 6.0 x 15 in
Wheel type . . . . cast aluminum
Tires . . . . . . Goodyear Eagle GT + 4 M + S, P215/65R-15
Test inflation pressures, F/R . . . . 30/30 psi

CAR AND DRIVER TEST RESULTS

ACCELERATION
	Seconds
Zero to 30 mph	2.9
40 mph	4.6
50 mph	6.9
60 mph	9.7
70 mph	13.0
80 mph	17.4
90 mph	24.3
100 mph	33.7
Top-gear passing time, 30–50 mph	4.6
50–70 mph	6.8
Standing ¼-mile	17.1 sec @ 79 mph
Top speed	106 mph

BRAKING
70–0 mph @ impending lockup . . . . 207 ft
Fade . . . . none **moderate** heavy

HANDLING
Roadholding, 300-ft-dia skidpad . . . . 0.75 g
Understeer . . . . minimal **moderate** excessive

COAST-DOWN MEASUREMENTS
Road horsepower @ 30 mph . . . . 6 hp
50 mph . . . . 16 hp
70 mph . . . . 35 hp

FUEL ECONOMY
EPA city driving . . . . **18 mpg**
EPA highway driving . . . . 27 mpg
C/D observed fuel economy . . . . **20 mpg**

INTERIOR SOUND LEVEL
Idle . . . . 45 dBA
Full-throttle acceleration . . . . 74 dBA
70-mph cruising . . . . 69 dBA
70-mph coasting . . . . 69 dBA

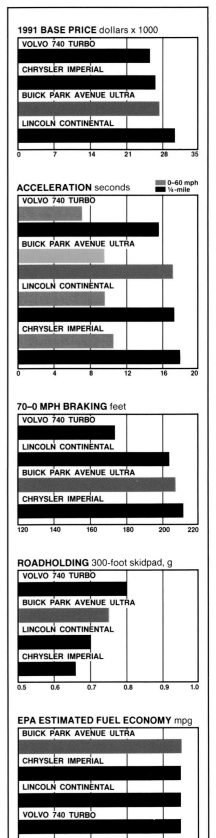

1991 BASE PRICE dollars x 1000
- VOLVO 740 TURBO
- CHRYSLER IMPERIAL
- BUICK PARK AVENUE ULTRA
- LINCOLN CONTINENTAL

0 7 14 21 28 35

ACCELERATION seconds
■ 0–60 mph ■ ¼-mile
- VOLVO 740 TURBO
- BUICK PARK AVENUE ULTRA
- LINCOLN CONTINENTAL
- CHRYSLER IMPERIAL

0 4 8 12 16 20

70–0 MPH BRAKING feet
- VOLVO 740 TURBO
- LINCOLN CONTINENTAL
- BUICK PARK AVENUE ULTRA
- CHRYSLER IMPERIAL

120 140 160 180 200 220

ROADHOLDING 300-foot skidpad, g
- VOLVO 740 TURBO
- BUICK PARK AVENUE ULTRA
- LINCOLN CONTINENTAL
- CHRYSLER IMPERIAL

0.5 0.6 0.7 0.8 0.9 1.0

EPA ESTIMATED FUEL ECONOMY mpg
- BUICK PARK AVENUE ULTRA
- CHRYSLER IMPERIAL
- LINCOLN CONTINENTAL
- VOLVO 740 TURBO

0 4 8 12 16 20

MERCURY CAPRI XR2

By John Phillips III

When the Mazda Miata appeared in the fall of '89, you can bet the farm that an entire floor of product planners at Ford were gulping Maalox and stomping around with bright-blue veins popping up at their temples. Mazda, it seemed, had stolen their thunder.

At the time, the Miata was hogging the covers of all sorts of magazines, from yours truly's to *Leisure Living in Leather* —even making the "CBS Evening News" and National Public Radio—while the idea for a born-again, back-to-basics roadster was Ford's. At least that was the thinking causing all those blue veins.

Six years earlier, long before Mazda's Bob Hall began doodling the characters "MX-5" on office notepads, Ford had unveiled a sports car called the Barchetta on the show-car circuit. It was a simple front-drive two-seater—using an engine and drivetrain already proved to be as reliable as a Stanley crowbar—and Ford was willing to bet it was what sporting America wanted. It was styled in Italy, used mechanicals from Mazda, and would be assembled in Australia.

That Ford roadster has at last arrived in Mercury showrooms. There are two versions: the 100-hp Capri with a 1991 base sticker price of $12,588, and a 132-hp turbo-charged and intercooled Capri XR2 for $15,522, which works out to an extra $91 for each additional horse.

Because we can't just say no, we lunged headfirst for the version with the most horsepower, the XR2.

Acceleration in a 2545-pound car with a 132-hp engine is substantial. No nosebleeds, but you can smoke the XR2's front tires for a full ten feet. Zero to 60 mph requires only 7.9 seconds, and that's 1.3 seconds quicker—a car-length or two—than the Miata. The blown Capri moves smartly through the quarter-mile in sixteen seconds flat, arriving at 86 mph (comparable to a Chevy Beretta GTZ). Top speed, with the soft top up, is 126 mph. Imagine the potential performance if the XR2 did not weigh 335 pounds more than the Miata.

Driving around town, the Capri's IHI turbo/intercooler installation goes unnoticed. From idle to peak torque (3000 rpm), the engine neither bogs nor lugs, failings common to many turbocharged powerplants. In fact, 90 percent of peak torque is available as low as 2500 rpm. This engine is so tractable that second gear can be used to pull away from stoplights, with only a bit of clutch slippage.

But in Bob Glidden–style sprints

Acceleration in this 2545-pound car, with its 132-hp engine, lets you smoke the front tires a full ten feet and do 0–60 mph in 7.9 seconds.

typical of turbocharged engines and old Buick Electras. The engine's lusty contralto song bursts through loud and clear thereafter, however. And you'll hear it often. This sixteen-valve Mazda powerplant rushes eagerly to its 6500-rpm redline (500 rpm beyond its power peak), and the excitement hasn't greatly diminished even when the electronic limiter triggers at seven grand.

Although the Capri is intended to be a hard-core sports car, its front and rear struts do a terrific job of dissipating impacts, and the ride is further softened by the conservative Dunlop SP Sport D8s. The front struts, in particular, feel as though they travel through long strokes. Our test car failed to fetch up against any pothole that fully compressed its springs. In Michigan, that's saying something.

In steady-state turns, you expect a front-drive car with 64 percent of its weight at the nose to understeer. And it does. The XR2's skidpad result of 0.77 g lags well behind the Miata's 0.82 g and puts it on par with far less ambitious cars, like the Plymouth Sundance RS. What you don't expect is the Capri's occasional habit of suddenly wagging its bespoiled tail—noticeable if you turn in too abruptly or upset the car's balance in mid-

through first and second, torque steer is evident, particularly on bumpy roads or through sharp turns. Although it won't nose the Capri into the nearest drainage ditch, it is sufficiently pervasive that you quickly find yourself disciplining your right foot until both front wheels are pointed straight down a billiard-table-smooth piece of pavement.

Up to 4000 rpm, the XR2's exhaust makes that whispery, whooshing noise turn. A stab of brakes will cause it. So will scabrous pavement. This quirk is not dangerous but will surprise the pants off a few dental hygienists. Practice your trail-braking techniques and you can intentionally rotate the Capri's tail a few fun degrees, but work on this caper cautiously. Remember, we're dealing here with the previous-generation chassis from a 1988 Mazda 323GT. If this conservative, ride-biased platform were a wine, vintners would comment, "It pours well"—a remark reserved for workmanlike spirits about which there is utterly nothing else to say.

The Capri's rod-actuated shift linkage, although not as fast or direct as the Miata's, is nonetheless fine. A little more resistance at each gate would be better, so we'd know sooner when we'd engaged a gear. The clutch is light, with silky take-up. Our only complaint is that the Capri's throttle and brake pedals, like the Miata's, ought to be a half-inch closer to facilitate easier heal-and-toeing.

Tuned for city driving, the standard power-assisted steering is light but remains linear and nicely weighted in the critical 45-to-65-mph range, where most twisty-road touring is accomplished. Fat and wrapped in leather, the steering wheel feels great, too. But in place of the ride-conscious Dunlops, we wish the Aussies had opted for tires more concerned with handling tasks.

One of the Capri's strong suits is the way it tracks down the Interstate. Its supple suspension and fuss-free steering made possible a 290-mile trip from Ann Arbor to Indianapolis without the need to stop even once for a leg stretch. (A trip we made, by the way, on one 11.1-gallon tank of fuel.) The same jaunt in the more nervous Miata would have required at least one, and maybe two, coffee-and-relaxation breaks.

Four-wheel discs are standard, but the brakes are difficult to modulate. You wouldn't expect the fronts to lock prematurely on a car with this weight distribution, but they do. In fact, you'll need to locate 209 feet of uncluttered highway to stop from 70 mph. That's three feet more than is required for a Lincoln Continental. Anti-lock brakes might alleviate this problem but are not offered.

The Capri XR2's single most glaring flaw is cowl shake—a lack of structural rigidity. The Australian engineers buttressed the platform at six sites, but it wasn't enough. Even on roads not partic-

ularly rough, the A-pillars jiggle and the steering wheel shudders in your hands. (Glance in the rear-view mirror and you can see the spoiler on the trunk appear to move laterally in one direction as the mirror itself moves in the other.) And the doors creak and moan at their latches. These character faults do not inspire confidence. What sorts of rattles and twisted trim bits will appear at, say, 30,000 miles?

Structural rigidity doesn't count in the showroom, of course, where one of the XR2's charms is that its buyer need not tick a single option box. Standard stuff includes power windows and twin electric remote-control mirrors (neither available on a Miata), a clever but flimsy height adjustor for the driver's seat, air conditioning, cruise control (which, on our car, obstinately kicked in 5 mph below our request), power door locks, a driver-side air bag, and an AM/FM/cassette player. We tried the optional upgraded sound system ($280), but the Capri's cockpit (the Miata's, also) is too noisy to make out whatever it is that 2 Live Crew is saying to inflame mothers everywhere, particularly in Texas.

But it is otherwise a civilized and practical cabin. You can store two full-size Samsonite suitcases in the back seat or, briefly at least, force-fit one adult back there—if the front passenger agrees to move his seat forward. For roadside naps, the front seats recline nearly horizontal, rare in a sports car (we took a successful two-hour doze in the Capri). There are extra-storage hidey-holes under the trunk floor. The trunk itself will swallow four five-gallon jerrycans. And you can stick your skis through a clever 27-by-8-inch

In sprints through first and second gear, torque steer is evident on sharp turns, making you watch your right foot.

Highs: *Good cargo space, cushy ride, blowered brawn.*
Lows: *Dubious rigidity, dull handling, unexciting body.*
The verdict: *Plush and quick, the thirty-something roadster.*

trap door that leads through the soft-top storage nacelle and into the back seat, which itself folds flat. A useful layout.

The secondary controls are easy to reach and simple—with the lone exception of the headlamp switch, which is a weird two-position recessed rocker that requires a lot of groping in the dark. The cockpit's one clear ergonomic flaw is the ignition-key release button on the lower left-hand side of the steering column. Removing the ignition key requires two hands.

Some features are delightful. A flash-to-pass stalk, for example, raises the pop-up headlamps almost instantly. The seat fabric has a handsome herringbone-tweed look and is as good at dissipating heat as it is at hiding dirt—definite considerations in a convertible. There's a tonneau lid made of steel for those of us who cannot resist the temptation—yes, yes, some

danger is involved—to sit on the rear deck with our feet planted on the rear bench seat. (You never know when you'll be asked to ride back there in a Shriners' parade.)

Lowering the Capri's vinyl, cotton-backed top is a seven-step operation for which you must get out and work. With practice, we managed the job once in just over 90 seconds. Top-down motoring is noisy and windy, but fierce buffeting of the back of your head—a condition that makes you wish you were wearing a baseball cap—does not begin until 50 mph.

Turbo notwithstanding, we expected the Capri to pale in the Miata's popular glow. But they are surprisingly different cars. If you overlook its annoying body flex, the Capri is a nicely finished and well-rounded car that may, as Ford predicts, find its way into the garages of many buyers who never expected to wind up in roadsters. The Capri is set up for ride comfort over handling, and it's true it doesn't deliver the visceral driving excitement of the Miata through the neighborhood esses. But it's better at covering long distances and more comfortable in the reality of daily traffic jams.

Think of the Capri XR2 as a Mazda 323GT with a flip top and a tiny back seat. The new Mercury sportabout passes muster as primary transportation, working as well for picking up groceries as it does for top-down after-dinner drives to view the sunset. A bit subdued for our tastes, perhaps, but the deal—it's $1700 less than the Miata—includes a grin-to-dollar ratio surpassed only by nitrous oxide.

THE CAPRI VERSUS THE MIATA

They won't look you in the eye when they say it, but Mercury's marketing guys insist that the Capri doesn't compete with Mazda's Miata. But that doesn't affect passersby, and sooner or later they will ask the inevitable out loud: "How's it compare with the Miata?"

Here's the answer.

Styling: As the Lotus Elan of the nineties, the Miata looks smarter and fresher than Jamie Lee Curtis at her high-school graduation. On the other hand, the Capri's lines are knife-edged and angular, its deck spoiler is a fussy tack-on, and its removable hard top (a $1200 option) has a formal roofline inappropriate for a sporty roadster. Advantage: Miata.

Interior: The Capri's cockpit beats the Miata's in fit and finish and in its lineup of standard amenities. Power windows, door locks, and side-view mirrors make the Capri a more comfortable place to play. Moreover, under full throttle and at 70-mph cruising/coasting, the Capri makes less noise. Advantage: Capri.

Packaging: With its back seat, its spe-

COUNTERPOINT

I'll tell you my big problem with the new Capri: it's so homely it could stop a Timex. Its every line seems to scream, "I wish I were a sedan, a very *sensible* sedan."

What's going on here? I thought Ford's designers had all the right pen strokes in their repertoire. Sports cars are supposed to be fun, frivolous devices—four-wheeled pieces of costume jewelry that make you look good and feel better. How could the organization that turned out such elegant machines as the Probe, the Taurus, and the Thunderbird have lost sight of that?

Even the Capri's interior dampens my enthusiasm. A sports car ought to fit you like a custom-made suit; the Capri seems baggy around the edges. The view out front is blocked by a high cowl and a dash that towers over you. And no amount of fiddling with the seats can make you feel as if you're in a low-slung sportster.

The XR2 is anything but a disappointment to drive, but that's only half of its mission in life. If a sports car is going to elicit an involuntary "I gotta have one," it had better pump out plenty of voltage just sitting at the curb. —*Rich Ceppos*

Its cowl shimmies more than a last-act stripper, but the Capri runs like hot barbecue sauce. So I nicknamed this little sweetie "Shake 'n Bake."

Mazda's much-heralded Miata offers less shake but also a lot less bake. It's more than a matter of power: it's the difference between a runabout and a real car. The Capri skips the Miata's endearing tininess—the zippiness evident in its minuscule dimensions—but wins as an everyday automobile.

The Capri lacks no necessities, yet it's also outfitted with many niceties. Its comfort lasts all day and more. Its steering, tracking, handling, and braking give you the feeling that this is one of those rare cars that takes care of its business, leaving you free to take care of yours. The bare bones of mere transportation have been covered in a modicum of muscle, very little lard, and a fetching skin. The Capri may not be as cootchy-cootchy cute as the Miata, but it's a more complete piece. When it comes to companionship, it's pretty tempting to wind up with both shake and bake. —*Larry Griffin*

It almost goes without saying that if you want a great color TV, you buy a Sony. Sure, there are other sets that offer as good a picture, more features on the remote, and a lower price tag. But if you want the best, the industry standard, the TV that you look at even when it's off, you buy a Sony. Easy.

In the world of affordable two-seat convertibles, the Mazda Miata is a Sony and the Mercury Capri XR2 is a worthy also-ran. I'm not going to debate their respective merits; each has its virtues and drawbacks. But the Miata is clearly the pacesetter—a stylish, high-quality machine that exhibits attention to every detail. Let's be honest here: do you really think any Miata buyers are going to look longingly at the Capri and say, "You know, I wish I'd bought that little Mercury?" But you can bet that more than a few Capri buyers are going to feel a wave of envy when a Miata rolls by.

Whether you're shopping for a color TV set or a two-seat convertible, you don't *need* the best. But if you *want* the best, the choice is obvious.
—*Arthur St. Antoine*

cial soft-top storage nacelle, and its bigger trunk, the Capri is the hands-down winner for anyone who has to carry clubs to the links or Rex to the vet's. Advantage: Capri.

Convertible top: The Capri's hard tonneau wins points for its sharp, uncluttered good looks. But retracting the Miata's top is half as complicated as retracting the Capri's, and it can be done from the driver's seat. Advantage: Miata.

Visibility: With its top up, the Capri has a big blind spot in what passes for the C-pillar area. The Miata has it, too, but it's smaller. Advantage: Miata.

Primary controls: The Miata's steering and shifter are both faster and more direct than the Capri's. Advantage: Miata.

Structural rigidity: Even with 35,000 miles on its legs, the Miata exhibits less cowl shake than the Capri did with just 4000 miles on its odometer. Advantage: Miata.

Acceleration: Maybe it looks like the fix is in, because it wouldn't be fair to compare a turbocharged Capri with the normally aspirated Miata. But because you asked, here's the deal: the XR2 is 1.3 seconds quicker to 60 mph, rolls through the quarter-mile 0.8 second sooner, and has a 10-mph-higher top speed. Advantage: turbo.

Handling: The Miata has a half-g better grip on the skidpad, offers almost 50/50 front/rear balance (in part because of its appealing rear-drive layout), doesn't understeer as resolutely as the Capri, and more readily encourages its driver to toss it into turns. Advantage: Miata.

Freeway manners: The Miata's ultrafast steering, its tiny 89.2-inch wheelbase, and the ease with which it is yanked off course by pavement irregularities make it a nervous, fatiguing partner on Interstate jaunts. Advantage: Capri.

Linescore: Miata 6, Capri 4.

Our conclusion: The Capri is the more practical, civilized car, a roadster that will work as day-to-day transportation. With the Capri, you won't need a "grown-up" car in the garage as a backup. The Miata, on the other hand, is a no-compromises sports car that feels more solidly built.

It's the difference between, say, the Honda CRX Si and the Civic Hatchback Si —both are fun to drive and they are mechanically similar, but they have slightly different missions. Think of the Miata as a back-to-basics sportster—the car you want for the Angeles Crest Highway. Think of the Capri as a soft-top runabout —the car you want for errand-hopping and commuting. —*JPIII*

MERCURY CAPRI XR2

Vehicle type: front-engine, front-wheel-drive, 2+2-passenger, 2-door convertible

Price as tested: $16,157

Options on test car: base Mercury Capri XR2, $15,522; sound-system upgrade, $280; freight, $355

Standard accessories: power steering, windows, and locks, A/C, cruise control

Sound system: Ford Premium Sound AM/FM-stereo radio/cassette, 4 speakers

ENGINE
Type . . . . turbocharged and intercooled 4-in-line, iron block and aluminum head
Bore x stroke . . . . 3.07 x 3.29 in, 78.0 x 83.6mm
Displacement . . . . 98 cu in, 1598cc
Compression ratio 7.9:1
Engine-control system . . . . Mazda electronic with port fuel injection
Emissions controls . . . . 3-way catalytic converter, feedback fuel-air-ratio control
Turbocharger . . . . IHI RHB5
Waste gate. . . . . integral
Maximum boost pressure . . . . 8.6 psi
Valve gear . . . . belt-driven double overhead cams, 4 valves per cylinder, hydraulic lifters
Power (SAE net) . . . . .132 bhp @ 6000 rpm
Torque (SAE net) . . . . 136 lb-ft @ 3000 rpm

DRIVETRAIN
Transmission 5-speed
Final-drive ratio 3.85:1

Gear	Ratio	Mph/1000 rpm	Max. test speed
I	3.31	5.1	33 mph (6500 rpm)
II	1.83	9.1	59 mph (6500 rpm)
III	1.23	13.6	88 mph (6500 rpm)
IV	0.97	17.3	112 mph (6500 rpm)
V	0.80	20.9	126 mph (6050 rpm)

DIMENSIONS AND CAPACITIES
Wheelbase . . . . 94.7 in
Track, F/R . . . . 54.9/56.0 in
Length . . . . 166.1 in

Width . . . . 64.6 in
Height. . . . . 50.2 in
Frontal area . . . . 19.0 sq ft
Ground clearance . . . . 4.9 in
Curb weight . . . . 2545 lb
Weight distribution, F/R 63.5/36.5%
Fuel capacity . . . . 11.1 gal
Oil capacity . . . . 3.2 qt
Water capacity . . . . 6.3 qt

CHASSIS/BODY
Type . . . . unit construction
Body material . . . . .welded steel stampings

INTERIOR
SAE volume, front seat . . . . 46 cu ft
          rear seat . . . . 19 cu ft
          luggage space . . . . 6 cu ft
Front seats . . . . bucket
Seat adjustments . . . . fore and aft, seatback angle, height, lumbar support
General comfort . . . . poor fair **good** excellent
Fore-and-aft support . . . . poor **fair** good excellent
Lateral support . . . . poor **fair** good excellent

SUSPENSION
F: . . . . ind, strut located by a control arm, coil springs, anti-roll bar
R: . . . . .ind, strut located by 1 trailing link and 2 lateral links, coil springs, anti-roll bar

STEERING
Type . . . . rack-and-pinion, power-assisted
Turns lock-to-lock 3.2
Turning circle curb-to-curb . . . . 32.5 ft

BRAKES
F: . . . . 10.2 x 0.7-in vented disc
R: . . . . 8.7 x 0.4-in disc
Power assist . . . . .vacuum

WHEELS AND TIRES
Wheel size . . . . 5.5 x 14 in
Wheel type . . . . cast aluminum
Tires . . . . Dunlop SP Sport D8, P185/60HR-14
Test inflation pressures, F/R . . . . 32/29 psi

---

CAR AND DRIVER TEST RESULTS

ACCELERATION
	Seconds
Zero to 30 mph	2.5
40 mph	3.9
50 mph	5.6
60 mph	7.9
70 mph	10.6
80 mph	14.0
90 mph	18.3
100 mph	23.9

Top-gear passing time, 30–50 mph 11.3
          50–70 mph 10.2
Standing ¼-mile . . . . 16.0 sec @ 86 mph
Top speed . . . . 126 mph

BRAKING
70–0 mph @ impending lockup . . . . 209 ft
Modulation . . . . poor **fair** good excellent
Fade . . . . **none** moderate heavy
Front-rear balance . . . . .poor **fair** good

HANDLING
Roadholding, 300-ft-dia skidpad . . . . 0.77 g
Understeer. . . . . minimal **moderate** excessive

COAST-DOWN MEASUREMENTS
Road horsepower @ 30 mph . . . . 5 hp
          50 mph . . . . 13 hp
          70 mph . . . . 27 hp

FUEL ECONOMY
EPA city driving . . . . **23 mpg**
EPA highway driving . . . . 28 mpg
C/D observed fuel economy . . . . **24 mpg**

INTERIOR SOUND LEVEL
Idle . . . . 50 dBA
Full-throttle acceleration . . . . 84 dBA
70-mph cruising . . . . 77 dBA
70-mph coasting . . . . 76 dBA

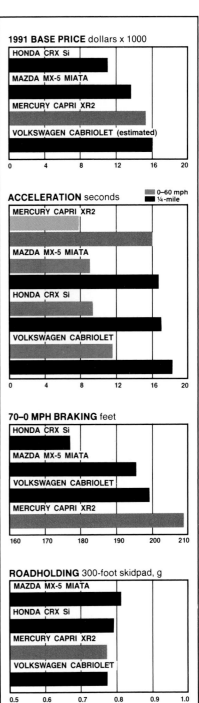

1991 BASE PRICE dollars x 1000

HONDA CRX Si
MAZDA MX-5 MIATA
MERCURY CAPRI XR2
VOLKSWAGEN CABRIOLET (estimated)

0   4   8   12   16   20

ACCELERATION seconds
(0–60 mph / ¼-mile)

MERCURY CAPRI XR2
MAZDA MX-5 MIATA
HONDA CRX Si
VOLKSWAGEN CABRIOLET

0   4   8   12   16   20

70–0 MPH BRAKING feet

HONDA CRX Si
MAZDA MX-5 MIATA
VOLKSWAGEN CABRIOLET
MERCURY CAPRI XR2

160   170   180   190   200   210

ROADHOLDING 300-foot skidpad, g

MAZDA MX-5 MIATA
HONDA CRX Si
MERCURY CAPRI XR2
VOLKSWAGEN CABRIOLET

0.5   0.6   0.7   0.8   0.9   1.0

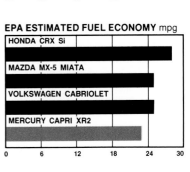

EPA ESTIMATED FUEL ECONOMY mpg

HONDA CRX Si
MAZDA MX-5 MIATA
VOLKSWAGEN CABRIOLET
MERCURY CAPRI XR2

0   6   12   18   24   30

MITSUBISHI 3000GT VR-4

By Arthur St. Antoine

You know about Swiss Army knives. The chunky little contraptions are bursting with blades and tools and usually a corkscrew, too. Pack one and you're ready for any exigency. Now take a look at the 1991 Mitsubishi 3000GT VR-4 on these pages. What we have here is nothing less than the Swiss Army knife of sports coupes.

Feel a need to blow off that unruly two-seater in the next lane? *Flick:* you've got 300 hp under your right foot. Want to impress the neighborhood? *Flick:* just give 'em a look at this outlandish body. Are the roads buried in snow? *Flick:* you've got full-time four-wheel drive to pull you through. Just had a truck jump out in front of you? *Flick:* you've got anti-lock brakes to help you stop and a driver-side air bag to protect you if you can't. Want to crack open a bottle of '61 Châ-

teau Latour when you reach your destination? Sorry: you're going to need your Swiss Army knife for that one.

The 3000GT VR-4 may not be able to uncork vintage Bordeaux, but it's equipped to do almost anything you could ask of a sports coupe. From a driver-adjustable shock-absorber system, to an auto-adjusting rear wing and air dam, to a variable-noise exhaust system, to four-wheel steering—this Mitsubishi brims with technological wonders. Make no mistake: this is not an elegant, super-polished GT in the vein of the Nissan 300ZX Turbo. But the VR-4 is unquestionably the most hardware-packed entry in its class.

That fact is evident the moment the Mitsu strides onto the scales. The VR-4's numerous fixtures plump its curb weight to 3800 pounds, which is 300 pounds past

the ZX Turbo's, 400 pounds past the base Corvette's, and up into the weighty realm of the BMW 735i sedan. Build a car equipped with everything but a corkscrew and you can expect that kind of obesity.

Still, the 3000GT VR-4 is no laggard. The engine room sports a 300-hp 3.0-liter V-6 fortified with twin cams, 24 valves, and twin turbochargers and intercoolers —a powerful antidote to the poison of mass. Last month we tested the 3000GT's near twin, the Dodge Stealth R/T Turbo (which Mitsubishi builds in Japan for the American maker), and found that it accelerates from 0 to 60 mph in 5.9 seconds and reaches a top speed of 151 mph. The VR-4 feels every bit as quick.

Because the VR-4 is fast despite its weight, you can revel in its full-time four-wheel drive without feeling guilty about the added pressure it puts on the scales. Indeed, the four-wheel-drive system— equipped with three differentials and viscous couplings in the center and the rear —is what singles out the VR-4 in the high-power sports-coupe ranks. Not only is the VR-4 easily able to put its power down in the dry, but it can continue to romp when

the weather turns sour. The 3000GT VR-4 is a year-round supercar.

The four-wheel drive system feeds four fat 245/45ZR-17 tires mounted on 8.5-by-17-inch alloy wheels. They help provide face-distorting dry-road grip and, in concert with the four vented disc brakes and anti-lock system, contribute to outstanding braking ability. The 3000GT VR-4's test-track abilities rank with the class's best.

The Mitsu's high-octane bodywork— less innovative than the Stealth's but also, we think, less ostentatious—is sure to be a strong draw for buyers. With its sleek shape, slotted side strakes, and movable rear wing, the car *looks* like a piece of high-tech wizardry. (The 3000GT's "Active Aero" system, which adds downforce above 50 mph by automatically shifting the angle of the rear wing and lowering the front air dam, is not available on the Dodge Stealth.) The interior is noteworthy, too: a mostly successful blend of easy-to-reach controls and appealing materials.

And yet, much as we like the car, we find that the blades in its portfolio aren't as sharp as they could be. The turbo-

This sports coupe does 0–60 in 5.9 seconds and offers full-time four-wheel drive, a driver-adjustable shock-absorber system and much more.

charged six-cylinder engine is powerful, no question, but it's not as smooth or as eager to rev high as the 300ZX's turbo six. The Getrag-developed five-speed (no automatic is offered with the turbocharged 3000GT) lacks the fluid, positive action that's so essential to the day-to-day enjoyment of a sports car. Even with the electronically adjustable shock absorbers set in the soft "Tour" position, the car hammers noticeably over road imperfections. And the interior, attractive and functional as it is, doesn't rank with the Z's in style and efficiency. Don't misunderstand: not one of our criticisms is cause for a thumbs-down overall rating. But there's a noticeable absence of all-of-a-piece, buttoned-down finesse in this automobile.

What the VR-4 lacks in refinement it attempts to make up for in class-leading value. Final prices had not been set as we went to press, but Mitsubishi expects the base price of the 3000GT VR-4 to come in around $31,000. Included in that sum are all the performance pieces we've mentioned so far, plus a long list of luxuries. Among the standard fitments: a six-way power driver's seat, an automatic climate-control system, a 100-watt AM/FM/cassette system with six speakers, and power mirrors, windows, and locks. The only options are a CD player, leather seats, and a sunroof. (Shoppers who like the 3000GT but can't make the stretch for the turbocharged VR-4 can choose between two 222-hp, normally aspirated, front-drive versions.)

If you're hunting for a sports coupe, this Swiss Army knife of a car definitely deserves your consideration. It offers amazing value and versatility. True, there's no corkscrew included. But, well, only a barbarian would open a bottle of '61 Château Latour with a car.

MITSUBISHI 3000GT VR–4
Vehicle type: front-engine, four-wheel-drive, 2 + 2-passenger, 3-door coupe
Estimated base price: $31,000
Engine type: twin-turbocharged and intercooled DOHC 24-valve V-6, iron block and aluminum heads. Mitsubishi electronic engine-control system with port fuel injection
Displacement . . . . .181 cu in, 2972cc
Power (SAE net) . . . . 300 bhp @ 6000 rpm
Transmission 5-speed
Wheelbase . . . . 97.2 in
Length . . . . 180.5 in
Curb weight . . . . 3800 lb
EPA fuel economy, city driving . . . . 18 mpg

The interior is a mostly successful blend of easy-to-reach controls and appealing materials. The engine is a 300-hp 3.0-liter V–6 with twin cams, 24 valves, and twin turbochargers and intercoolers.

PHOTOGRAPHY BY AARON KILEY

TOYOTA PREVIA LE

By John Phillips III

Okay, sure. This *is* the most technically fascinating minivan extant, what with its twin-cam engine prostrate, heeled over at a radical 75-degree angle and situated about an inch below the walkway between the front seats. (Every time we ambled to the rear of the van, we'd get all adolescent: "Okay, here I go; right now I'm walking on top of the engine.") But the wholly hidden four-cylinder powerplant isn't what you notice when the Previa passes on the highway, is it? And the mid-engine layout isn't what prompts neighbors to *demand* you turn off the lawn mower so they can ask about the vehicle parked in your driveway. No, sir. What they want to talk about is how neat this minivan looks. And what they want to hear is whether it works.

We have here a minor breakthrough in packaging. And the best part is that it's okay to be all patriotic and teary-eyed, because the Toyota Previa was styled in America—well, at the CALTY design studio in California, which is pretty close to being in America.

With a drag coefficient of only 0.34, the Previa qualifies as aerodynamic. It has a steeply raked windshield, like GM's APVs, yet the distance from the Toyota's steering wheel to the base of its windshield is eight inches less wasteful. And the luscious jellybean curves are in such perfect proportion that the Previa *looks* like the smallest minivan on the market. It isn't. In fact, it still swallows lots of four-by-eight-foot sheets of plywood. Or, with its bench seats locked in place, it seats seven adults —giving these folks in the middle seats, by the way, more than two inches more headroom than they'd enjoy in a Pontiac Trans Sport.

Climb inside and it gets even better.

The Previa's lovingly assembled interior stands as a high-water mark for minivan tastefulness and functionality. The A-pillars and their angled supports are expensively upholstered. The admittedly large dash—with a center bulge that makes it look pregnant—is finished in a brushed gray plastic that looks like titanium. The defroster outlets are so painstakingly countersunk and pressure-fitted into the dash that the two appear to have come from the same injection-molded piece. The backs of the door grab-bars are covered in a supple urethane that feels like ultrasuede. The retractors for both front seatbelts are hidden within flush, upholstered wall panels. The soft-drink holder, ashtray, and center storage bin (the latter a perfect place to hide a radar detector or eight stereo cassettes) are so cleverly integrated they're almost hidden. All of the switch gear is up high, located where you expect to find it. (One of the benefits of the pregnant dash is that the radio and ventilation controls are thrust within ten inches of the right edge of the steering wheel.) And the sliding cargo door opens with less resistance than the passenger doors on many luxury cars.

There's more. Get down on your hands and knees and you'll notice that the upholstered left-side wall panel, a huge thing that runs from directly aft of the front seats all the way to the tailgate, is a single piece. So is the liftgate liner. So is the downy headliner. So is the carpet. Not only do these one-piece trim panels eliminate a lot of cutlines and visible fussiness in the interior, they also reduce the potential for rattles.

One of Toyota's goals was to build "the sports car of minivans," which motivated the company to pursue a mid-engine—rear-drive layout. That lends the Previa a low center of gravity, reduces polar movement of inertia, and distributes weight evenly. In theory, at least. When we weighed our Previa LE, its weight distribution worked out to about 53/47 front/rear. That's a good figure, but the front-engined Ford Aerostar and the rear-engined Volkswagen Vanagon are every bit as well balanced.

On the skidpad, the Previa doesn't exactly wade into sports-car territory, clinging to Mother Earth with 0.70 g of grip. That's not as much as is generated by either the Pontiac Trans Sport or the Mazda MPV, but perhaps the trade-off is ride comfort. The Previa jostles its occupants far less fervently than the Pontiac. Still, we wish the Toyota were fitted with fatter, lower-profile rubber.

And yet, on twisty two-lanes, this most modern of minivans *does* feel better-balanced and more agile than any of its competitors, save the Trans Sport. Behind the wheel, you detect no twitches that reveal whether this is a front- or rear-drive vehicle. The Previa tracks determinedly

down the road, its path unaltered by scabrous pavement or truck ruts. It takes a confidence-inspiring set through corners, requiring a minimum of corrections. The steering, in fact, is the best of any minivan on the market: nicely weighted, eager to self-center, and almost perfectly linear.

Understeer appears earlier than we'd prefer. And although lateral body motions are satisfactorily damped, dive and squat are not. A sudden braking induces unnecessary forward pitching.

At the test track, our Previa required only 198 feet to bring itself to a halt from 70 mph. And it didn't even have ABS. We consider that very good stopping performance for a minivan.

The Previa interior is a winner, from its dash designed for driver convenience to appointments surrounding its seven seats.

The "pregnant" dash places radio and ventilation controls within finger-tip reach.

The engine, top photo, is located under the driver's seat. This mid-engined, rear-drive layout results in a low center of gravity and a good 53/47 front/rear weight distribution.

The chief drawback to the mid-engine layout is that the cubbyhole is big enough for only a four-cylinder engine. Yes, Toyota's 138-hp, sixteen-valve powerplant is a fine piece of work—or it would be fine if it were installed in, say, a Celica, where you could plumb its charms in the 4000-rpm-and-beyond range. But when you're driving a minivan, what you want is plenty of torque at step-off, and the Previa simply can't supply it. A foot-to-the-floor brake-torque launch won't even chirp the tires. The 0-to-60-mph sprint requires 12.2 seconds, which isn't exactly disastrous; three of the Previa's V-6-powered competitors make the same trek in the high-eleven-second range. It's just that the Toyota's four-cylinder engine huffs and puffs and screams its guts out, making surprisingly raucous, unrefined noises. Moreover, to keep the engine on the boil, the four-speed automatic kicks down at the slightest provocation and with more harshness than we expect from Toyotas.

There are a couple of other detail imperfections that merit attention. The en-gine's idle, for example, bogs and surges as the air-conditioner compressor kicks in and out. (As an aside, we discovered that, with the A/C running, a light application of the throttle induces an annoying whistle from a vacuum line. Toyota confirms an identical problem in about half of the Previas shipped to date, and dealers will reroute the line "for any owner who complains.") And on its high-speed setting, the rear ventilation blower, mounted on the headliner just aft of the front seats, sounds like a Huey gunship on takeoff.

Previas are available with more seating variations than Madison Square Garden: a base version with no rearmost bench seat, mid-line models with the twin-bench, seven-passenger layout (version tested here), others with two swiveling captain's chairs mounted amidships. Previa prices: the manual-transmission Deluxe ($13,998), the full-time four-wheel drive Deluxe All-Trac ($16,608), the LE ($18,698), and the flagship LE All-Trac ($21,308).

The rear-drive LE model promises to

become the best-selling Previa. Standard equipment is exhaustive. Were we ordering the vehicle for ourselves, the only options we'd specify would be ABS ($1130), power windows and mirrors ($380), and —forgive us for this, but we can't help ourselves—the gargantuan power sunroof ($1370) above the middle seat. We usually sneer at sunroofs, but this one is a jewel, offering a 32-by-40-inch hole. What's more, Toyota adds 30mm of extra roof height to all Previas (Previi?) with sunroofs, so that interior headroom is unmolested.

All of which brings the price of our wish-list Previa LE, including freight, to $21,843. That's $2128 more than our "Best Buy" Mazda MPV V6 3.0i, a machine we still regard as the most versatile and carlike minivan on the planet. Of course, the Mazda MPV can't compete with the Previa's inspired styling, nor can it match the fit and finish of the Previa's cockpit, which seems to have been hand-assembled by 30 or 40 Japanese craftsmen who have no regard for Toyota's profits and have never punched a clock in their lives.

All that the Previa needs now is a six-cylinder engine. But unless somebody ships a load of acetylene torches to Toyota's indefatigable product planners, that's an improbable upgrade. Hold on. How much *are* acetylene torches?

COUNTERPOINT

The year 2000 is fast approaching, and Toyota is ready. The Previa is the best example of forward thinking in minivan design thus far. This package shows off a sleek and seductive skin, complemented by an amalgam of futuristic and exciting shapes inside.

Sitting in the driver's seat is like being on the bridge of the starship *Enterprise.* Although spartan, the instrument panel looks space-age; its sweeping and sculptured contours are very pleasing. And all of the Toyota's panel textures feel good to the touch.

The Previa is as capable as it looks. It has a good ride, predictable handling, and delicious steering. I would like it more if it had a larger, more powerful flat-six engine and a tachometer. But for now, the Previa is as good as minivans get.
—*Nicholas Bissoon-Dath*

When I go vehicle hunting, two of my priorities are versatility and adaptability. I think the clever (but expensive) Previa meets these criteria better than any other minivan. And I would really like Toyota's slick new people-and-stuff mover if it weren't for one glaring shortcoming of minivans in general: utter nerdiness.

Some research supports my view. Chrysler, which sells the most minivans these days, says minivan buyers are more like owners of wood-sided, whitewalled station wagons than any other shoppers.

One reason these buyers enjoy minivans is height—the vehicles are tall enough to provide a view over traffic. But once minivans and sport-utility vehicles pack our roads, nobody will be able to see over anybody. Already, from the seat of an MR2 you can't see through the tinted windows of a Previa in front of you. And it's going to get worse. My fear is as gripping as walking down the hall in high school beleaguered by seven-foot-tall chess-club members all wearing pocket protectors. No doubt they arrived at school in Previas.
—*Phil Berg*

I haven't been this excited about a van since the original VW Microbus limped its way down the back roads of my anti-establishment consciousness more than twenty years ago. That old VW said "screw you" to everyone with conventional ideas about transportation, and the Previa does the same—albeit in a much friendlier way.

Friendliness, in fact, is what the Previa is all about. From its friendly ladybug shape to its user-friendly space-pod control clusters, it carries out its mission of utility with consummate pleasantness. Toyota has made sure that passengers are well cared for and that cargo is swallowed whole—and that converting from people mover to cargo hauler is a nearly effortless task. All this and a thoroughly artful interior make the Previa a low-stress, high-pleasure transporter.

The Previa demonstrates the kind of future-think that GM's new minivan triplets hint at but can't deliver. Toyota's New Age design does more than just look good, it advances the minivan science to a new plane of . . . friendliness. As I used to say about the VW Bus: "It's far out, man, far *out.*"
—*Rich Ceppos*

Toyota Previa LE

Vehicle type: mid-engine, rear-wheel-drive, 7-passenger, 4-door van

Price as tested: $20,995

Options on test car: base Toyota Previa LE, $18,698; rear spoiler and power moonroof, $1370; power package (includes power windows and mirrors), $380; deluxe sound system, $190; floor mats, $92; freight, $265

Standard accessories: power steering and locks, A/C, cruise control, tilt steering, rear defroster and wiper

Sound system: Toyota 16401 AM/FM-stereo radio/cassette, 6 speakers

ENGINE
Type	4-in-line, iron block and aluminum head
Bore x stroke	3.74 x 3.39 in, 95.0 x 86.0mm
Displacement	149 cu in, 2438cc
Compression ratio	9.3:1
Engine-control system	Toyota TCCS with port fuel injection
Emissions controls	3-way catalytic converter, feedback fuel-air-ratio control, EGR
Valve gear	chain- and gear-driven double overhead cams, 4 valves per cylinder
Power (SAE net)	138 bhp @ 5000 rpm
Torque (SAE net)	154 lb-ft @ 4000 rpm

DRIVETRAIN
Transmission	4-speed automatic with lockup torque converter
Final-drive ratio	4.30:1

Gear	Ratio	Mph/1000 rpm	Max. test speed
I	2.45	7.0	42 mph (6000 rpm)
II	1.45	11.8	71 mph (6000 rpm)
III	1.00	17.1	101 mph (5900 rpm)
IV	0.73	23.4	104 mph (4450 rpm)

DIMENSIONS AND CAPACITIES
Wheelbase	112.8 in
Track, F/R	61.6/61.2 in
Length	187.0 in
Width	70.9 in
Height	69.9 in
Ground clearance	7.1 in
Curb weight	3858 lb
Weight distribution, F/R	52.6/47.4%
Fuel capacity	19.8 gal
Oil capacity	5.8 qt
Water capacity	12.3 qt

CHASSIS/BODY
Type	unit construction
Body material	welded steel stampings

INTERIOR
SAE volume, front seat	56 cu ft
middle seat	51 cu ft
rear seat	49 cu ft
luggage space	28 cu ft
Front seats	bucket
Seat adjustments	fore and aft, seatback angle
General comfort	poor fair good **excellent**
Fore-and-aft support	poor fair **good** excellent
Lateral support	poor **fair** good excellent

SUSPENSION
F:	ind, strut located by a control arm, coil springs, anti-roll bar
R:	rigid axle located by 4 trailing links and a Panhard rod, coil springs

STEERING
Type	rack-and-pinion, power-assisted
Turns lock-to-lock	3.7
Turning circle curb-to-curb	37.4 ft

BRAKES
F:	10.9 x 15-in vented disc
R:	11.4 x 0.7-in disc
Power assist	vacuum

WHEELS AND TIRES
Wheel size	6.0 x 0.9 in
Wheel type	stamped steel
Tires	Bridgestone SF-406 Steel M+S, P215/65HR-15
Test inflation pressures, F/R	35/35 psi

CAR AND DRIVER TEST RESULTS

ACCELERATION
	Seconds
Zero to 30 mph	4.1
40 mph	6.2
50 mph	9.1
60 mph	12.2
70 mph	17.0
80 mph	23.5
90 mph	35.0
Top-gear passing time, 30–50 mph	5.7
50–70 mph	9.2
Standing ¼-mile	19.0 sec @ 73 mph
Top speed	104 mph

BRAKING
70–0 mph @ impending lockup	198 ft
Modulation	poor fair **good** excellent
Fade	none **moderate** heavy
Front-rear balance	poor fair **good**

HANDLING
Roadholding, 300-ft-dia skidpad	0.70 g
Understeer	minimal **moderate** excessive

COAST-DOWN MEASUREMENTS
Road horsepower @ 30 mph	6 hp
50 mph	17 hp
70 mph	38 hp

FUEL ECONOMY
EPA city driving	**18 mpg**
EPA highway driving	**22 mpg**
C/D observed fuel economy	**20 mpg**

INTERIOR SOUND LEVEL
Idle	47 dBA
Full-throttle acceleration	79 dBA
70-mph cruising	72 dBA
70-mph coasting	71 dBA

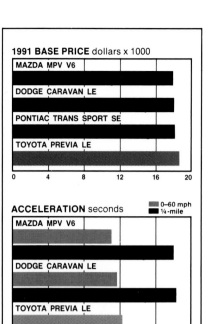

1991 BASE PRICE dollars x 1000

(MAZDA MPV V6, DODGE CARAVAN LE, PONTIAC TRANS SPORT SE, TOYOTA PREVIA LE — scale 0 to 20)

ACCELERATION seconds (0–60 mph / ¼-mile)

(MAZDA MPV V6, DODGE CARAVAN LE, TOYOTA PREVIA LE, PONTIAC TRANS SPORT SE — scale 0 to 20)

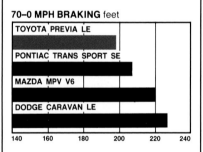

70–0 MPH BRAKING feet

(TOYOTA PREVIA LE, PONTIAC TRANS SPORT SE, MAZDA MPV V6, DODGE CARAVAN LE — scale 140 to 240)

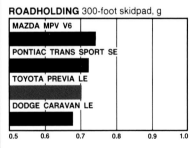

ROADHOLDING 300-foot skidpad, g

(MAZDA MPV V6, PONTIAC TRANS SPORT SE, TOYOTA PREVIA LE, DODGE CARAVAN LE — scale 0.5 to 1.0)

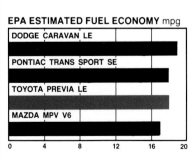

EPA ESTIMATED FUEL ECONOMY mpg

(DODGE CARAVAN LE, PONTIAC TRANS SPORT SE, TOYOTA PREVIA LE, MAZDA MPV V6 — scale 0 to 20)

MERCEDES-BENZ 500E

By Pete Lyons

The Mercedes-Benz engineers responsible for this car are so proud of it they can't keep their faces straight. Carelessly refer to it as their "baby Hammer" and they'll interrupt you with broad grins and emphatic fist-pounding. *"Nicht* 'baby!' This is adult hammer! Steam hammer!"

What the M-B engineers have perpetrated here is a Stuttgart factory hot rod. They have taken the normal, everyday 300E sedan bodyshell and stuffed it full of all the important goodies found in the 500SL sports convertible: its tires, wheels, brakes, suspension, four-speed automatic transmission, and—most important—its 322-horsepower, four-cam, 32-valve 4973cc V-8 engine. The result is a car slightly bulkier than the SL two-seater but substantially lighter—a car that goes like, well, like a combat jet off a carrier's steam catapult.

It's called the 500E. Starting in the 1992 model year, as many as 5000 U.S. buyers will have a chance to call one their own. The price has yet to be determined, but get in line now anyway. The car is that good.

In its role as a mild-mannered passenger car, the 300E—Mercedes-Benz model-type W124—has won critical acclaim for its refinement, comfort, and handling stability. An "outstanding transportation tool," *C/D* has called it. As sold in U.S. specification, it lists for $45,950. It's built on a 110.2-inch wheelbase and rides on V-rated 195/65R-15 tires. Curb weight is now 3315 pounds. Its SOHC, two-valve-per-cylinder engine puts out 177 hp at 5700 rpm and 188 pound-feet of torque at 4400. When we last tested the 300E, in August 1986, it accelerated from 0 to 60 mph in 8.3 seconds, ran the quarter-mile in 16.3 seconds at 87 mph, and reached a top speed of 136 mph.

From this car sprang the Hammer—the creation of Hans-Werner Aufrecht, proprietor of the German aftermarket company AMG. In December 1987, we tested an original Hammer, which was similar in concept to the production 500E that Mercedes is now preparing to unveil. The primary difference: AMG used its own twin-cam, four-valve-per-cylinder heads atop the longer stroke Mercedes 560 V-8 engine. Horsepower was estimated at 360 at 5750 rpm. With a curb weight of 3600 pounds, the Hammer scorched from 0 to 60 mph in 5.0 seconds and through the quarter-mile in 13.2 seconds at 108 mph. Top speed: a mighty 181 mph. Those of us who got to drive the AMG Hammer three years ago are still talking about it. Talking is all we've done, though, because Aufrecht's U.S. agents wanted $160,000 apiece when Hammers were available. (Recent emissions regulations pushed the Hammer out of the U.S. market.)

Since the Hammer's introduction, it's been easy to picture little knots of Mercedes-Benz factory guys gathered around the water coolers talking about how they could do a better Hammer of their own. They soon included their colleagues at Porsche in their talking. As the program was finalized, M-B did the engineering and Porsche carried out test and development duties. Porsche will also assemble the production cars.

The heart of the new 500E is Mercedes' M119 engine. The heritage of its aluminum block goes back more than a decade, when it appeared in 5.0-liter form with single-cam heads in the 1978 450SLC 5.0 —a model never officially imported to America. In 1979, Mercedes put a twin-turbocharged version in the back of its C111/IV streamliner. Tuned for about 500 hp—a limit established by the available tires—it lapped the 7.82-mile track at Nardo, Italy, at an average speed of 250.803 mph. That was good for the world closed-course speed record.

Five years after that, Swiss driver and

constructor Peter Sauber talked the factory into supplying him with engines for a Group C racing effort. Gradually, Mercedes took on more and more elements of the project—when a trio of Sauber-Mercedes C9 coupes went to Le Mans in 1989, they wore German racing silver. Equipped with four-valve-per-cylinder heads and twin turbos, the C9's engine was capable of about 830 horsepower, although at Le Mans it was tuned for about 750 hp at 7000 rpm to meet the fuel-consumption requirement of 51 liters per 100 kilometers (4.6 mpg). Torque was just under 600 pound-feet at 3500 rpm. In practice, one of the Sauber-Mercedes team cars was timed on the Mulsanne straight at 249.826 mph.

In the race, despite losing two-thirds of the blades on one turbo impeller when it swallowed an errant bolt, one Sauber-Mercedes car won, covering 3271.49 miles in the 24 hours. Another took second, even though its transaxle locked itself in top gear in the last hour. A third C9 was fifth. On teardown in Stuttgart, ac-

cording to Mercedes, none of the three V-8s showed more than nominal wear.

Minus the turbos and some racing modifications, this was the engine introduced to street duty later that summer in the 500SL two-seater. Its main features: low weight (claimed to be 456 pounds), compact size, and an electromechanical advance mechanism for the intake camshafts, which broadens the torque curve.

Stuck into the type W124 body, the M119 engine brings the 500E's all-up *fahrfertig* (driving-ready) weight to about 3750 pounds, according to preliminary factory figures. Call it a good ten percent lighter than the 500SL. Also, the 500E's final-drive ratio is shorter than the SL's—2.82:1, versus 2.65. The result is a claimed 0-to-62-mph time of 6.1 seconds. (It may in fact be even quicker: we typically find that Mercedes perform better than the factory claims.) The 500SL managed a 6.3-second 0-to-60-mph run for our December 1989 issue.

Cosmetically, the 500E's Z-rated 225/

What factory engineers proudly call "The Hammer" is a Mercedes 300E sedan bodyshell packed with the important goodies of a Mercedes 500SL Sports Convertible.

55-16 tires require small fender bulges that add 2.2 inches to the car's overall width. These bulges were on the prototype we drove and photographed, as was an AMG-style painted radiator shell. According to early information, production 500Es will have normal chrome-plated shells and also will get big SL mirrors on both sides. U.S. cars will feature a license-plate valance panel, the inevitable high-mounted rear brake light, and all-leather upholstery. Unlike AMG, Mercedes doesn't seem to feel its supercar needs a ducktail spoiler.

It does seem to feel the 500E needs ASR, M-B's traction-control system. The prototype was equipped with it. Mercedes says ASR may be one of the few 500E options. If so, buyers are going to have to think hard about whether to order it or not, because it probably won't come with an off switch.

Functioning much like similar systems on other cars, ASR senses wheelspin at the drive wheels and both cuts engine power and drags the proper brake to stop it. It really works. Snow was unavailable to us during our test drive in Germany, but there was no shortage of rain. Our test: maneuver the 500E off pavement onto a forest track, make sure the rear wheels are standing on squishy mud, and stamp all 322 horses deep into the ground. What happens? Nothing. The huge, exotic Le Mans–winning V-8 simply chugs softly, tenderly nursing the fat rear tires forward through the goo.

Impressive, in the sense it's interesting to watch an autopilot fly a plane. No doubt there are innumerable situations in everyday driving when traction control can save your hide, or at least a fender. But if you suspect there are other situations, times when the ASR's "Get your damn hands off, I've got it" personality might cut into the fun factor, you're right. On a rain-slick Hockenheim racetrack, we found it balked at our every attempt to boot the tail out with power as God and Gottlieb Daimler intended. All we got was persistent, piggish push.

Going into bends, though, the prototype's tail felt a little wayward, a touch tricky. A 500SL we tried was steady at the same points. Oh, and at the end of our few laps we blotted our copybook with our hosts by clouding the pit lane with stinky white brake-pad smoke. This car isn't a racer.

But otherwise . . . well, wow. The 500E may be a factory hot rod, but the hot-

rodding was done by a factory justifiably famous for doing its work with obsessive, serious-minded thoroughness. There are no raw edges on the Mercedes-Benz 500E. As a transportation tool, it's strictly presentation-quality.

Though it's not meaningfully bigger than the 300E, somehow the 5.0-liter car seems as though it commands twice as much space on the road. The seats in the prototype lock you firmly and prominently into your proper place behind the magnificent steering wheel. The car rides tautly, is quick-steering, and feels bull-powerful—a meaty delight in the hands. The engine is like good blue-cheese dressing: creamy-cool with lots of satisfying little chunks of V-8 pulse in it. The neo-Hammer simply storms down the road, gathering way like a steam locomotive that's snapped loose from its train. On Hockenheim's return straight, it's no trick at all to see 210, 215, maybe 217 on the kilometer scale before you have to shut off for a curve. Later you work it out—almost 135 mph. In pouring, streaming, swishing rain. Wow again. It felt as solid and comfy as hurtling along inside a rocket-assisted, leather-lined gun safe, if you can imagine such a thing as being pleasurable.

A long autobahn holiday in this machine would be first-class travel indeed. Truly. Oh, baby.

The heart of the beast is aluminum. A twin-turbocharged version, tuned for 500 hp, once powered the fabled C111/IV streamliner.

MERCEDES-BENZ 500E

Vehicle type: front-engine, rear-wheel-drive, 5-passenger, 4-door sedan

Estimated base price: $65,000

Standard accessories: power steering, windows, seats, locks, and sunroof, A/C, cruise control, rear defroster

Sound system: Mercedes-Benz AM/FM-stereo radio/cassette, 10 speakers

ENGINE

Type	V-8, aluminum block and heads
Bore x stroke	3.80 x 3.35 in, 96.5 x 85.0mm
Displacement	303 cu in, 4973cc
Compression ratio	10.0:1
Engine-control system	Bosch KE-5-Jetronic with port fuel injection
Emissions controls	3-way catalytic converter, feedback fuel-air-ratio control, EGR
Valve gear	chain-driven double overhead cams, 4 valves per cylinder, hydraulic lifters
Power (SAE net)	322 bhp @ 5500 rpm
Torque (SAE net)	332 lb-ft @ 4000 rpm
Redline	6000 rpm

DRIVETRAIN

Transmission . . . . 4-speed automatic
Final-drive ratio 2.82:1

Gear	Ratio	MPH/1000 rpm	Speed in gears
I	3.87	6.7	40 mph (6000 rpm)
II	2.25	11.5	69 mph (6000 rpm)
III	1.44	18.0	108 mph (6000 rpm)
IV	1.00	25.9	155 mph (6000 rpm)

DIMENSIONS AND CAPACITIES

Wheelbase	110.2 in
Track, F/R	60.3/59.9 in
Length	187.2 in
Width	70.7 in
Height	56.3 in
Frontal area	22.4 sq ft
Curb weight	3750 lb
Fuel capacity	18.5 gal
Oil capacity	8.5 qt
Water capacity	15.9 qt

CHASSIS/BODY

Type . . . . unit construction with 1 rubber-isolated crossmember
Body material . . . . welded steel stampings

INTERIOR

SAE vol. . . . . front seat 50 cu ft, rear 40, luggage 15
Front seats . . . . bucket

SUSPENSION

F: . . . . ind, strut located by a control arm, coil springs, anti-roll bar
R: . . . . ind, 2 lateral links and 3 diagonal links per side, coil springs, anti-roll bar

STEERING

Type	recirculating ball, power-assisted
Turns lock-to-lock	3.2
Turning circle curb-to-curb	36.7 ft

BRAKES

F: . . . . 11.8 x 1.1-in vented disc
R: . . . . 10.9 x 0.4-in disc
Power assist . . . . vacuum with anti-lock control

WHEELS AND TIRES

Wheel size	8.0 x 16 in
Wheel type	cast aluminum
Tires	Dunlop SP Sport D40, 225/55ZR-16

MANUFACTURER'S PERFORMANCE RATINGS

Zero to 62 mph	6.1 sec
Top speed	155 mph

This high-strung racer is barely tame enough for the streets, but it's legal.

FERRARI F40

By Rich Ceppos

Here are twelve things you should know about the Ferrari F40:
- Its sticker price is about $400,000.
- But dealers are getting about $700,000 for one, a bargain from last summer's peak price of $900,000 and change.
- The price does not include a spare tire or a jack. Neither is available.
- The price does include a free trip for two to the Ferrari factory in Italy for the purpose of showing the buyer how to drive it.
- It goes 122 mph in the quarter-mile.
- Flat out, it goes 197. You have our word.
- Insurance costs about $15,000. *Every six months.*
- The F40 meets all U.S. emissions and safety regulations. In short, it's legal.
- As soon as he got his, Formula 1 driver Nigel Mansell sold it.
- It pulls 1.01 g on the skidpad.
- Financed over five years, the monthly payment on an F40 runs about $12,000 a month.
- One buyer took no chances. Without even driving it, he sealed up his new F40 in the safest place available: his living room.

At *Car and Driver*, Rule 1 for test drivers is this: Be Cool. Rules 2 through 10 are equally simple: Remain Cool.

Sad to report, a wrecking ball called the Ferrari F40 has just put big crow's feet on our stony editorial face. Tough as it is to admit, the F40 has made our knees tremble involuntarily, our hearts do little stutter steps, and it made our palms disgustingly wet. Doctor, doctor! Maybe the editorial feet are touching ground, maybe not—we'll get back to you on that a little later.

After two days on the road and an afternoon at the test track, we can report that nothing we've ever driven can match the mix of sheer terror and raw excitement of earth-scorching around in someone else's three-quarter-million-dollar toy. (Our privately owned test car came to us thanks to the kind assistance of Ferrari dealer Rick Mancuso, who owns Lake Forest Sports Cars, in Lake Forest, Illinois. Understandably, the F40's owner wants to remain anonymous.)

Piloting an F40 is like, well, imagine being blindfolded in a pitch-black closet with Michelle Pfeiffer, Cher, and Ellen Barkin and having to guess their identities without talking—but, sorry, you're married. Imagine standing alone in center field at Dodger Stadium while the crowd cheers. But also imagine riding around with a million bucks in your trunk and a three-foot neon sign on the roof reading: "Million Dollars in Trunk." That's what driving an F40 is like.

A deep breath here and we'll attempt to explain further. You see, a Ferrari F40 isn't like other current exotic cars. In the last twenty years, the cars with the mile-high price tags and headache-inducing acceleration have gone through a remarkable metamorphosis: they've become thoroughly domesticated. They have power windows and respectable air conditioners and enough room for six-footers now. You can see out of them well enough to change lanes without saying Hail Mary first. You can hop into almost any of them and drive cross-country reasonably assured of emerging of sound mind and body.

Not so the F40. It harks back to a time —the late 1950s and before—when makes like Ferrari, Maserati, Jaguar, and Porsche built sports and GT cars for the road that could be raced with a minimum of modifications. Some started life as high-strung racers and were barely tamed for the street. We're talking about cars like

Highs: *Zenith of speed with a body like Venus.*
Lows: *Price tag causes heart flutters even when car is parked.*
The verdict: *A religious experience.*

the original Testarossa, the Jag C- and D-types, the Porsche 550 Spyder. The Ford GT40 Mark III is the lone American car that follows this blueprint. None of them were comfortable, tractable, or reliable. What they offered was unvarnished excitement—the raw, elemental race-car experience for the street.

The F40 is like that. It looks like a race car that made a wrong turn at the end of pit lane. Its nose droops to shovel air out of the way. Its Kevlar body is pockmarked with enough air scoops to inhale a flock of sheep. A wing fit for a Formula 1 car sprouts from the rear deck—no wimpy spoilers here. The F40's midship-mounted, twin-turbocharged 2.9-liter V-8 is on display under a lightweight plexiglass rear window that's been slotted to allow hot engine-compartment air out. Know of any other street car with a rear window like that? The F40 has height-adjustable suspension, too. There are two positions, one about two inches lower than the other. You have to unbolt the entire suspension to move it but, hey, you have a pit crew, right?

When you pull open the door, you are confronted with an interior as stark as any endurance racer's. Ferrari could have glued some leather to the door panels and

put some carpeting on the floor—it would have added only a couple of pounds. But that would have killed the racing ambience.

Instead, what you see is the glare of nude black-and-tan Kevlar mat on the doors and floor. A thick bead of ugly green sealer runs along the fender-well joint. A single strap opens each door from the inside. The rudimentary dash is covered in gray flannel, apparently to cut glare. The pedals are drilled metal plates. A roll bar nestles behind the seats, hidden by some interior panels. Its Kevlar-covered support tubes run down between the doors and the seats, blocking easy entry. The mil-spec monotone is broken only by a pair of deeply contoured racing-style bucket seats with almost no padding, covered in iridescent orange Nomex fireproof cloth. Amid all of this go-fast seriousness, you'll find an air conditioner, which is standard equipment.

Everything about the F40 feeds your Mario Andretti fantasies. Driving a real race car is a big production; you just don't hop in and buzz out onto the track. Same with the F40. You squirm your way past the roll-bar brace and twist and wriggle your legs around the front wheelhouse and under the steering column; only then —providing you haven't pulled any muscles—can you drop into the deep seat. Inevitably, you sit on the seatbelts. Our U.S.-spec car was fitted with a six-point racing harness that has to be dug out and clicked together laboriously. The steering wheel is up and away, requiring an awkward arm's-out reach. Your legs are cramped too close to your chest.

Turn the ignition key and . . . nothing. The F40 has a starter button. (It's a race car, remember?) When our test car did

fire off, it belched clouds of oily smoke. "Something's wrong," said The Owner, blipping the throttle and looking concerned. "I think the plugs are fouled." He had his foot to the floor, but the engine barely oozed through the rev range, as if it were filled with molasses.

Calls were placed to Lake Forest Sports Cars. Could be fouled plugs, they said. It was also a 25-degree morning, and the F40 apparently doesn't cotton to that. It figured: normal cars don't foul plugs in these circumstances, and if they did they wouldn't pass the emissions standards. Race cars, on the other hand, eat plugs for breakfast, lunch, and dinner. The Ferrari guys must have been very crafty to coax the F40 over the EPA's hurdles.

"Drive it for a while," Lake Forest advised, so we did. About ten miles into the trip, your faithful servant at the wheel, the engine decided to clear out. Make that *CLEAR OUT*—with a belch and a shudder and a pop. Then it lunged at a Corolla that tooled along in front of us like it wanted to ingest it. Oh wow. We backed off in second, then squeezed the throttle again. See that car up ahead? Zap, we were there.

The noise coming from behind our shoulder blades was deafening. You can't talk in an F40 in full assault mode—not that you'd want to. You want to look straight ahead—far ahead. The noise is deafening but magic. It growls, it whooshes, it whirs. The twin turbos add a jet-engine whistle. It has 478 horses back there, which feels, each time you poke the accelerator, like someone firing off a 5000-pound Roman candle strapped to the back bumper.

The Kelvar body is pockmarked with enough air scoops to inhale a flock of sheep. The lightweight plexiglas rear window is slotted to allow escape of engine-compartment hot air.

We headed for a two-lane road. The F40 responds like a race car: directly, instantaneously. The grip in the corners is tenacious—1.01 g, our skidpad test revealed, better than any production car we've ever tested. We pushed harder. It felt like the tires were rolling in foot-deep grooves in the road; there was no side-slip, even at sensational cornering speeds. Where's the limit?

An F40 owner had told us, "When the gold-chain set tries to drive an F40 in the rain, it's all over." He made a spinning motion with his hand.

Better be careful in the dry, too. As we've noted, it is the most powerful American-spec production car we've ever tested. It's the quickest to 60 mph (just 4.2 seconds), the quickest through the quarter-mile (12.1 seconds at 122 mph), and the all-out fastest (197-mph top speed). Don't even think about giving it full throttle in first or second gear unless you're pointing straight ahead. Coming out of one 70-mph second-gear bend, the boost came up a little too fast and the tail stepped sideways in a blink. Big adrenaline rush. Okay, that's close enough.

This is an expert's car. It begs to be put on a racetrack, where you can work up to its limits gradually. The F40's massive power, sudden boost, and incredible grip make various things happen very suddenly on the road. The gold-chain set isn't ready for this car.

This F40 is best taken in small Sunday-morning doses. No one will mistake it for a long-distance cruiser. The car pounds across tar strips and takes the big swells stiffly. The steering hunts nervously on uneven pavement. The unassisted brakes require a hefty push. (Our test car's only shortcoming involved braking. Early rear lockup stretched its stopping distance to 218 feet. Since the average econobox can beat that, we must conclude that something was amiss.)

Anyway, here's the most fun thing you can do in an F40: Ease along in first gear at fifteen miles per hour, then squeeze the throttle down to the floor and hang on. Before you can count one-one-thousand, the boost kicks in, the rear tires break loose and the back end fishtails, and the F40 hurtles ahead. You know those in-car camera shots of Alain Prost smoking out of the Ferrari pits after a tire change? You just experienced it. We nominate first-gear blasts in an F40 as the drug of choice for the 1990s. It's certainly expensive enough.

Here's the least fun thing you can do with a Ferrari F40: drive it 60 miles on a traffic-choked freeway. Pure terror. Since the rear cabin window is plastic, the view is distorted, so you can't watch for cops, or see the crazies weaving in for a closer look. Rear-quarter vision is bad too, so lane changes require leaps of faith. The door mirrors are not much help; they're mostly full of rear fender. Seating is so low you look directly into the rear license plates of Taurus wagons. Other cars tower over this one, making it difficult to anticipate slowing traffic ahead. Prayers are offered that the driver of that semi in the next lane sees you and doesn't come over unannounced. And this certainty: every Porsche, Corvette, and Mustang driver will offer that silent challenge, so you will be called upon to ceremonially smoke them all off and you wrestle with the absolute, overmastering compulsion to dip into the *whoosh* every time the traffic clears but you can't pass anyone too fast because they might pull out on you and you have to keep a vigilant eye for road debris because the front end is so incredibly low and don't forget to slow down for those steep driveways and keep the revs above 4500 so the plugs stay clear and don't do anything stupid because if you mess up *this is someone else's THREE-QUARTER-OF-A-MILLION-DOLLAR CAR.*

Arrive, finally. Palms wet. Squeeze out of the cockpit. It's safe at last, safe at last. Glad that's over with. Gawd, how to get more? More!

Ferrari's best guess is that it will ship about 200 U.S.-legal F40s to America. That may be just about enough. There probably aren't a whole lot more people who can take this much pressure.

Ferrari F40

Vehicle type: mid-engine, rear-wheel-drive, 2-passenger, 2-door coupe

Price as tested: $399,150

Options on test car: base Ferrari F40, $395,000 (includes $1850 gas-guzzler tax); freight, $4150

Standard accessories: A/C

Sound system: none

ENGINE
Type . . . . twin-turbocharged and intercooled V-8, aluminum block and heads
Bore x stroke . . . . 3.23 x 2.74 in, 82.0 x 69.5mm
Displacement . . . . 179 cu in, 2936cc
Compression ratio 7.7:1
Engine-control system . . . . Weber-Marelli IAW with port fuel injection
Emissions controls . . . . 2 3-way catalytic converters, feedback fuel-air-ratio control
Turbochargers . . . . 2 IHI RHB53 LWs
Waste gate . . . . Ferrari
Maximum boost pressure . . . . 16.0 psi
Valve gear . . . . belt-driven double overhead cams, 4 valves per cylinder
Power (SAE net) . . . . 478 bhp @ 7000 rpm
Torque (SAE net) . . . . 424 lb-ft @ 4500 rpm

DRIVETRAIN
Transmission 5-speed
Transfer-gear ratio 1.33:1
Final-drive ratio . . . . 2.90:1, limited slip

Gear	Ratio	Mph/1000 rpm	Max. test speed
I	2.77	7.0	54 mph (7750 rpm)
II	1.71	11.3	88 mph (7750 rpm)
III	1.23	15.8	122 mph (7750 rpm)
IV	0.96	20.2	157 mph (7750 rpm)
V	0.77	25.4	197 mph (7750 rpm)

DIMENSIONS AND CAPACITIES
Wheelbase . . . . 96.5 in
Track, F/R . . . . 62.8/63.2 in
Length . . . . 171.6 in
Width . . . . 77.6 in

Height . . . . 44.3 in
Frontal area . . . . 19.9 sq ft
Curb weight . . . . 3018 lb
Weight distribution, F/R 38.9/61.1%
Fuel capacity . . . . 26.4 gal
Oil capacity . . . . 9.5 qt
Water capacity . . . . 18.0 qt

CHASSIS/BODY
Type . . . . plastic panels bonded to steel-tubing space frame
Body material . . . . Kevlar- and carbon-fiber-reinforced plastic

INTERIOR
SAE volume, front seat . . . . 46 cu ft
luggage space . . . . 4 cu ft
Front seats . . . . bucket
Seat adjustments . . . . fore and aft, seatback angle
General comfort . . . . poor fair **good** excellent
Fore-and-aft support . . . . poor fair **good** excellent
Lateral support . . . . poor fair good **excellent**

SUSPENSION
F: . . . . ind, unequal-length control arms, coil springs, anti-roll bar
R: . . . . ind, unequal-length control arms, coil springs, anti-roll bar

STEERING
Type . . . . rack-and-pinion
Turns lock-to-lock 2.9
Turning circle curb-to-curb . . . . 38.1 ft

BRAKES
F: . . . . 13.0 x 1.2-in vented disc
R: . . . . 13.0 x 1.2-in vented disc
Power assist . . . . none

WHEELS AND TIRES
Wheel size . . . . F: 8.0 x 17 in, R: 13.0 x 17 in
Wheel type . . . . Speedline 3-piece modular aluminum, center-lock hubs
Tires . . . . Pirelli P Zero, F: 245/40ZR-17; R: 335/35ZR-17
Test inflation pressures, F/R . . . . 44/44 psi

CAR AND DRIVER TEST RESULTS

ACCELERATION
	Seconds
Zero to 30 mph	1.8
40 mph	2.5
50 mph	3.6
60 mph	4.2
70 mph	4.9
80 mph	5.7
90 mph	7.2
100 mph	8.3
110 mph	9.5
120 mph	11.0
130 mph	13.5
140 mph	15.6
150 mph	18.0
160 mph	21.3
170 mph	26.3
Top-gear passing time, 30–50 mph	12.1
50–70 mph	12.2
Standing ¼-mile	12.1 sec @ 122 mph
Top speed	197 mph

BRAKING
70–0 mph @ impending lockup . . . . 218 ft

Modulation . . . . poor fair good **excellent**
Fade . . . . **none** moderate heavy
Front-rear balance . . . . **poor** fair good

HANDLING
Roadholding, 300-ft-dia skidpad . . . . 1.01 g
Understeer . . . . **minimal** moderate excessive

COAST-DOWN MEASUREMENTS
Road horsepower @ 30 mph . . . . 5 hp
50 mph . . . . 14 hp
70 mph . . . . 30 hp

FUEL ECONOMY
EPA city driving . . . . **12 mpg**
EPA highway driving . . . . 17 mpg
C/D observed fuel economy . . . . **9 mpg**

INTERIOR SOUND LEVEL
Idle . . . . 78 dBA
Full-throttle acceleration . . . . 95 dBA
70-mph cruising . . . . 89 dBA
70-mph coasting . . . . 88 dBA

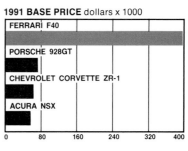

1991 BASE PRICE dollars x 1000

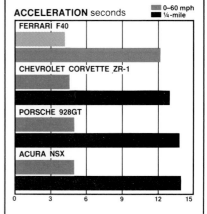

ACCELERATION seconds

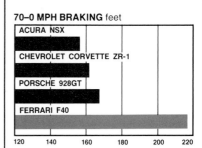

70–0 MPH BRAKING feet

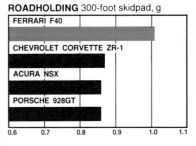

ROADHOLDING 300-foot skidpad, g

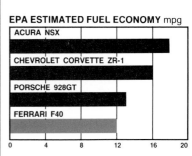

EPA ESTIMATED FUEL ECONOMY mpg

BEST SEDANS
IN THE WORLD

By William Jeanes

What we're about to do here is tell you about the Best Sedan in the World, Regardless of Price. What we're not going to do is bore you with disclaimers that say choosing the winner took so much effort that it wasn't any fun. After all, how could spending a week with four cars worth nearly $350,000 *not* be any fun?

Mind you, when you're driving something that costs more than some condominiums, there's a compulsion to look both ways with greater care than you would with lesser cars. It's one thing to explain how you got shopping-mall acne on the door of a Dodge Colt and quite

another to explain away dings on a Bentley that weren't there when you borrowed it.

But we overcame these concerns—and a few others you're going to hear about—in an effort to name what we believe to be the best four-door luxury transportation you'd ever be able to find. You should note that the "value" category you normally see in our comparison tests is absent. Price, in other words, doesn't matter. Only excellence.

The BMW 750iL won, so you can stop right here if you aren't interested in what it's like to drive cars that really rich people get to drive and if you don't care how

With price no object, we determine which car offers the best four-door luxury transportation. From left: Lexus LS400, Bentley Turbo R, Mercedes-Benz 560SEL, BMW 750iL.

we reached that conclusion. But, on the assumption that you're as curious as we were when we started this project, we'll continue to elaborate on what we learned and how we learned it.

The first thing we found out when we tried to assemble a Bentley Turbo R, a BMW 750iL, and a Mercedes-Benz 560SEL is that the Bentley people don't want to part with their cars. Well, they do *want* to part with their cars, but so many wealthy Americans are hammering on their dealers that they sell them all. They told us to hang on—there'd be a car for us to test soon.

When the day finally came, nine months after we'd started asking, the Bentley man got run into by a truck as he was on his way here with the car. By then, of course, we were too far into this exercise to quit. Our friend Rick Mancuso, proprietor of Lake Forest Sports Cars near Chicago, saved the day by arranging for us to borrow a valued customer's Turbo R. Richard Templer's Bentley was, however, a 1989 model and did not have the new electronic suspension. Right there, we were in trouble.

We next decided to include a $44,700 Lexus LS400 in the test. The inclusion of a car with a base price half that of the Mercedes-Benz may look dumb, but it wasn't. The Lexus went into the mix as a control car because it won our "Showdown" luxury-sedan comparison test in December 1990, besting six worthy competitors. We felt, therefore, that the Lexus could help us find out how good is good. Much as you would send a Triple-A shortstop up to the majors to see if he's got the stuff to play with the big guys.

The Lexus has the right stuff, so now you know that. But if you want to know about the Bentley and the Mercedes-Benz and how they compared with the Maximum Bimmer and the light-on-the-wallet Lexus, keep reading.

BENTLEY TURBO R
4TH PLACE

If you are a person to whom status means everything and to whom the making of an automotive statement means more than your mother or your firstborn, write out your check for $170,852 (our 1989 Bentley cost $149,500), take the Bentley home, and forget about reading beyond this sentence.

You could be seen sneaking Kim Basinger into your home, or you could be seen parking a gloss-black Bentley Turbo R in your driveway. Either act will gain you all the respect and slavering envy you've ever coveted from your neighbors.

We immediately noticed that the Bentley had, without question, the best paint job most of us had ever seen on a production car. You rarely see an automotive finish that makes you look at BMWs and Mercedes and wonder if their paint got put on with a towel. That's how good our Bentley's exterior finish was.

Open the big door and climb into the Bentley and we'll guarantee that the cabin will remind you of the bar at Claridge's in London. The difference, of course, is that more care and money have been lavished on the Bentley. The seats are big and sofalike, though not overly spacious in front, and you feel as if you were sitting at one end of a dining table, gazing through glass at the far end, about twenty yards distant.

In your hand, the leathered wheel feels a bit thin in diameter, but not off-putting. The instruments, which you can easily see, have about them that air of efficiency from another time—think of those great brass instruments you see in movie scenes set in a ship's engine room—but they are thoroughly modern and complete.

In the rear, that hidebound haven for hedonists, there's a ton of space, including ample legroom but not-so-ample headroom. The carpets are of good wool, clipped short but not too short, and over the entire compartment wafts the good-leather smell that only the English seem able to create. (This is true, actually, and it has to do with the tanning process and the chemicals employed therein; the Lexus development team duplicated this, which is why the Lexus smells like a Jaguar inside.) Getting into the rear compartment is so easy that it will remind you of entering a minivan.

Under way, the 5124-pound Bentley will astound you with its responsiveness. It is so unexpectedly quick for such a heavyweight that, as you drive by the peasants trying to look like you're a Bentley owner, a grin of surprise repeatedly crinkles the face that you're trying to keep straight. Zero to 60 mph in 7.7 seconds and a standing quarter-mile of 16.0 seconds at 87 mph are impressive numbers for this mastodon. Astonishingly, the Bentley turned in the shortest braking distance from 70 mph, a surprising 179 feet.

Not only does the big, 325-hp turbo V-8, with its 450 pound-feet of torque at

The Bentley Turbo R is far faster than anything its size has a right to be. It also has the only interior we've seen lately that would justify a stiff initiation fee and the payment of dues.

3200 rpm, move things along with strength and dispatch, but the three-speed automatic's electric shifter is as silky as any we've ever experienced, and the turbo boost comes on so smoothly as to go almost unnoticed.

The Bentley—and this is the 1989 model, remember—did not absorb the sharp, annoying bumps that characterize many of our roads here in the Midwest. We experienced severe pothole feedback through the steering wheel and an overall shudder in the chassis over small bumps. Larger imperfections were handled quite nicely, however. We also witnessed visible hood shake—surprising in such a car, even after accounting for the length of the

Bentley's hood. At freeway speeds, the Turbo was stable and had more immediate throttle response above 70 mph than the others, but it also had far more wind noise, leaving us with mixed feelings about its worth as a long-distance freeway cruiser.

As a statement, however, it excels.

Lexus LS400
3rd Place

You've heard a lot about the Lexus, and we've written a lot about it. What you've heard and what we've written have been, preponderantly, favorable comments. This unfair matchup only serves to re-qualify the Lexus LS400 as a true automotive achievement.

In refinement, the Lexus LS400 takes a back seat to none of our gang of four. In back-seat room, it takes...well, a back seat. But keep in mind that the Lexus marketers never intended to position the car as a top-of-the-line luxury machine. Remembering that, and remembering that the Lexus folks definitely consider it a workable *alternative* to expensive luxury cars, the LS400 emerges as a fox in the henhouse.

"I can't believe that this car compares so well to the expensive cars," was a comment heard more than a few times during our testing days.

There were, of course, indications that the Lexus was a bit of a social climber. For one thing, its 7.9-second 0-to-60-mph time was the slowest of this bunch. For another, there's too much plastic in the interior. "But it's *good* plastic," said one of the testers, and he was right. Still, there's an undeniable lack of presence—heritage, if you will—to the interior. It's like some other experiences in life, sensational in the dark but not so memorable in the cold light of day. We may never utter these words again, but just a touch more wood inside might help the ambience.

We considered the four-speed automatic transmission the best of our bunch,

Bentley Turbo R
Highs: *More prestige than the queen and an incomparable interior.*
Lows: *Chassis shudder, hood shake, and a price as high as a cat's back.*
The verdict: *Hard to top as head-turning evidence that you're rich.*

though one of us thought it might have downshifted more readily. Otherwise, it contributed to a driveline so quiet that the tire thump constituted the only intrusive noise, and there was precious little of that.

The ride is the consistency of a firm marshmallow, but with some bump-thump and a touch of vertical body motion. The handling, even under pressure, is capable and controlled, despite the modest 0.73 g of grip provided by its all-season tires. And the Lexus is the most placid of the four on the freeway, for which it seems heaven-sent.

The combination of a comfortable interior, a silky 250-hp double-overhead-cam V-8, and an almost supernatural attention to detail makes the LS400 at home in any company, including this aggregation. What can we say? We were surprised, and then again, not so surprised. The Lexus may not be the car you want to arrive in, but it may be the car you'd like to drive there in.

Lexus LS400
Highs: *Smoothness, speed, overall silkiness, outstanding value.*
Lows: *Close-quarter rear seat, embryonic prestige factor.*
The verdict: *An excellent value that will improve with age.*

With by far the lowest sticker price in this test, the Lexus compared well in major categories.

Mercedes-Benz 560SEL
2nd Place

In our three editors' overall ratings, the Mercedes-Benz finished four points behind the 750iL. We'd say that most of the difference is attributable to age: the Bimmer is a younger design and benefits from newer technology and construction. (The new S-class Mercedes arrived in U.S. showrooms in late 1991.)

Of our four luxury sedans, the Mercedes wins the rear-seat award. That's no small matter, because a true luxury car must have a large rear compartment in order to merit the designation. The 560SEL is unquestionably the car that we'd like to be driven in, assuming a competent and aggressive chauffeur is at the wheel.

Not that this car is unpleasant to drive yourself. We've always believed that the S-class Benzes are among the best long-legged cruisers ever, and our test car upheld the tradition. Its 238-hp aluminum V-8 launches the Mercedes to 60 mph in seven seconds flat. The car will cruise forever at 125 mph—if only we had the roads, and the permission, to do it—and its every act sends a clear message that, with a big Mercedes, performance never takes a back seat to luxury.

"This car doesn't get fazed by much of anything," one of us wrote in the 560SEL's notebook. And that's a good way to look at the S-class flagship. The minute you're seated in the big, comfortable seat, the car surrounds you with an aura of an all-enveloping mass, a kind of battering-ram-solid sense of security. The combination of security, safety, and speed is, of course, a Mercedes hallmark, and it's a mighty comforting piece of baggage to have along.

The fit and finish inside leave no doubt that the absolute best of every material went into the car's construction. The interior is stark compared with the Bentley's, but it treats its occupants with respect from the twin standpoints of visual satisfaction and tactile comfort.

In town, the Mercedes feels generally docile, if not downright dull. But a vigorously applied right foot sends it into level-one aggressiveness. The engine is noisier and more perceptible to the foot than the Lexus's or the BMW's, but there's enough satisfaction in the smooth application of power to overcome that.

On highways, there's always enough power in reserve to ensure passing without panic, but the traditional Mercedes

Mercedes-Benz 560SEL
Highs: *Strength, security, and a rear seat big enough to live in.*
Lows: *A palpable but unavoidable air of old age.*
The verdict: *Excellent for driving or being driven in, in style.*

bump-thump now makes the car seem older than its other qualities would suggest. This is more sound than feel, but it nonetheless seems out of place in the stratospheric layer of luxury in which this car competes.

The driving position fit every size editor, though some wished for a lumbar support. The steering felt unnecessarily heavy but wasn't uncomfortable. Directional stability was very good, and the prospect of expending a full tank of fuel at one sitting seemed more attractive than not.

"The Mercedes," wrote one editor, "hauls itself around like an All-Pro defensive end—a little ponderous but able to cover an amazing amount of real estate." As it's covering this ground, the car's ride is absorbent to the point of convincing you that it's mushy—yet it never gets wobbly. The car does just about anything you ask of it with surprising agility.

In sum, for a car that's in the final years of a distinguished career, the big S-class Mercedes is little short of amazing. That the word "class" is a part of its name seems altogether right.

BMW 750iL
1st Place

If you can grasp that any number of auto writers, including ours, called the 750iL "the best car in the world" and nobody laughed, then you have an inkling of the level of automotive excellence present in history's finest BMW sedan. What Dom Perignon is to champagne, the 750iL is to luxury sedans.

It is not a showy car. Yet the 750iL commands attention and respect in equal quantities wherever it appears. It's close enough to its 7-series relatives not to appear terribly radical, and it isn't as traditional as the Bentley. But it leaves no doubt in the minds of onlookers that they're in the presence of an automotive heavyweight.

The 296-hp 5.0-liter V-12 leads our field in the number of cylinders and is second in horsepower only to the Bentley (which outweighs the Bimmer by a mere 877 pounds). In that all but indefinable area if integration—the feel of a car's thousands of parts working in concert—there may never have been a better car than the BMW 750iL.

The wonder of all this excellence is that the car is enormous fun to drive. It's fast, it's responsive, it's comfortable, and every piece of it works with every other piece to redefine the concept of a "precision instrument."

The 750iL doesn't redefine taste and restraint and quality, but it demonstrates why writers need those words to describe automobile interiors. Sitting behind the wheel, you look around at finely stitched leather that covers just about everything in sight but the floor—which is covered in carpeting that probably costs almost as much as the hides. The seats, front and rear, are comfortable, supportive, heated, and electrically adjustable. The rear-seat headrests position themselves automatically once the seatbelt is engaged. Over your head, more work has gone into seeing that the headliner is properly fitted and finished than some companies invest in whole cars. Throughout, you're willing to believe that nothing's been left undone and that even less has been left to chance.

Under way, the car exudes smoothness in every mode, from hard acceleration (0 to 60 mph in 6.5 seconds) to hard braking (70 to 0 mph in 182 feet). We attained a governor-limited top speed of 158 mph— fastest of the group—and did so with ease. At all speeds within reason, the

BMW is silent, stable, and satisfying.

Our quibbles were, as you might guess, few: the steering wheel is not adjustable, the climate controls are not as "automatic" as they ought to be, the transmission occasionally downshifts abruptly; and there seems to be less interior space than in the Mercedes.

We liked the supple, well-controlled suspension and the resulting ride, which was the firmest in our foursome. The proper amount of firmness, in our book, goes with high performance and in BMW's book, high performance is deemed synonymous with luxury. This makes the 750iL, as if it didn't have enough going for it, the best driver's car of the four. We call that an unbeatable combination . . . so there you are: a winner of a Bimmer.

It must be godawful nice to be rich.

BMW 750iL
Highs: *Its aura of automotive unity, its style, and its speed.*
Lows: *A too-quiet exterior, our inability to afford it.*
The verdict: *A lesson in what a great touring car ought to be.*

BMW's 750iL is slick, taut, tantalizing, and too good to be believed. It's an exercise in excellence that's an example to all automakers. The clear winner.

C/D Test Results

	acceleration, sec						top speed, mph	braking, 70–0 mph, ft	roadholdi 300-ft skidpad,
	0–30 mph	0–60 mph	0–100 mph	1/4-mile	top gear, 30–50 mph	top gear, 50–70 mph			
BENTLEY TURBO R	2.7	7.7	22.4	16.0 @ 87 mph	3.8	5.4	130	179	0.71
BMW 750iL	2.5	6.5	16.2	14.8 @ 96 mph	3.0	4.4	158	182	0.78
LEXUS LS400	3.0	7.9	20.1	15.9 @ 90 mph	3.6	4.7	150	188	0.73
MERCEDES-BENZ 560SEL	2.6	7.0	19.6	15.5 @ 90 mph	3.8	5.0	140	185	0.78

Vital Statistics

	price, base/ as tested	engine	SAE net power/torque	transmission/ gear ratios:1/ maximum test speed, mph/ axle ratio:1	dimensions, in			
					wheel-base	length	width	hei
BENTLEY TURBO R	$149,500/ $149,500 (1989)	turbocharged and inter-cooled V-8, 412 cu in (6750cc), aluminum block and heads, Bosch MK-Motronic electronic engine-control system with port fuel injection	325 bhp @ 4000 rpm/ 450 lb-ft @ 3200 rpm (C/D estimates)	3-speed auto/ 2.50, 1.50, 1.00/ 52, 87, 130/ 2.69	120.5	207.4	79.0	5
BMW 750iL	$70,000/ $72,860	SOHC V-12, 304 cu in (4988cc), aluminum block and heads, 2 Bosch Motronic electronic engine-control systems with port fuel injection	296 bhp @ 5200 rpm/ 332 lb-ft @ 4100 rpm	4-speed auto with lockup converter/ 2.48, 1.48, 1.00, 0.73/ 56, 93, 138, 158/ 3.15	116.0	197.8	72.6	5
LEXUS LS400	$36,000/ $44,700	DOHC 32-valve V-8, 242 cu in (3969cc), aluminum block and heads, Toyota electronic engine-control system with port fuel injection	250 bhp @ 5600 rpm/ 260 lb-ft @ 4400 rpm	4-speed auto with lockup converter/ 2.53, 1.53, 1.00, 0.71/ 48, 79, 121, 150/ 3.62	110.8	196.7	71.7	5
MERCEDES-BENZ 560SEL	$73,800/ $78,865	SOHC V-8, 338 cu in (5547cc), aluminum block and heads, Bosch KE-III-Jetronic electronic port fuel injection	238 bhp @ 4800 rpm/ 287 lb-ft @ 3500 rpm	4-speed auto/ 3.68, 2.41, 1.44, 1.00/ 49, 75, 125, 140/ 2.47	121.1	208.1	71.7	5

	interior sound level, dBA			fuel economy, mpg		
	full throttle	70-mph cruising	70-mph coasting	EPA city	EPA highway	C/D 500-mile trip
	76	70	69	10	13	14
	74	67	67	12	18	17
	70	67	67	18	23	17
	75	66	66	13	17	14

curb weight, lb	weight distribution, % F/R	fuel tank, gal	interior volume, cu ft			suspension		brakes, F/R	tires
			front	rear	luggage	front	rear		
24	52.9/47.1	28.5	49	43	15	ind, unequal-length control arms, coil springs, anti-roll bar	ind, semi-trailing arm, coil springs with nitrogen-over-oil hydraulic leveling units, anti-roll bar	vented disc/disc; anti-lock control	Avon Turbospeed CR27, 255/65VR-15
47	50.8/49.2	24.0	54	51	13	ind, strut located by 1 leading link and 1 lateral link, coil springs, anti-roll bar	ind, semi-trailing arm, coil springs, automatic-leveling shock absorbers, anti-roll bar	vented disc/disc; anti-lock control	Pirelli P600, 225/60ZR-15
37	52.9/47.1	22.5	56	41	14	ind, unequal-length control arms, air springs, anti-roll bar	ind; 1 trailing link, 2 lateral links, and 1 control arm per side; air springs; anti-roll bar	vented disc/vented disc; anti-lock control	Goodyear Invicta GA M+S, 205/65VR-15
35	53.8/46.2	23.8	51	47	15	ind, unequal-length control arms, coil springs, anti-roll bar	ind, semi-trailing arm, coil springs, automatic-leveling shock absorbers, anti-roll bar	vented disc/disc; anti-lock control	Pirelli P6, 205/65VR-15

Editors' Ratings		engine	trans-mission	brakes	handling	ride	ergo-nomics	comfort	room	fit and finish	luxury features	refine-ment	fun to drive	OVERALL RATING
	BENTLEY TURBO R	9	8	8	7	7	7	8	9	9	9	7	7	83
	BMW 750iL	10	9	10	10	9	9	9	9	10	9	10	10	96
	LEXUS LS400	10	9	9	9	9	10	9	8	10	9	9	9	91
	MERCEDES-BENZ 560SEL	10	9	10	8	9	10	10	9	10	9	9	8	92

Three editors rated the vehicles in each of thirteen categories; the scores presented are averages. A 1-to-10 scale (10 being best) was used for all categories except the Overall Rating, where a 1-to-100 scale was used. The Overall Rating for each vehicle was assigned independently; it is not a summation of the vehicle's points in the other categories.

PHOTOGRAPHY BY AARON KILEY

HOW WE TEST CARS

By Csaba Csere

Because so many of you have asked, and because it's important to you, we're going to reveal the secrets of how we test cars—and why we do it. And first off, we'll ask you to put aside your initial impression of our rock 'n' roll test team shown here. We were just kidding; at *Car and Driver,* the business of instrumented performance testing is serious work. We take cars to the test track for one reason: to get the facts, and just the facts. And to share those with you.

Evaluating cars without objective testing is at best guesswork, and you deserve more than seat-of-the pants guesstimates. Objective analysis—instrumented performance testing—alone can reveal the infinitesimal, incremental improvements that form the foundation of successful automotive development. Just saying that a

car feels fast isn't enough. You need to know how fast is fast.

Objective testing will also lay bare the deceptions inherent in subjective observations. For instance, the sudden kick produced by some turbocharged engines may feel more forceful than the steady pull of a well-tuned four-valve-per-cylinder engine, but that doesn't always mean that the turbo has better acceleration.

Objective performance testing adds the substance to a trained test driver's perceptions. It provides a solid framework upon which the driver can hang the countless subjective observations that produce a comprehensive vehicle evaluation—what you know as a *Car and Driver* road test.

Some automotive publications publish manufacturers' performance data, an approach with many pitfalls. The vested interest an automaker has in its product sometimes transforms in-house performance figures into little more than wishful thinking. Moreover, even when in-house testing is conducted with the best of intentions, differences in procedures can yield inconsistent results. Consider curb weight, for example. Ferrari's official curb weight for the 1984 GTO was 2557 pounds, while the figure we measured on our scales was 2880 pounds. The difference? We made our weight measurements when the car was fully loaded with gasoline and fluids; Ferrari no doubt produced its figure by weighing the car with its fluid reservoirs as dry as dust and then "adjusting" that number with a certain amount of optimism.

To avoid such inconsistencies, we at *Car and Driver* have spent years developing and refining our test procedures. By administering these tests ourselves, we can provide you with the most accurate and consistent performance figures you can find. Anywhere.

Because these performance data provide the backbone for all *Car and Driver* road tests (we conduct instrumented tests on more than 150 vehicles each year), we want you to know how we go about getting them.

THE TEST GEAR

The most important piece of test equipment in our arsenal is a Correvit EEP-4 optical fifth wheel. Actually, "fifth wheel" is a misnomer. Built by Datron-Messtechnik GmbH in West Germany, this exotic device accurately measures time, speed, and distance without a single part touching the ground. There's not a wheel anywhere on it.

The heart of the system is the Correvit-L sensor, which obtains speed measurements by projecting a beam of light onto the ground and electronically scanning the illuminated spot through a series of lenses, optical splitters, and photo transistors. The result is a speed figure accurate to one-half of one percent from 0 to 150 mph. Simple calibrations of the sensor allow us to measure speed on wet pavement, snow, ice, and even dirt.

Using this speed signal and a built-in crystal-controlled clock, the Correvit's small on-board computer calculates distance; it then computes and prints out the final acceleration, braking-distance, and coast-down data. We file the tapes.

This German-made Correvit computer is connected to the "fifth wheel," shown next page. The box computes and prints out final acceleration, braking distance, and coast-down data. We file the tapes.

On occasions when the Correvit is being used at a different site, we perform our instrumented tests with a Lamar Instruments fifth wheel. Rather than using an optical sensor, the Lamar system measures distance with a twenty-inch-diameter wheel and an optical encoder that creates 100 precise electronic impulses for each foot traveled. An internal computer then performs calculations similar to the Datron's; however, the older Lamar device provides less flexibility in test programming.

Each of the systems, the Datron and the Lamar, fits in its own compact, custom-made case. Each case also includes a sound-level meter, a skidpad timer, measuring tapes, and a small weather station (a barometer, an anemometer, and a sling psychrometer—used to monitor temperature and calculate relative humidity).

Some exotic test vehicles—most racing cars, for example—produce so much electrical interference that neither of our fifth wheels functions effectively. In such cases, we use a sophisticated radar-transponder system produced by Micromet, of Ann Arbor. This system feeds a precise radar-gun-generated speed signal to a strip-chart recorder, from which we can distill the test results. If the Micromet transponder cannot be attached to a particular test vehicle, we use our Kustom Signals HR-4 radar gun, which has been modified to perform a similar function—albeit at shorter range.

Test tracks are also vital tools of our trade. Some readers may envision us happily lapping our own private test track, but in fact we perform the majority of our evaluations—on rented time—at the Chrysler proving grounds in Chelsea, Michigan. A twenty-minute drive from our Ann Arbor headquarters, the CPG contains every venue we need to conduct a full round of tests: a long, flat straightaway; a 4.7-mile high-speed oval; and a huge vehicle-dynamics area that looks like the world's loneliest parking lot and contains a 300-foot-diameter skidpad. We also test at various drag strips throughout the country and at proving grounds around the world.

This is the Correvit outboard portion of the computer shown on the previous page. This "fifth wheel" measures time, speed and distance without a single part touching the ground. There's no wheel on it.

ACCELERATION

To most of our readers, the numbers obtained from our 0-to-60-mph and quarter-mile tests are the most important found on our specifications pages. These tests are also the most fun to perform. But before we burn any rubber, we fill the test car to the brim with fuel whose octane is no lower than the manufacturer's specification. We also set the tire pressures to the manufacturer's recommendations for light load and high speed (if available).

All testing is performed with windows up and power-robbing accessories (such as air conditioning) turned off—even when testing in the sweltering August heat of Phoenix. This procedure not only assures that each car delivers its best performance but also standardizes the procedure.

A quick start is the key to a good acceleration time. To achieve the most effective launch, we experiment with starting techniques. With manual-transmission cars, the best procedure usually involves dropping the clutch while the engine rpm is held at some elevated point below the redline. The goal is to spin the wheels just enough to ensure that the engine is in the heart of its power band when the tires hook up. Cars that have more traction than power—most full-time four-wheel-drive cars, for example—cannot be made to develop significant wheelspin. In such cases, slipping the clutch usually works best.

Most cars equipped with automatic transmissions benefit from brake torquing —applying the brakes with the left foot while simultaneously pressing the throttle with the right foot. This raises engine rpm just before launch, providing better off-the-line response. Brake torquing is unnecessary when testing cars with lots of low-end torque (Corvettes, for example), but it's especially effective for avoiding lag in turbocharged cars. To be certain that we get the best from an automatic, we also try upshifting manually.

We do our utmost to extract the best performance from our test cars, but we always lift off the throttle and disengage the clutch during shifts and we never exceed the engine's redline. In fact, if the engine's peak power and torque are concentrated at low rpm, it doesn't pay to wind the engine to the redline at all.

We run all of our acceleration tests to at least 100 mph (unless the vehicle can't go that fast). With faster machines, we continue to 150 mph—if our test track is long enough.

Because a car's performance changes with variations in the weather—cars run better on cold days with high barometric pressure, for instance—and because we test year-round, all over the world, we correct our test results to consistent atmospheric conditions (29.92 inches of mercury, 60 degrees Fahrenheit, and zero humidity). That ensures that the acceleration numbers you see on our spec page are comparable car-to-car, month-to-month, and year-to-year.

TOP-GEAR ACCELERATION

Standing-start acceleration performance is primarily a reflection of a car's power-to-weight ratio. Even a car whose engine is weak at low rpm can usually generate good acceleration times following a high-rpm clutch drop. That's why our top-gear acceleration tests measure a powertrain's flexibility when it is forced to pull from low rpm. This test gives you a good idea of how much passing power is on tap if you choose not to downshift manually.

We perform this test in two speed ranges: 30 to 50 mph and 50 to 70 mph. For each test, we shift into the vehicle's highest gear and stabilize its speed at the lower end of the test range. Then we floor the throttle and simultaneously press a hand-held button that starts a clock on our test equipment. We perform two runs in two directions for each test. The published figure is the average of the results —corrected to standard weather conditions, of course.

Cars with automatic transmissions naturally kick down in this test, giving them a decided advantage. But that merely reflects what happens in the real world. With either kind of transmission, good top-gear acceleration combined with good off-the-line acceleration translates into power when you need it. Or just want it.

TOP SPEED

Estimating a car's top speed based on its claimed power, drag coefficient, and other physical characteristics is a low-accuracy crapshoot. That's why we take every car we test to a high-speed oval or a long stretch of track and keep our right foot down until the vehicle stops accelerating or reaches its redline in its highest gear. This test requires lots of real estate and a skilled driver (especially when testing a 231-mph Callaway Corvette). But we feel that "getting the number" is worth the effort, because manufacturers' top-speed claims are traditionally unreliable—or just unavailable. *Car and Driver* is the only automotive publication in the U.S. that conducts top-speed evaluations on every test car. There's no other way to answer the question, "What'll it do?"

Our Datron and Lamar fifth wheels cannot be used for top-speed tests, because the added aerodynamic drag of the equipment might well cost a few mph. Instead, we measure the time a car needs to cover a known distance, which is never less than 0.5 mile. On the few occasions when that's not possible (testing a prototype on a restricted track for example), we use our instruments to calibrate the vehicle's tachometer or speedometer at a lower speed and then calculate a top-speed figure.

To minimize any wind or grade effects, we perform all top-speed tests in two directions and average the results.

BRAKING

We measure stopping ability with the same equipment we use in acceleration tests. We perform six stops from 70 mph, driving approximately one mile between runs to cool the brakes, and we publish the second-shortest stopping distance.

Our procedure is to accelerate to just above 70 mph, stabilize the car's speed, and firmly apply the brakes—holding the tires on the verge of lockup. (We avoid lockup during stops because locked wheels add to the stopping distance, reduce directional control, and leave embarrassing flat spots on the tires.) A pressure switch on the brake pedal signals the test equipment to record the speed at which the brakes were first applied; si-

multaneously, the equipment zeroes a distance counter. When the car comes to a stop, the equipment prints out the time elapsed and the distance covered. During data processing, we normalize the result to produce a stopping distance from exactly 70 mph.

Anti-lock brakes make our job easier, but even with ABS we experiment with pedal pressure. Some ABS systems produce the shortest stopping distance when you slam your foot against the brake pedal; others are most efficient with just enough pedal pressure to engage the ABS slightly.

The tester also gauges fade (degradation in stopping power as the brakes heat up in hard use), front-rear balance (which tires lock up first, the fronts or the rears?), and modulation (how well the brakes respond to changes in pedal pressure as the tires approach lockup). These are subjective evaluations, but the ratings become clear after several stops at maximum deceleration.

HANDLING

The fundamental objective handling test is roadholding—a car's absolute grip on the road. We perform this test on a skidpad, driving around a 300-foot-diameter circle and measuring our lap times with a photocell-activated stopwatch. The procedure is simple: we drive as quickly as we can while keeping the vehicle centered on the line of the circle. We take the average time of four laps—two in each direction—and then calculate the final maximum lateral-g figure ("max lat" in engineering jargon).

Almost every car understeers to some extent when pushed to the limit of adhesion on the skidpad. (Understeer means the front tires run out of adhesion in a turn before the rears do.) We subjectively categorize the understeer and report it on

To test stopping time and distance, we accelerate to just above 70 mph, stabilize the car's speed, and firmly apply the brakes—holding the tires on the verge of lockup, but avoiding lockup, which would add to stopping distance.

our spec page. This test also provides an ideal opportunity to evaluate the lateral support of the driver's seat.

Roadholding is a steady-state test. To measure transient handling—a car's ability to change direction—we use a slalom test. We lay out a course using eleven cones spaced 100 feet apart in a straight line and drive a serpentine path through them as quickly as possible. An onboard observer times the runs. Repeatable performance in the slalom test requires a high degree of driver skill, so we use this tool only when we have a group of cars that can be tested together by one driver under identical conditions.

SOUND LEVEL

Noise—or, more specifically, the lack of it—is an important component of driving comfort. We measure the overall sound level in a vehicle with a Brüel & Kjaer Type 2225 sound-level meter coupled to a microphone at the driver's right ear. The sound level is measured in decibels using the A-weighting scale.

We take our measurements at idle, during full-throttle acceleration between 0 and 70 mph, and while cruising and coasting at 70 mph. The last two measurements determine the powertrain's contribution to the overall noise at that fixed speed. All measurements are the averages of runs in two directions—to minimize wind effects—and are taken with all noise-generating devices (radio, heater fan, vents, wipers) turned off.

COAST-DOWN

A coast-down is the most direct way of measuring a vehicle's overall drag. In the test, we let the vehicle coast on a flat road from 60 to 20 mph with its transmission in neutral; as the vehicle slows, we take measurements of elapsed time at specific speeds. The final result is a speed-versus-time curve that we mathematically massage to extract the vehicle's aerodynamic and frictional drag components. From these we calculate road horsepower, which is the power required to overcome the drag of the vehicle at any specific speed. We publish the figures for 30, 50, and 70 mph.

FUEL ECONOMY

We do not have the resources to measure fuel economy under consistent driving or

On the skidpad, the front tires of most cars run out of adhesion before the rears do. This phenomenon is called understeer. *The skidpad also lets us evaluate lateral support in the driver's seat.*

environmental conditions. Therefore, we rely on the Environmental Protection Agency for precise fuel-economy data. One may quibble about the makeup of the EPA's city and highway driving cycles, but the tests are performed under highly regulated conditions, and every car certified for sale in the country must undergo them. So, if nothing else, they are consistent.

For reference, we publish the actual fuel economy our test cars achieve while in our custody. Though our cars are driven under a variety of conditions by many different drivers, they are all driven hard. Our results generally correspond to the EPA's tough city-cycle figures. Your actual mileage, as they say in the commercials, may vary—but unless you drive like a New York cabbie, it'll probably be better than ours.

And there you have it, testing fans. We realize that we've probably told you one or two things more than you wanted to know, but we hope that by so doing we've given you a clear picture of how we test, why we test, and why it's important to us as well as to you.

Just don't do any of this to your mom's or dad's car (or to your son's or daughter's) unless you take the owner along.

AARON KILEY

ILLUSTRATION BY MIKIO OKAMOTO

Above is artist's rendering. Below is photo of clay model.

1995 CORVETTE

By Rich Ceppos

The countdown to the next-generation Corvette is under way, and the human machinery is whirring up to full speed. These days, hundreds of people at the Chevrolet Division of General Motors—designers, engineers, product planners, and financial analysts—are huddling around their computer workstations and meeting in big, windowless conference rooms to decide the fate of the next two-seat Chevy.

In a few years, the first pre-production 1995 Corvettes are expected to begin trickling off the assembly line in Bowling Green, Kentucky. For that to happen on time, strategic decisions must be made now.

Normally, a news brief like this one would end right here. No film at eleven, no hourly updates. The press is not a welcome guest at the Corvette group's long-range planning sessions. The people in the know want to discuss their secret new models with automotive journalists about as much as they want to show up at work in their underwear.

But they don't have to talk. We have pictures. Spy pictures. And we were granted access to the CERV III (Corporate Experimental Research Vehicle), the single greatest influence on the technology that will be woven into the next Corvette. All of this, taken together, points like a weather vane in the direction of the 1995 Corvette.

First, the physical evidence. The silvery apparition you see below is not the 1995 Corvette—at least not yet. At this point it is the leading design proposal for the new car, sculptured full-size in clay and covered with a thin silver coating to give it added realism. With years of work ahead,

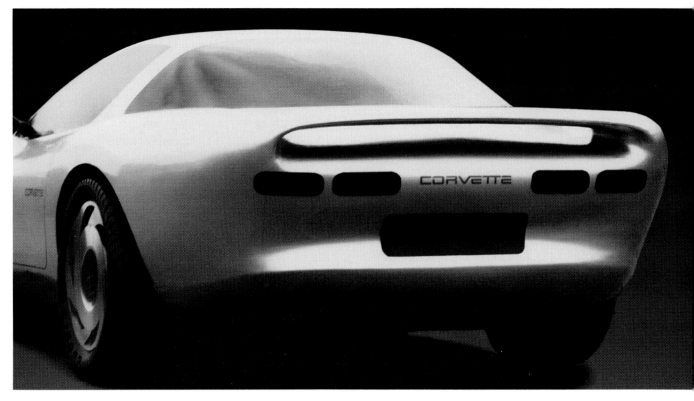

An integral spoiler on the rump will reduce aerodynamically induced rear-end lift at high speeds. The taillights evidence a strong family resemblance to those of the ZR-1.

the designers are still feeling their way, searching for the nuances of the final form, indicating some but not all of the details.

The new shape is most striking—and most believable—in side view, but other angles reveal several features that look right enough to make it onto the final product. The prow-like front end is a recurring theme on recent Chevy show cars, and something a lot like it will adorn the front end of the 1994 Camaro. The prototype Corvette's tail shows a strong family resemblance to the current ZR-1's, with the trademark rectangular taillights stretched taut.

Fastback shapes like the Corvette's are notorious for their aerodynamically induced rear-end lift at high speeds, so an integral spoiler, such as the one seen on the rump of the prototype, makes sense. Removable roof panels are likely to continue as well—the prototype shows cut lines indicating the familiar targa-style top.

As for the skin itself, you can bet your alloy wheels it won't be steel. Tradition dies hard. The Chevy folks cherish their 35 years of building Corvettes from fiberglass. Expect some sort of composite (reinforced plastic) panels bonded to a steel skeleton, much as is done now.

A slinky body alone does not a new Corvette make, of course. We need to know about the guts of the new machine: will the next Vette have performance to lust for? Will it handle like a four-wheeled Baryshnikov? Will it corner hard enough to rip chunks out of the asphalt?

In looking for the answers, our inquiry unearthed almost enough evidence for a conviction. The key was the CERV III, which turned up on the Chevrolet stand at this year's auto show in Detroit wearing a Corvette badge. That led a lot of people to believe they were looking at the 1995 Corvette.

The CERV III is unequivocally not the next Corvette. It is, however, exactly what its name says it is: a corporate experimental research vehicle. The CERV's mission is to explore all of the technological possibilities available for pushing performance and handling beyond anything available in today's high-performance machines. That it does, but no one at GM's Advanced Vehicle Engineering group is about to share the hard-earned information gleaned from the CERV with the rest of the world's carmakers.

Still, we've managed to learn enough through other channels to have a good idea about which of the CERV's advanced systems show promise—so we'll conduct our own briefing right here. Running down the CERV's technology menu, here's what you can expect when the next Corvette pops out of the oven.

Basic configuration: The CERV is a mid-engined car with a complicated four-wheel drive system. The new Vette, however, will have its engine in front, driving the rear wheels.

Engines and transmissions: The CERV is powered by a 650-hp turbo-charged version of the 32-valve LT5 V-8 from the ZR-1. The '95 Corvette will offer two 32-valve all-aluminum V-8s: the current LT5—tweaked to about 400 hp—and a new base engine, code-named "LT1." The LT1 will displace between 4.2 and 5.0 liters and will develop 300 hp. This powerplant could either be supplied by Isuzu (a prototype of such an engine was unveiled at last year's Tokyo Motor Show) or be an adaptation of the GM Northstar 4.5-liter V-8 coming on the 1992 Cadillac Seville. Transmissions will include the current Vette's six-speed manual gearbox and an automatic.

Chassis hardware: The CERV incorporates a mind-boggling array of computer-controlled chassis pieces, including active suspension, four-wheel steering, traction control, and anti-lock brakes. All those systems are interactive—linked by powerful computers that enable them to work together to enhance handling and control. If sensors detect the tail sliding in hard cornering, the system will automatically reduce power to the rear tires and steer the rear wheels to help counter the slide.

Active suspension is not in the production plan at this point. It continues to be expensive and unreliable. Its place could be taken by the so-called fast shocks rumored to be under development. Fast shocks are quick-reacting, automatically adjusting dampers that sense bumps and switch to the optimum setting for precise control of body motions—a quicker version of the smart system used on the plush-riding Lincoln Continental.

Four-wheel steering is a good bet, because the hardware is relatively straightforward; it's the software that's complex. The CERV's system can steer the rear wheels up to nine degrees, and it can even compensate for crosswind gusts. It slows down steering response at high speeds and endows the CERV with uncanny stability, we're told. It should do the same for the 1995 Vette.

One of two traction-control systems will be incorporated as standard equipment. The first, an adaptation of current systems, allows you to choose from two settings: a minimal-slip program for the street and a performance calibration that allows more rear-tire slip—which is optimal for autocross or racetrack use.

The second system, explored on the CERV, reduces wheelspin with something called a "pedal pusher." When the drive wheels start to spin, a mechanism in the throttle linkage simply pushes the pedal back. If you want the wheels to spin, you push through this resistance.

The anti-lock brakes on the CERV employ a similar pedal-pusher arrangement. But, today's anti-lock systems are so well worked out it's unlikely that the CERV's will ever see production.

Structural materials: The CERV III's body shell is made from the same kind of exotic space-age materials used on Formula 1 cars—Kevlar, carbon fiber, aluminum honeycomb. Its disc brakes (two per wheel) use carbon-fiber rotors and pads. Unfortunately, all of this stuff is also space-age expensive, so don't expect to see more than a few pounds of it on the 1995 Corvette. The driveshafts and the

central torque tube connecting the gearbox and the differential could be made of carbon fiber, but that's about it. As a result, the 1995 Vette will weigh the same as today's car—about 3300 pounds.

Everything we've been able to uncover points to a Corvette with much better performance and handling—no complaints here. But more speed and better grip aren't the only items on our wish list. Today's Corvette is lagging in fit-and-finish quality and structural integrity. It squeaks and rattles and feels more trashy by the mile. What the next Corvette needs is buckets of sweat lavished on details.

Conquering the Vette's massive quality problems will go a long way toward boosting the proud plastic flyer up to the front of the sports-car class. After all of the behind-the-scenes technological horse-trading is finished, let's hope Chevrolet management has the collective will to bless the 1995 Corvette with the kind of craftsmanship it deserves.

The CERV III (Corporate Experimental Research Vehicle) will have great influence on the technology in the next Corvette.

PHOTOGRAPHY BY AARON KILEY

DODGE VIPER

By Patrick Bedard

Unreasonable. That is the word François Castaing uses to describe the Viper. It's not his only word, for sure, but it's the one word he keeps coming back to again and again. "Unreasonable."

Castaing is a 45-year-old Frenchman—a grown-up sixties activist, the architect of Amedée Gordini's turbo racers, and a former manager of Renault's Formula 1 team. His is the résumé of a guy drawn to heat, to making things happen.

So the U.S. is where you'll find him now. In Detroit. At the Chrysler Corporation. Behind the desk in the office reserved for vice president, vehicle engineering. And when he says the Viper is unreasonable, well, who's to argue with the engineering vice president?

Who *could* argue?

Besides, what else could you say about

a 1992 two-seater powered by an 8.0-liter V-10 engine?

What else could you say about a $50,000 car that doesn't have side windows?

What else could you say about a body so voluptuous, so overstuffed, so evocative of zaftig hips and supple loins that you'd swear it's Jayne Mansfield coming back as a sports car?

The Viper is a *perfectly* unreasonable car. And that's why Castaing and Chrysler Motors president Bob Lutz and a hand-picked group of some 50 get-it-done guys within the company love it so much. The Viper makes a statement, and what it says is that the Lamborghini Countach is just another two-door hardtop.

"When we tell people about this car," Castaing says, "some of them don't under-stand at all. We think that's good. If every-body liked it, we wouldn't be pushing far enough."

This conversation is taking place in the middle of Arizona, where there's still room left to drive. Chrysler is showing its 1991s to the automotive press—and, what the hell, if you had something like the Viper project on the boil in your shop, could you resist showing off a little? So Chrysler packed a harlot-red example into a truck and sent it west.

"This is not a prototype," Bob Lutz says, "We're not that far yet. This is an engi-neering mule."

Lutz has a résumé, too: General Motors, BMW, Ford of Europe, Ford of Dearborn. Now, at 59, he's recently become presi-dent of the Chrysler Corporation. After all those years of jockeying for his chance to sit in the big chair at some car company, he finally has his job. So it's time to show the world what he can do. He's not wasting a minute. The Viper is his way of raising the Jolly Roger. Now everybody can see that the Chrysler Corporation is under new management.

This time, "new management" means more than just changing the names on the reserved-parking slots. It means a whole new way of creating cars. The 50-man Viper group was selected from volunteers within the corporation, largely on the basis of personal want-to. Those 50 guys are completely responsible for the car, right down to sourcing the production parts. "It's a small, dedicated team of people behaving as if they were the owners of the Viper Car Company," Lutz says. "They have goals and budgets, and so long as they stay within that framework, they're their own bosses."

There's a lot of talk in the business world these days about taking the entrepreneurial approach, but few presidents are brave enough to loosen the reins as much as Lutz has with the Viper group. To avoid the appearance of second-guessing them, he hasn't even driven the car in several months. That is, until this week. Now, under the guise of giving rides to

magazine writers, he's getting his first seat time in the V-10 (initial test cars had 360 V-8s).

If Lutz cares a fig what anybody says about him, he sure doesn't show it. He's wearing faded brown Levi cords and a blue windbreaker; his white hair fringes out from under a black IROC cap. There are no handlers in his entourage. He's out front because that's the kind of guy he is, and he talks easily with the writers gathered around the red car.

Chrysler's financial straits are well known. How can the company, in a time like this, spare the cash to develop a car that's unreasonable? Lutz recounts a conversation he had with a young guy in charge of Viper purchasing. The suppliers wanted some money up front before they'd start developing parts. Lutz asked him what he'd do if it were his own project, financed with his own money. Well, he'd try to get every parts builder believing in the project, taking a share of the risk, buying into the mission by supplying development parts at his own cost in order to get a piece of the action later. Lutz told him to do that for the Viper. And if he found any suppliers who absolutely wouldn't go along, then the president would meet them for lunch.

With exhaust ports under each door, driver and rider each hear half of the engine, sounding like an even-five cylinder instead of a V-10.

"I've had only two lunches," Lutz says.

The Viper may look like a sports car, but it's a lot more than that to Chrysler. Earlier, in a quiet conversation, Castaing called it a rebellion. "Like in the sixties, we are trying to show our parents we can do it our own way." This is a rebellion against the big-corporation procedures that don't work anymore, the Harvard B-school methods, the same old ways that always seem to pull Chrysler back to only a half step ahead of its creditors. The Viper is supposed to jolt the internal organization every bit as much as it piques the auto market.

Castaing went on to describe a small group working quickly and efficiently, responding to the needs of the mission rather than to rigid engineering-department procedures or the dictates of the "beanies." "We need to have a few cars out by Christmas 1991 to prove we can do it in three years, and we need to prove we can make a profit on a small volume of cars," he said. "The pride of Chrysler engineering rides on the Viper."

There aren't many gas stations in Arizona's high country, and the mule has only a small tank. So pit stops are frequent. Chrysler technicians are pouring fuel from red 2.5-gallon cans into a big opening on the Viper's back, just under the roll bar, right where racing sports cars of old had their flip-open lids. The engine man, Dick Winkles, has his black box tapped into the V-10's computer, just checking, the auto engineer's version of an EKG. Lutz answers more questions. The price will be less than $50,000. Once under way, production will be 15 to 25 cars a day. But Dodge won't run ahead of demand. "The worst thing that could happen would be a Dodge dealer with a sign out front, 'Vipers in stock, all colors, immediate delivery.'" He wants the car to be scarce, but not a scalper's ticket.

The technicians tell him the mule is ready. Now it's your author's turn in the right seat. Four-point competition belts await, draped over the buckets. The footwell angles my legs outward, away from the car's center line, a reminder that this is a front-engined car. The instruments take me back to the Cobra: round dials in a simple array. A few of the dials have redlines made of tape across their faces. Stuck in the center of the dash is a handwritten crib sheet showing road speed in the gears at various tach readings.

Lutz pulls down his black cap and lets out the clutch. "This car is extremely easy

Like race cars of old, the Viper has its gas cap just behind its roll bar and lacks side windows.

to drive," he says. "We have a six-speed, but the engine doesn't care what gear it's in." To prove his point, he shifts to fifth at what seems a dog trot. Sure enough, the engine shrugs its brawny shoulders. So he shifts to sixth, and even he seems surprised by the indifference under the hood. The V-10 just seems to shuffle along.

The side exhausts position one outlet down under my door. In effect, I hear half an engine. It sounds like an even-fire five, rather mumbly at part throttle, turning to a hard buzz as Lutz pushes wide open. We're following a route that generally encircles Mormon Lake. As we crest a hill, the lake becomes a panorama off to the left. The road ahead bends into a huge sweeper. "Look at that," Lutz says, and it takes me about too clicks to realize he doesn't mean the lake.

He double-clutches down two gears and charges into the bend, building the g's. He's crowding the power—I can hear it in the exhaust—his foot pressing down, then giving back some, aching to get the pedal to the metal, feeling for the right time. The man is motivated. Now the buzz

Pushing the tach in higher gears in this open-top shreds reporters' notebooks.

goes full hard and we depart the sweeper in a defiant blast of V-10 unreasonableness. He flicks into fifth. Wind buffets through the cockpit. We both pull our caps down. The Viper feints left, then right, in response to the morning's gusts. His foot stays down. Nonchalantly, I try to check the speed. The lever is in sixth. The fluttering dash chart shows 119 mph at 3000 rpm. I look over at the tach. We're somewhere north of there and climbing.

I had in mind to take some notes, about the swelling of the hood into what looks like a red horizon, about the immensity of the transmission tunnel, about the grip of the Goodyears. But the wind is shredding my notebook. So I give up on that and turn my mind toward the white-haired man beside me, the one who thrusts this extroverted hunk of car into every bend and immediately begins crowding the power, playing the forces, calling up the g's.

That the president of an American car company would drive like this, is even *able* to drive like this, is a revelation. After years of Motor City insularity and decline, of presidents who did all their hard driving with golf clubs, we've finally got one who stands on the gas.

Foreign competition has finally awakened the giant. I'm considering the implications as Lutz steers into the parking lot, next to the red cans, and cuts the engine. One of the technicians checks his watch. "Sixteen miles in eleven minutes," he announces.

A chuckle of satisfaction comes from the president. The Viper may be unreasonable, but not to him.

VIPER INNARDS

"The Viper exists purely for the fun of driving," says François Castaing. So all compromises have been made to that end. The point of the exercise is a husky, open car with a colossal engine. And Castaing says it will weigh less than 3000 pounds —even if the engineers have to use a pinned, lift-off hood (as on the mule) to save the weight of hinges.

The Viper will have side curtains instead of roll-up windows. The top will be a take-off-and-fold-up affair (perhaps it won't even be standard equipment; the decision is pending). A rear window will pop in place under the roll bar.

As in the mule, the exceptionally wide body (75.7 inches) will be made of fiber-reinforced plastic over a frame of rectangular steel tubing. The suspension will consist of unequal-length control arms with anti-roll bars and coil-over shocks on both ends.

Brakes will be four-wheel discs. An anti-lock system will not be offered, it being contrary to the spirit of elemental driving fun.

Castaing speaks of cornering capability in the range of 1.2 to 1.3 g's. That means sticky tires. Big sticky tires. The mule was equipped with Goodyear Eagle tires: 275/40ZR-17s on 11.0-inch rims in front, 335/35ZR-17s on 13.0-inch rims in back.

Because passenger cars these days are made of wimpy, weight-watcher parts, very little is transferable into an Attila sportster. So the Viper team will borrow where possible from Chrysler's truck division. The standard-equipment power rack-and-pinion steering will be a truck-based part, as will the basic pushrod V-10 engine. But the Viper version will be cast entirely in aluminum, and the heads will get enhanced porting. Port fuel injection and Chrysler's distributorless ignition will also be used. Despite these breathing aids, though, the V-10's personality will remain akin to a truck engine's. Torque is projected to be tremendous: 450 pound-feet in a curve that's quite flat in the 2000–3000-rpm range. The target horsepower of 400 is also expected to arrive at relatively low revs.

With so much output so low in the range, the six-speed Getrag box will be more a gesture to driving fun than to serious motion. You won't have to use all the gears if you don't want to.

In fact, you don't have to care at all about this car. It's meant only for those few drivers who need it bad. Chrysler is counting on them to know who they are.

The pushrod V-10 will be cast in aluminum, heads with advanced porting. Torque is projected to a tremendous 450 pound-feet in the 2000–3000-rpm range.

DODGE VIPER

Vehicle type: front-engine, rear-wheel-drive, 2-passenger, 2-door roadster

Estimated base price: $50,000

Standard accessories: power steering

Sound system: none

ENGINE
Type .... V-10, aluminum block and heads
Bore x stroke .... 4.00 x 3.88 in, 101.6 x 98.6mm
Displacement .... 488 cu in, 7990cc
Compression ratio 9.2:1
Engine-control system .... Chrysler electronic with port fuel injection
Emissions controls .... 3-way catalytic converter, feedback fuel-air-ratio control, EGR, auxiliary air pump
Valve gear .... pushrods, hydraulic lifters
Power (SAE net) .... 400 bhp
Torque (SAE net) .... 450 lb-ft

DRIVETRAIN
Transmission 6-speed
Final-drive ratio .... 3.07:1, limited slip

DIMENSIONS AND CAPACITIES
Wheelbase .... 96.2 in
Track, F/R .... 59.6/60.6 in
Length .... 175.1 in
Width .... 75.7 in
Height .... 44.0 in
Curb weight .... 3000 lb

CHASSIS/BODY
Type .... plastic panels bolted to steel-tubing space frame
Body material .... fiber-reinforced thermoset plastic

SUSPENSION
F: .... ind, unequal-length control arms, 1 coil-shock unit per side, anti-roll bar
R: .... ind, unequal-length control arms and a lateral link, 1 coil-shock unit per side, anti-roll bar

STEERING
Type .... rack-and-pinion, power-assisted

BRAKES
F: .... vented disc
R: .... vented disc
Power assist .... vacuum

WHEELS AND TIRES
Wheel size .... F: 11.0 x 17 in, R: 13.0 x 17 in
Wheel type .... cast aluminum
Tires .... Goodyear Eagle ZR; F: 275/40ZR-17, R: 335/35ZR-17

MANUFACTURER'S PERFORMANCE TARGETS
Zero to 60 mph .... 4.0 sec
Zero to 100 mph .... 10.0 sec
Zero to 100 mph to zero .... 14.7 sec
Top speed .... 188 mph

GLEAMS IN THE EYE

By Phil Berg

Auto companies make great efforts to keep their future models out of public view until ready for sale. Yet since these cars receive track and street tests, vigilant photographers sometimes manage to take "spy photos" for us. Some photos are shot at night or in a hurry, so the results are often too blurry or are otherwise unsuitable for publication. In those instances, we ask illustrators to render them. Here then is a mix of photos and renderings, giving a taste of the future.

BERNIE SOLO

1992 HONDA CRX
Here's is a new version of Honda's cute and cheap sports coupe. This model, about which Honda kept its traditional super-secrecy, is powered by a twin-cam, 1.6-liter four cylinder that features variable valve timing. It's said to produce as much as 150 horsepower, which is 42 hp more than the previous model.

CHRYSLER SPORTS MINIVAN?
Stylists at Chrysler produced this minivan design, anticipating what buyers might want next in a people mover. The recently introduced second-generation of Chrysler minis is the most popular in the little-van market. However, the car itself is not as exciting looking as this rendering. One possible powertrain for this van would be a twin-cam version of the 3.0-liter V-6 currently available, and driving all four wheels.

BERNIE SOLO

1993 MERCEDES
Expected to go on sale in summer 1992, this is an evolution of Mercedes' smallest sedan, the 190 series. This car was photographed during testing in Germany. The top-of-the-line 190E model pictured will be powered by a 200-horsepower 2.8-liter in-line six cylinder.

PORSCHE 962

This street-legal version of Porsche's Group C 962 racing car was the German sports car maker's entry into a growing pool of street racers that became the rage in mid-1990. Latest word is that Porsche will not produce the car, though former racer Vern Schuppan is selling street-legal versions of the 962 for $1.6 million.

FERRARI 12-CYLINDER COUPE

Although Ferrari is testing this sleek convertible, word as we go to press in 1991 is that the car might not carry a Ferrari badge. This Italian sports car company is owned by Fiat, which also owns Lancia, which may wind up with this four-seater. In Ferrari guise, the car would be powered by a 5.0-liter twelve-cylinder engine. The scoops on the hood and other body disguises (shown) are unlikely to appear on the production version.

MERCEDES C112

This is how Mercedes envisions a street-legal model of its quick Group C race car, driven successfully by the Peter Sauber team. This version is called the C112, though the racer's potent turbocharged V-8 engine would likely be replaced by the more docile non-turbocharged V-12 that Mercedes is readying for its new large sedans.

TOYOTA COROLLA GT

Although Corolla advertising boosted the car's success by promoting economy, this view of the future two-door GT model indicates a shift toward high performance. This Corolla GT is powered by a five-valve-per-cylinder, 1.6-liter four cylinder that produces 170 horsepower. A supercharged model is said to produce 200 hp, and rev safely to 9000 rpm. These engines, plus the new curved sheetmetal, should call a new kind of buyer to the former economy car.

CHEVROLET MONTE CARLO

It's possible that General Motors might want to give Ford's rear-drive Thunderbird some competition in the two-door luxury-car market. In that case, Chevrolet has already designed a new Monte Carlo, based on the rear-drive platform of the Caprice. This car would use GM's 5.7-liter V-8 engine. Yet, so outfitted, it might cut into the market for Chevrolet's 210-hp Lumina Z34. Latest word is that the Monte Carlo won't be manufactured.

GIANCARLO PERINI

MASERATI SPORTS COUPE

This mid-engine sports car was drawn by famed Lamborghini designer Marcello Gandini and will become a new Maserati soon. It may be powered by the 3.2-liter V-8 that is currently in use in Maserati's Shamal coupe or by a V-10 engine developed by Alfa Romeo.

1992 HONDA PRELUDE

Honda's newest Prelude, which is the fourth generation of sporty coupes from Honda, will continue to be powered by a 2.0-liter four-cylinder engine. However, rumor says the new coupe will be powered by a turbocharged version of the Prelude's current engine, which will also have variable valve timing. Rumor also suggests four-wheel-drive, which would be appropriate for transmitting the turbo motor's 230 hp to the road.

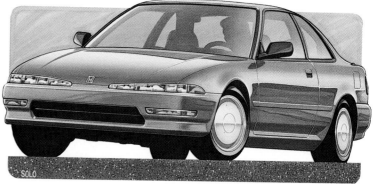

BERNIE SOLO

HANS LEHMANN

BMW 5-SERIES COUPE

This two-door sedan is approximately the same size as BMW's slick 5-series mid-range four-door. However, every body panel is new and much more aggressively styled. Spies have also observed the testing of a tamer version of a two-door 5-series BMW.

1994 FORD MUSTANG

Enthusiasts have been waiting for a car in which to evaluate Ford's robust new overhead cam V-8, which currently resides only in Lincoln's Town Car. This heavily restyled Mustang may be the car. It would employ the current ponycar's rear-drive chassis. With double overhead cams, such a Mustang should produce about 300 hp. Alas, sages suggest we'll need to wait until 1994 for it.

BERNIE SOLO

BERNIE SOLO

MERCEDES 190

A small roadster built from the mechanical pieces of Mercedes' 190 sedan may join the German maker's lineup as soon as 1993. Besides boosting the conservative image of the small sedan line, the new roadster should appeal to sport-oriented buyers, like those who prefer BMW's Z1 roadster. The Benz will have a 160-hp four-cylinder or a 200-hp 2.8-liter six.

JAGUAR TWR XJR-15

You can buy this car for about $1 million, but you have to agree to race it in the JaguarSport International Challenge. If you don't wreck it on the track, you can then use its 6.0-liter, 450-hp motor around town. About thirty such cars were built in 1991.

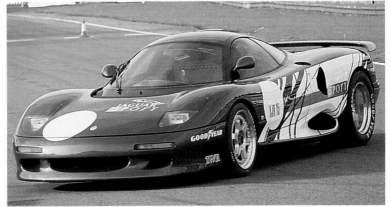

RAY HUTTON

STOP PRESS! SYNDICATION

PORSCHE 911

By 1995 or 1996, Porsche may have a new sports coupe to replace its venerable 911. In keeping with tradition, the new coupe will have a shape similar to the 28-year-old Porsche. The engine will also be mounted in the rear, though we hear that a 4.2-liter V-8 will replace the current 3.4-liter flat six.

CHEVROLET CONCEPT CAMARO

General Motors' Advanced Concept Center in California created the convertible you see here, which looks much like a drawing-board Camaro that the company revealed at the 1989 Los Angeles Auto Show. That car was built on a Camaro chassis and was rear-drive. Perhaps GM is thinking of competing with Dodge's new Viper roadster.

PONTIAC PROTOSPORT4

What about a four-door Firebird for under $25,000? This is what Pontiac offers as one way of building a future four-seat sports sedan. It is rear drive and is powered by a 4.0-liter V-8 that makes 250 horsepower. All four wheels steer, and the body is made of carbon fiber.

FORD CONTOUR

A remarkable new in-line eight-cylinder engine is mounted transversally in the front of Ford's newest concept car, the Contour. Power from the new engine is directed through gears located in the center of the crankshaft. This arrangement leaves room to fit a large engine under a very short hood and leaves space enough for six passengers.

MOE PARE

DODGE NEON

This little number sports a 1.1-liter three-cylinder two-stroke engine under a minimal hood. The rest of the car is big enough for four people, four doors, and a unique trash compactor between the two front seats. The front seats are hammock-style canvas for rear-seat legroom. The Neon's wheels are recycled aluminum.

YESTERYEAR

JEFFREY G. RUSSELL

AMERICAN DREAMCARS

By Brock Yates

PHOTOGRAPHY BY JEFFREY G. RUSSELL

Purists, cover your eyes. Send your children out of the room. We are about to deal with a subject so sacrilegious, so vile and upsetting to your sensibilities, that it may send you screaming into the night hugging your latest issue of *Hemmings.* Let's call it a peek at some automotive soft porn. Better yet, let's call it "Invasion of the Retro Rockets."

Here's the deal. It seems as if everybody is hooked on nostalgia. Vintage racing is hot. Collectors are snapping up rusty Italian coupes with zoomy multi-cam engines. Air shows featuring World War II planes propelled by giant, thumping powerplants attract enormous crowds, as do drag and stock-car races—both of which headline machinery powered by monster V-8s designed in the 1950s and 1960s. Street rods flaunting body styles of the 1930s and 1940s are immensely popular, and good 1960s muscle cars are selling at as much as twenty times their original cost. Otherwise responsible business executives now contemplate selling their teenage daughters into white slavery to pay for throwback Harley-Davidsons with V-Twin engines designed when the Oakland chapter of the Hell's Angels was still a pack of Cub Scouts.

Perhaps this phenomenon is connected to the prospects of the Brave New World,

where smooth-edged androgyny will prevail and all zaniness, originality, and latent irresponsibility may well be crushed under a tide of conformity and collectivism. Whatever the reason, we are looking backward with increasing sentimentality, turning to old machines to reassure us that irrationality in the human species is alive and well.

It was thus all but inevitable that American DreamCars would be created. This new company's products are totally restored but not authentic muscle cars of the 1960s that handle better, stop better, steer better, and almost perform better than those predators that roamed America's streets 25 years ago. In a cavernous building inside a nondescript industrial park in the flight path of Cleveland's Hopkins Airport, a gang of twenty-odd mechanics busily re-create a gaggle of resurrected Oldsmobile 4-4-2s, Pontiac GTOs and Trans Ams, Chevrolet Chevelles and Camaros, and Ford Mustangs for speed-crazed, aging teenage punks.

What they produce are near-perfect new old automobiles: throwback muscle cars with updated drivetrains and better paint and detailing than the originals. No claim is made that the machines are gen-

uine. Quite to the contrary, in fact. Larry Taylor, general manager of manufacturing of the fledgling Cleveland operation, makes a point of noting that each DreamCar is sold with a package of written material describing all the modifications made to the automobile. "Anybody dumb enough to buy one of these and think it's an original deserves what he gets," says the 43-year-old engineer with more than twenty years in the car business. "One look under the hood tells anyone with any understanding of the subject that these aren't classic, original cars with matching serial numbers."

But hang in there. Don't people buy 1960s tire-burners as collector's items, as precious investments to be hauled to car shows on sunny Sundays? Perhaps. But that's not why they buy American DreamCars. "Our customers want a no-brainer," says Taylor. "They don't want the hassle of restoration, of chasing parts, of the constant fiddling with old stuff and the endless repairs. They want to walk out to the garage, climb in, and drive off in what is essentially a brand-new car."

Exactly. Does your basic 44-year-old divorced orthodontist, haunted by the midlife crazies and seeking a few simple hours re-creating life as a hot rodder, want to worry about changing a water pump before he takes a shot at his 23-year-old secretary? *"Jennifer! Get me American DreamCars on one!"*

Okay. Granted that there is a certain group of potential customers who'd love to own one of the machines that made them occasionally drop *Playboy* to read the drag mags when they were kids. Granted that they will pay upwards of 30 grand for a perfect replica with paint, detailing, reliability, and handling superior to the original. Granted that they don't give a hoot that the car is a purist's nightmare, a blatantly bogus knockoff of the original. Granted all of that. The question remains: how, as we careen into the 1990s, does one build a brand-new 25-year-old automobile?

Not easily, it turns out. First, you've got to find original examples (so-called core cars) that form the basis for the restoration. Rust-free models with complete trim and instrumentation are the most desired (red convertibles command a premium), although a vast source pool for replacement bits has been created. "Our ideal candidate is an unrestored but complete car with a blown engine," says the laconic Taylor. "We replace the engine and transmission anyway, so their condition is meaningless to us." The worst cars are those that have been partially restored. ("We have to undo most of what has been done") or—quite obviously—badly wrecked or rusted hulks. "Our best cars often come from the South, although we get the good convertibles from the North, mainly because they were stored for the winter months," Taylor notes.

Once the old crock is hauled to Cleveland, it is stripped to the frame in a so-called dirty room separate from the final assembly hall. The frame and the major body panels are "dry-stripped" to bare metal using plastic pellets that leave the surfaces unharmed. They are then primed and repainted in the company's body shop. A two-stage polyurethane paint process is employed for the final coat; it is vastly superior to the coats worn by the original cars.

While the large components are being restored, an endless list of such niggling items as instruments, upholstery trim, chrome headlight bezels, ashtray liners, foot-pedal rubber, taillight lenses, win-

Left is general manager of manufacturing Larry Taylor. Below, an Oldsmobile 4–4–2 convertible nears completion.

dow cranks, door latches, scuff plates, emblems, etc., is being run down by materials manager Ken Peffer, who spends most of his waking life with a phone plugged into his ear. "We do a lot of business with General Motors," he says. "They have an amazing inventory of parts for these cars, although it's spotty. You might find they have inner fender liners for the right side of a certain model but none for the left. It's stuff like that that makes the job interesting." The toughest part? "Bumpers," Taylor jumps in without hesitation. "In those days, they were all chromed and prone to rust and damage. A lot of them got thrown away."

On the positive side is the vast potential inventory of pieces spread around the nation. Recall that the great muscle machines of the sixties were for the most part simply trim and performance upgrades of basic intermediate and compact models—hotted-up General Motors A-body Pontiac Tempests, Oldsmobile Cutlasses, Chevrolet Chevelles, etc. Says DreamCars public-relations chief Tim Cline: "When you consider that Detroit built about 500,000 of these cars a year for six or seven years, and that a ton of them are still around, the potential for parts is considerable."

Still, some models are extremely rare. The 1969 Mustang convertible, for instance—for which almost no spares exist. Both Taylor and Cline agree that the hardest cars to restore are Chrysler products, due to the ragged quality control of that era and their unit-body construction. DreamCars has yet to tackle a Mopar product.

Once Peffer has accumulated the missing bits and the body and frame have been repainted, reassembly begins. Now commences the part that upsets the purists. Tempests, for example, become GTO's simply by the application of fresh labels and trim. Oldsmobile 4-4-2s arise miraculously from aged Cutlasses. Chevy Chevelles become "SS" upgrades in a wink.

The drivetrain is the easy part. Rather than try to rebuild a variety of original muscle motors, DreamCars uses 350-cubic-inch Chevrolet engines that have been totally rebuilt by the massive Jasper company in Jasper, Indiana. Each engine receives a slightly hotter camshaft than stock and, as a gesture to authenticity, its block is painted with an original factory color. Also, a new aluminum Edelbrock intake manifold is mounted; it wears a four-barrel carburetor from the same noted West Coast manufacturer. Output is 245 hp (with no catalytic converter—remember, these are pre-1971 automobiles) and 350 pound-feet of torque.

The engine is hooked to a rebuilt GM Turbo 350 three-speed automatic transmission, although a four-speed Muncie transmission with a Hurst linkage can be special-ordered. Perhaps the most critical changes are made to the steering, the suspension, and the brakes. A contemporary GM variable-rate power-steering unit reduces the original riverboat wheel ratios to three turns lock-to-lock. Power-assisted GM 9.5-inch vented disc brakes are fitted to the front; the rears are re-shoed drums. KYB shock absorbers are hung on all four corners ("We'd use American makes if we could," Taylor says, "but for some reason only the Japanese make the right sizes for these cars"). A larger rear anti-roll bar is added to quell the notorious understeer of these solid-axle monsters of yesteryear. But no one will ever confuse a DreamCar's handling—even in updated form—with that of any modern automobile.

Once Taylor and his small staff have reassembled all the primary pieces, such details as carefully reproduced upholstery and external trim are fitted. The instrument panel—on most models simply a speedometer and a gas gauge plus a collection of idiot lights—remains untouched, save for the conversion of the old clock to a quartz movement and the addition of a Pioneer AM/FM/cassette system. Air conditioning is a standard DreamCar add-on, a large, single unit mounted under the center of the dashboard. Perhaps the most jarring alteration is the steering wheel, a small, contemporary three-spoker with a rubberized rim. Gone are the gaudy, cartwheel-sized beauties of the sixties with their chromed horn rings and garish colors. Taylor explains that with quicker-ratio power steering, such massive units are simply superfluous.

Factory fifteen-inch wheels are refurbished and fitted with modern rubber. Most DreamCars get a set of Goodyear Eagle GT 215/65R-15 radials—which are light-years ahead of the old 1960s bias-ply Goodyears and Firestones that came as original equipment. All of this—the teardown, the painting, and the reassembly—takes about ten to fourteen days. Each vehicle is then road-tested and hauled off, in an enclosed trailer, to one of the nine franchised DreamCar dealers around the nation. There the cars will be sold for about $25,000 to $30,000 (the cheapest recommended 1990 retail price is $21,295 for a Buick Skylark GS coupe; the most popular machines so far are red GTO convertibles at $25,995). The dealer outlets are established franchises for a variety of brands—including Mercedes-Benz, Porsche, and several domestics—where, Taylor says, the flashy retro rockets do wonders as traffic builders. DreamCars issues a 12-month/12,000-mile warranty for the entire car, with an additional 36/36,000 warranty for the drivetrain. The car is sold as a spanking-new machine (which it is), and thus the company shows no reluctance to back it with a proper guarantee.

So far, demand has been brisk. Dozens of cars have been sold. And DreamCars is increasing its production. Most of the cars will carry the standard General Motors 350 powerplant, but several custom cars have already been delivered, including a lovely black Olds 4-4-2 with a freshly rebuilt but original 455-cubic-inch engine and a Chevelle SS with its potent 396-incher in place. "No two cars will be exactly alike," says Taylor, "although we do our best to keep the result as original as possible while adding contemporary reliability and handling."

So now you know how an American DreamCar is made. But where did the idea come from? The notion for American DreamCars sprang from the fertile brain of Joseph Bianco, an ex-Yale law student whose enthusiasm for automobiles led him away from law, investment banking,

and several successful high-tech businesses to form Lotus Performance Cars, Inc., in 1983. When General Motors bought Lotus in 1987, Bianco sold his interest in the operation and began to seek a way to reinvest his profits in the burgeoning world of performance cars.

He linked up with Bob Seasonwein, a fortyish attorney with extensive experience in the automobile industry (Ford, VW, Range Rover), and out of their discussions came the genesis for American DreamCars. "It was pretty clear from the start," says Seasonwein, "that we had this giant pool of baby-boomers who were fascinated with cars of their youth. They somehow wanted to recapture those times, and in that sense we are selling a dream, not an automobile." Seasonwein and Bianco were both aware of the fact that nostalgia trips can be deceivingly seductive. As with childbirth, the pain is soon forgotten. Memories of the sound and fury of 1960s muscle cars generally overwhelm the stark fact that they handled like runaway Kenworths, rattled like cracker boxes, and possessed pre-electronic ignitions that stayed in tune like a rented guitar. Says Seasonwein: "We recognized that people wanted only the happy memories, not all the bad stuff with the brakes, the body rust, the fouled spark plugs."

Once a business plan was in place, a corporate headquarters was established in Bethesda, Maryland, and a manufacturing facility opened in Cleveland. (Why Cleveland? How about a good labor pool and access to masses of automotive after-

DreamCars restores from old-timers, preferably rust-free. Most cars come from the South, where roads aren't salted in winter. Convertibles, like this Olds 4–4–2, often come from the North where they've been garage-kept in winter.

market sources and technical supports?) The fledgling company built three prototype cars for the 1990 National Automobile Dealer Association show, and they were a hit. Serious inquiries from 160 dealers around the nation poured in. The first customer car was delivered in March of 1990, and Seasonwein is seeking larger quarters. "Provided the economy doesn't receive a major shock," he says, "I look for us to be able to produce 25 to 30 cars a month. Based on that economy of scale, we can be quite profitable."

What is one to make of all this? Are the purists correct when they grump that American DreamCars produces counterfeits intended to deceive the public? Is it sufficient that the company makes open disclaimers that their products are modified and cannot be construed as originals? The same question might be asked of the makers of Ethan Allen colonial furniture or the mass-marketers of women's clothing who copy the European couturiers. Surely anyone purchasing an Ethan Allen dinette set with the notion that it is a valuable museum piece deserves to be bilked. So does anyone sufficiently dimwitted to believe a DreamCar GTO with a modern drivetrain and no matching serial numbers is an authentic restoration. (Besides, if you want to get technical, Pontiac's "GTO" moniker is itself a shameless rip-off of the fabled Ferrari coupe—so what's the problem here?)

Any American DreamCar is exactly that: a fantasy machine by which a small cadre of wealthy, semiserious motorists can attempt to recapture some of the raffish adventures of their youth. In this sense, who cares if the car is not museum quality? Who cares if the purists sneer? Will this minor violation of automotive dogma affect the potential of what appears to be a viable business—provided, of course, that the economy stays on track and Taylor and company continue to round up enough usable parts and pieces?

What are dreams made of, anyway?

DreamCars 4–4–2 replica has a 350-cubic-inch GM V-8, a rubber-rimmed steering wheel, a beefy air-conditioning unit, and a modern AM/FM/cassette system.

Driving the New Old Olds 4-4-2

This *is* your father's Oldsmobile. Lest you let your reverie for 1960s muscle cars overwhelm you, please understand that they were large, heavy, ungainly automobiles that generated performance through the rather mindless application of unseemly numbers of cubic inches. The original 1967 4-4-2 Oldsmobile—so named, in a spasm of marketing genius, because it featured a four-barrel carburetor, a four-speed transmission, and dual exhausts—carried a 400-cubic-inch V-8 developing 350 hp SAE gross (something under 300 hp by today's standards). It was an immense automobile, only two inches shorter than the 1991 Buick Park Avenue Ultra and more than two inches wider! At around 3700 pounds, it also weighed about as much as the Buick, so any illusions that these muscle cars of yore were taut, svelte road rockets must be instantly dismissed.

Upon planting your butt on the broad, flat, vinyl-covered seat of a DreamCar 4-4-2 replica, you are greeted by the jarring presence of the nonadjustable, upright, rubber-rimmed steering wheel. You automatically reach for the key on the steering column, only to recall that every mid-1960s American car had a dash-mounted ignition switch.

Thanks to modern electronics, the 350-cubic-inch GM V-8 lights instantly, emitting a pleasant grumble from its noncatalytic dual exhausts. There is absolutely no fuss from the engine: no lumpy idle, no reluctance to rev, no tendency to stall as the console-mounted shift lever is notched into Drive. The side mirrors, you forget, were tiny in the 1960s; the DreamCar Oldsmobile has Dixie Cup–sized versions that are authentic but essentially useless.

With its slightly larger than stock fifteen-inch radials, the DreamCar 4-4-2 stands perhaps an inch taller than the original. Otherwise, it looks so similar that even the most discerning of critics would have trouble identifying it. The paintwork, in shimmering red, is far superior to that on all but show-car candidates of the 1960s.

Driving the brute is an instant throwback to those woolly days of street racers and the Woodward Avenue Timing Association. The rebuilt Turbo 350 automatic transmission snaps home shifts with such authority than the tires chirp at even half throttle. The suspension—with precious little travel and crude geometry—refuses to be civilized by the updated shocks and tires. When the surface is flat and smooth, the behavior is acceptable. But bumps, expansion joints, and modest undulations prompt the rear tires to dance across the macadam like Gregory Hines on speed. The dreaded old bugaboo of axle tramp, long since forgotten in the lexicon of current handling nightmares, lingers in the background.

Happily, the magical, torquey bedlam of an open throttle on a big-inch V-8 is retained. Thanks to the big four-barrel, the aluminum manifold, the hotter cam, and the dual exhausts, the DreamCar Olds replicates perfectly that traditional banshee yowl of sucking air, thrashing pistons, and hammering exhausts. The entire machine seems to gather itself up for Neanderthal leaps away from stoplights.

During our drag-strip tests, the automatic insisted on making its one-two upshift at 2500 rpm, which caused 0-to-60-mph times to flatten out at 9.9 seconds and the quarter-mile to come up in a laggardly 16.9 seconds at 76 mph. But with everything operating in proper sync, it is entirely possible that the American DreamCar 4-4-2 might duplicate the

times of the original: 7.8 seconds to 60 seconds and a quarter-mile sprint of 15.8 seconds at 91 mph. Whatever the actual speed, you'll probably *think* you're going that fast.

Surely the 3.55:1 final-drive ratio is intended to enhance this short-burst capability, although the car behaves well at 65-to-70-mph freeway speeds. At 80 mph, the buzzy exhaust begins to drown out the sound system (already stressed inside the ragtop). Still, it's the Main Streets of America, not open Interstates, that are this car's bailiwick.

THE NEW OLDS

Vehicle type: front-engine, rear-wheel-drive, 5-passenger, 2-door convertible
Price as tested: $24,895 (base price: $24,495)
Engine type: V-8, iron block and heads, 1x4-bbl Edelbrock 1405 carburetor
Displacement .... 350 cu in, 5733cc
Power (SAE net) .... 245 bhp @ 3750 rpm
Transmission .... 3-speed automatic
Wheelbase .... 115.0 in
Length .... 203.2 in
Curb weight .... 3695 lb
Zero to 60 mph .... 9.9 sec
Standing ¼-mile .... 16.9 sec @ 76 mph
Braking, 70–0 mph .... 231 ft

CYRIL POSTHUMUS

La Jamais Contente *topped 60 mph before the turn of the century.*

RECORDWAGONS

By Csaba Csere

The pursuit of speed is as old as the automobile itself. Automotive pioneers used speed to demonstrate the worth of their inventions back when cars could barely outrun horses. The variety of automotive speed contests has grown over the years, but one quest has always remained simple and absolute. Which is the fastest car?

Today, with the street cars hitting 200 mph, it's difficult to get excited about land speed records that wouldn't attract a traffic cop. There was a time, however, when it was thought that anyone breathing in an airstream flowing faster than 20 mph would suffocate. Once upon a time engineers didn't know how to construct a tire that had a life expectancy of more than 20 miles. The principles of aerodynamics are a relatively modern fact of life.

Exceeding 100 mph without a seatbelt, helmet, or roll cage, in a machine built in someone's backyard at a time when the finest engineers in the world did not understand fundamental automotive principles, was as dauntless as surpassing 600 mph in *Thrust 2*. All of these recordwagons were once on the cutting edge of technology, and their drivers were daredevils of the first order. Examine these ten milestone machines that account for more than 90 years of land speed records and ask if you'd be willing to drive any of them.

1899 *La Jamais Contente*—65.79 mph

The world's first land speed contest was held near Paris in December 1898. A publication called *La France Automobile* organized it over 2000 meters of road. A Belgian, Camille Jenatzy, was an also-ran in the event, but he was bitten by the top-speed bug.

At right, the prehistoric Gobron-Brillié exceeded 100 mph. Above, the boatlike Babs boasted 26.9 liters and did 171.02 mph.

He returned the next year in the first car designed solely for speed. It was called *La Jamais Contente* ("The Never Satisfied"), and it was powered by two electric motors producing a total of 40 hp at the rear wheels. It weighed about 3200 pounds, 650 of which was batteries. Most of the hardware was encased in a cigar-shaped streamlined aluminum shell, but the tiller steering and other controls, as well as Jenatzy, sat fully exposed to the wind. Nevertheless, the vehicle became the first to break the 60-mph and 100-kph barriers.

1904 GOBRON-BRILLIÉ—103.55 MPH

Jenatzy's 65.79-mph record stood for almost three years before it was broken by a succession of powerful road-racing cars. The first to exceed the magic 100-mph barrier was a Gobron-Brillié in 1904.

Built in Paris, this Gobron-Brillié was a large and powerful car energized by an unusual four-cylinder engine displacing 15.1 liters. Each cylinder contained two pistons moving in opposite directions, whose motion was harnessed via a complex linkage to a single crankshaft.

With only 130 hp to push the large and unstreamlined bulk of the Gobron-Brillié through the air, driver Louis Rigolly did well to coax this 2150-pound machine to 103.55 mph at Ostend, Belgium, 1904.

1926 *BABS*—171.02 MPH

The land speed record gradually rose over the next two decades, and a Sunbeam driven by Malcolm Campbell achieved 150 mph in 1925. Recordwagons were evolving from souped-up track racers into highly specialized prototypes. One machine that bridged the transition was *Babs,* driven by Parry Thomas.

Purchased by Thomas for a mere 125

pounds from the estate of deceased racer Count Louis Zborowski, *Babs* was originally built to race at the banked Brooklands track. It was a strong car, powered by a 400-hp 26.9-liter V-12 Liberty aircraft engine. Thomas set about converting the racer to a record runner by rebuilding the engine and fitting a lower, more sloping radiator, a more sophisticated front suspension, a new clutch to lower the driveline, and relatively smooth bodywork.

Weighing about 4300 pounds, *Babs* needed space to realize its potential. So Thomas took it to the beach at Pendine in South Wales. He achieved great success with his low-budget project, raising the record 17 mph on April 27, 1926, and adding almost two miles per hour the following day. Malcolm Campbell broke *Babs*'s record in early 1927, and Thomas returned to the sand in March to reclaim it. He lost control at about 170 mph and was killed as *Babs* rolled and bounced its way to rest.

1927 SUNBEAM—203.792 MPH

Attempts to break 200 mph spawned a new age of huge and monstrously powerful record cars. The first of these was the Sunbeam "1000 HP."

The name was an exaggeration, but the Sunbeam was still the most potent recordwagon built to that point. It was powered by two 435-hp 48-valve 22.5-liter Sunbeam boat engines. They were mounted in tandem, with the cockpit between them. Both engines fed a three-speed gearbox located ahead of the cockpit, which in turn drove the rear wheels via chains. This mass of hardware was covered by a full envelope body with full fenders. All-up weight was slightly more than 8000 pounds.

By this time, Daytona Beach had become the favored place for record runs. Not only was the sand hard, relatively smooth, and ten miles long, but there was enormous spectator turnout for record runs. Driven by Sir Henry Segrave on March 29, 1927, the Sunbeam 1000 HP became the first car to exceed 200 mph.

1935 *BLUEBIRD*—301.129 MPH

"Bluebird" is perhaps the most famous name in land speed record cars. It was used by Sir Malcolm Campbell for seven of his record-setting runs and by his son, Donald Campbell, on his turbine-powered 1960s recordwagon.

The *Bluebird* that was the first vehicle to break 300 mph was a modified version of the elder Campbell's earlier cars. Power was provided by a Rolls-Royce R-type V-12 supercharged racing airplane engine displacing 36.5 liters and developing 2300 hp. The engine fed a rear axle fitted with two tires per side for improved traction—a problem in spite of *Bluebird*'s 11,000-pound weight. A sleek new body designed by Reid Railton covered the massive engine. The car had six wheels

Above, the Bluebird *topped 300 mph using a Rolls-Royce R-type V-12 supercharged racing airplane engine developing 2300 hp. The Sunbeam, at left, was powered by two boat engines that fed a three-speed gearbox, ahead of the cockpit, that drove the rear wheels via chains.*

and air brakes. To further reduce drag, the small radiator air intake could be blanked off at the peak of the run. For all its sophistication, however, *Bluebird* still had an open cockpit.

Campbell took *Bluebird* to Daytona in March 1935 and ran 276.82 mph on the hard sand. That was a 4-mph improvement on his existing record but short of his 300-mph goal. Within the fortnight, he journeyed to the Bonneville Salt Flats and, on the twelve-mile-long smooth surface, broke 300 mph.

1947 RAILTON—394.20 MPH

World War II interrupted a frenzied battle between two Brits, John Cobb and George Eyston, to conquer 400 mph at Bonneville. Eyston's *Thunderbolt* was big, heavy, and powerful. Cobb's mount, designed by Reid Railton, was smaller and more sophisticated.

The Railton matches most people's image of a land speed recordwagon. It was a completely smooth, flattened, and elongated teardrop, punctuated by carefully faired blisters for the driver's head and the four large tires. No radiator intake marred the clean lines. Cooling for the Railton's two supercharged Napier Lion engines came from a 75-gallon tank filled with ice. The engines were staggered side by side, with each engine driving each axle independently.

When the Railton first ran in 1938, its W-12 powerplants were ten years old and together produced only 2500 hp—barely half of Eyston's *Thunderbolt's* output. But they were feasible and strong enough to push the 7200-pound car to three world records. The last came in 1947, when Cobb strapped himself into the cockpit in the Railton's nose and ran to 394.20 mph, a record that would stand well into the 1960s.

1965 *GOLDENROD*—409.277 MPH

Compared with the huge battle-axes of

Top photo, the Railton's aerodynamics helped it set records. Middle, the Goldenrod *had four souped-up Hemis inside. Bottom, looking much like* Air Force One, *Craig Breedlove's* Spirit of America *dominated at Bonneville in the 1960s.*

the 1930s, *Goldenrod* was a slim rapier of a car. It was built by Bill and Bob Summers, a pair of Southern California hot rodders who understood that low drag contributes as much as high power to top speed.

The concept for *Goldenrod* was beautifully elegant. Rather than draw power from a bulky aircraft engine, the Summers brothers used four souped-up Chrysler Hemis arrayed in a single row. The arrangement produced more than 2400 hp in a body barely wider than one engine. All four engines were coupled together and fed two four-speed gearboxes, one driving each axle. The cockpit sat at the extreme rear of the machine, neatly integrated into a stabilizing fin.

On November 13, 1965, Bob Summers averaged 409.277 mph on his back-to-back runs and set a new wheel-driven land speed record. He never got into top gear, but his record still stands.

1965 SPIRIT OF AMERICA SONIC I— 600.601 MPH

One reason that *Goldenrod*'s record still stands is the arrival of jet and rocket-driven land speed record machines in the mid-1960s. Although the Bonneville Salt Flats are miles long, reaching speeds beyond 400 mph requires acceleration that exceeds the available traction. A machine that relies on thrust to propel itself neatly solves this problem.

In 1963, Craig Breedlove's *Spirit of America* became the first jet to break the land speed record. That mark was broken eight more times by jets in the next two years, ending again in Breedlove's possession with a second-generation *Spirit of America* called *Sonic I.*

Sonic I was essentially a jet engine on wheels. The powerplant was a General Electric J79 capable of developing 15,000 pounds of thrust (equivalent to 24,000 hp at 600 mph). Breedlove sat in a cockpit in front of the engine and below the flattened air intake. *Sonic I*'s four wheels were spaced no farther apart than needed to clear the engine, and the entire assembly was clothed in a smooth body with a prominent rear stabilizing fin. A pair of horizontal nose fins helped keep *Sonic I* from leaving the ground.

After breaking the 600-mph barrier in 1965, *Sonic I* and Breedlove both retired as the well-earned victors of the Bonneville jet battles.

1970 BLUE FLAME—622.407 MPH

Breedlove's record stood for five years before falling to the rocket-powered *Blue Flame.* Conceived by Reaction Dynamics, a group of rocket engine–focused racers, *The Blue Flame* was a much thinner machine than *Spirit of America Sonic I* because of its tiny powerplant.

Although it weighed only 750 pounds *The Blue Flame*'s rocket engine developed 22,000 pounds of thrust (equivalent to 35,200 hp at 600 mph). With no need for an air intake, *The Blue Flame* had a needle-nose rocket shape. Two closely spaced tires four feet in diameter supported the nose, and a pair of widely spaced open wheels buttressed the stern. Most of the body was filled with hydrogen peroxide—which provided the oxygen to sustain combustion—and liquefied natural gas for fuel. This unusual fuel choice and the machine's name were dictated by the main sponsor, the Institute of Gas Technology.

On October 23, 1970, with Gary Gabelich at the controls, *The Blue Flame*

The Blue Flame *used a compact rocket engine fueled by hydrogen peroxide and liquefied natural gas.*

blasted into the record books with a horrific run of 622-plus mph. Although it used less than two-thirds of its available thrust, it raised the record by more than 20 mph and was promptly retired.

1983 THRUST 2—633.468 MPH

Interest in the land speed record seemed to wane during the 1970s. Gabelich's record wasn't threatened until the Englishman Richard Noble put a serious effort together in 1981.

Noble's mount was *Thrust 2,* a jet-powered machine whose layout resembled Art Arfons's *Green Monster* of the 1960s. It was a boxy-looking device with the round outlines of its Roll-Royce jet engine running down the middle, flanked by a cockpit on either side. The driver sat on the right, and the left was available for any passenger daft enough to go along.

Bonneville suffered from flooding in the early 1980s, so *Thrust 2* ran at Black Rock Desert, north of Reno. The desert course was shorter than the Salt Flats, but that was not a big problem for *Thrust 2* and its 17,000-pound thrust. During a practice, *Thrust 2* hit 394 mph after a run of only three-quarters of a mile. Using the full length and full afterburner, Noble in 1983 went 633.468 mph.

It had taken thirteen years for *The Blue Flame*'s record to fall, and it was only beaten by 11 mph. Further increases in speed will require a car capable of breaking the sound barrier, and that will take sophistication, planning, and a great deal of money. We have no doubts that before long, all three key elements will come together to achieve the next land speed record milestone.

The Thrust 2 *had all the good looks of jet-powered kielbasa but in 1983 beat the record* The Blue Flame *(shown previous page) had held for thirteen years.*

CARS THAT SAVE GAS

Maybe we need a gas crisis every decade or so to remind us that (1) America still does not have a rational, foresighted energy policy, (2) we are still dependent on foreign crude oil, and (3) we are caught, seemingly forever, in the middle of a politically volatile situation in the Mideast.

, Since the early seventies, when oil-producing Arabs became aware of the political power of oil, the world has been a shakier place in which to live, not to mention drive. It's popular to place all the blame on Arabs. In 1990, the oil barons here at home used the Iraqi invasion of Kuwait to begin gouging their own customers at the pumps. Then the Administration made a clever move to head off this price escalation by flooding the market with our own reserves—except the flood was the equivalent of the country's fuel appetite for just 30 hours.

Consider this statistic from *Harper's Index* just before the Gulf War:

"Barrels of oil the U.S. imports from Iraq and Kuwait annually: 290 million.

"Barrels of oil that could be saved by raising U.S. auto efficiency standards by 2.75 mpg: 290 million."

Car and Driver's contribution to the cause are the six cars that prove there is life after your gas bill doubles. Following careful examination of the EPA's 1991 fuel-economy postings, we've anointed the outstanding machines in each of six categories, covering most of the market: luxury cars, minivans, sportsters, family sedans, sport-utilities, and economy cars.

Plus, we'll examine a sensational microcar that is solving space and fuel problems in Japan. Finally, some folks say they've seen the future and it's electric—the money spent on a GM-sponsored solar-car race was definitely serious, as were the future engineers who built the race cars.

About the cars. We had just one requirement: nominees for our crisis fighters had to get at least 20 mpg in the EPA city-driving cycle. Our own merry band of leadfoots often equals and sometimes betters the EPA ratings.

But fuel economy isn't everything. While these cars eat gas sparingly, they also make the most of it. Each of them is a kick to drive—we wouldn't have it any other way. And in the event our taste differs from yours, difficult as that is to imagine, we've also included a list of runners-up, all of which are definitely in the same league as our recommendations.

As they say, your mileage may vary.

MERCEDES-BENZ 350SDL

By William Jeanes

Even in times of crisis, it is important that certain entrants in the human race be permitted to move in a manner that befits their station, whether that station be real or self-assigned. Even in the cause of saving fuel, you must admit that it would somehow be wrong for the chairman of a vast corporation to roll up to the door of his skyscraper in a Daihatsu Charade sedan. Or for Jack Nicholson to be driven to the Academy Awards in a Subaru Justy. Or for any number of Third World diplomats to move humiliatingly about the UN's environs in cars of less than majestic mien.

Thank God, then, for Rudolf Diesel. This engine builder, who leaped (or was pushed) to his death from aboard a channel ferry bound for Ipswich in 1913, laid the foundation for such cars as the formidable Mercedes-Benz 350SDL Turbo to exist. One can all but hear the wheezes of gratitude from the canyons of Park Avenue and the frondy expanses of Palm Springs and Palm Beach. Yes, Cyril, it will be possible to move stylishly whilst saving the odd porringer of petrol. The Mercedes-Benz S-class has saved us and our kind.

Weighing in at 3800 pounds, the 350SDL is a genuine S-class Mercedes. Big, impressive, impeccably trimmed, and a signal to everyone that important persons are doubtless snugged in its leather interior. And not only might the occupants be snug, they are also likely to be smug. For does this behemoth not deliver stunning EPA ratings of 25 mpg highway, and 22 mpg city? It does indeed, with a debt to Dr. Diesel.

You will not, of course, be impressing the impatient among us with your 350SDL. The turbocharged single-overhead-cam in-line six requires a leisurely 11.4 seconds to attain a speed of 60 mph. But once momentum has been achieved, the big car will perform with surprising power and ease at highway speeds.

The behind-the-wheel experience in an S-class has always appealed to some of us here at *Car and Driver,* and though the 350SDL lacks the response delivered by the big V-8 gasoline engine in the 560SEL version of the car, we have no hesitation in recommending the 350SDL as an example of true luxury transportation. Particularly when the reasonable mileage figures are made a part of our deliberations.

The rear seat of the 350SDL won the first-place cup in our crisis-fighter luxury category. Here is a space that will carry three large adults in comfort, to be sure, but more important to

PHOTOGRAPHY BY TOM DREW

TURBO (DIESEL)

the true luxury customer, the rear seat provides a hospitable venue for those who wish to be driven rather than do the work themselves. No other luxury car in the over-20-mpg universe can provide that advantage. The 350SDL's cost will not embarrass those consumers devoted to the principles and pleasures of conspicuous consumption. Its base price of $57,800 leaves no doubt that the two-dollar punter has no business even thinking of such a car.

Or course, in addition to the fuel savings provided by the 350SDL, one also gets the high Mercedes safety standards. Few companies in history have devoted so willingly so many resources in the cause of safety engineering. A supplementary air-bag system protects both the driver and the passenger. Luxury, economy, safety, prestige, and all else that the public associates with Mercedes-Benz are yours with the 350SDL . . . a true crisis fighter.

Vehicle type: front-engine, rear-wheel-drive, 5-passenger, 4-door sedan
Base price: $57,800
Engine type: turbocharged SOHC 6-in-line diesel, iron block and aluminum head, Bosch mechanical fuel injection
Displacement . . . . 210 cu in, 3449cc
Power (SAE net) . . . . .134 bhp @ 4000 rpm
Transmission . . . . 4-speed automatic
Wheelbase . . . . 121.1 in
Length . . . . 208.1 in
Curb weight . . . . 3800 lb
EPA fuel economy, city driving . . . . 22 mpg

1991 HONORABLE MENTION

Mercedes-Benz 300D ($39,700): It's a bit slower (0 to 60 mph in 12.4 seconds) and less spacious than the 350SDL, but it's the only other car with truly parsimonious fuel consumption (27 mpg city, 33 highway) that can claim luxury status.

MODELS: MARY ANN PICKNEY, PHIL BERG, AND WILLIAM JEANES

MAZDA MPV

By Csaba Csere

Vans and fuel economy don't exactly go together like cheese and crackers. Vans are popular with those who want to carry a lot of people and things, and therefore are big machines fitted with boxy, swollen bodies. Unfortunately, a big machine that punches a large, blunt hole through the air is unlikely to be very fuel efficient—particularly if it's equipped with a V-6 engine for performance motives and the automatic transmission that most buyers prefer.

Only two vans available early in 1991 could meet our 20-mpg EPA-city-driving bogey and qualify as crisis fighters. They are the Mazda MPV (equipped with a four-cylinder engine and a manual transmission) and the Dodge Caravan/Plymouth Voyager (also powered by a four-banger, although one coupled to a three-speed automatic transmission).

Both vans are at the top of their class, but we give the nod to the MPV, due largely to its peppier powertrain. The Mazda 2.6-liter four develops 121 hp at 4600 rpm. Chrysler's 2.5-liter four puts out 100 hp at 4800 rpm. Moreover, the mandatory automatic transmission that accompanies the Chrysler engine absorbs more energy than the five-speed offered in the MPV.

Our four-cylinder MPV is probably not the best choice for an outing in the Rockies, but it is quick enough to accomplish most van tasks. The balance-shaft-equipped powerplant revs easily and willingly, without any pronounced boomy or buzzy regions in its operating range, although it does get steadily noisier as it winds beyond 4000 rpm. By carefully manipulating the smooth-shifting five-speed gearbox, however, one can keep the engine in the speed range where it generates more thrust than tumult. Given our druthers, we prefer Mazda's V-6, but if fuel is a priority we can certainly live with this powertrain.

We can also live with the rest of the MPV, which, even after the redesign of the Chrysler products and the introduction of the Toyota Previa and the GM APVs, remains one of the most desirable vans on the market.

The MPV's smooth, clean styling still looks good despite the competition's radical new profiles. Not only does the shape

yield a reasonably sleek 0.36 drag coefficient, but its fine detailing creates a strong impression of quality design and construction.

Remarkably, the Mazda rides and handles like a car. The suspension uses struts in front and a well-located live axle in the rear, and it provides a soft and supple ride. Bumps large and small are smothered whether the van is full or empty.

This absorbent suspension allows the MPV to roll considerably during hard cornering, but it always keeps the four tires well planted on the pavement. Although too soft and under-tired for seriously fast driving, the MPV responds accurately and predictably enough to satisfy even a demanding driver under most conditions.

The design and finish of the MPV's interior is also quite satisfying. All versions come with a nicely detailed dashboard equipped with full instrumentation, an AM/FM-stereo radio/cassette, and a clock. All versions also have a cloth headliner and upholstery, electric mirrors, tilt steering, and a rear wiper/washer. As far as bodies go, the standard five-passenger configuration comes with a three-passenger seat in the middle of the rear box, and an optional seven-passenger version has a second rear seat.

A five-passenger MPV with air conditioning and floor mats will run you $14,987. That price makes the MPV as much a bargain to buy as it is to run. If,

however, your tastes run along more hedonistic lines, you can equip a four-cylinder MPV with a full complement of power options, dual air conditioners, and alloy wheels and run the price tab beyond $21,000. Either way, the four-cylinder MPV is the best van around for the hard times that may be coming.

Vehicle type: front-engine, rear-wheel-drive, 5-passenger, 4-door van
Base price: $13,715
Engine type: SOHC 12-valve 4-in-line, iron block and aluminum head, Mazda electronic engine-control system with port fuel injection
Displacement .... 159 cu in, 2606cc
Power (SAE net) ....121 bhp @ 4600 rpm
Transmission............................... 5-speed
Wheelbase .... 110.4 in
Length .... 175.8 in
Curb weight................................ 3500 lb
EPA fuel economy, city driving .... 20 mpg

1991 HONORABLE MENTION

Dodge Caravan/Plymouth Voyager ($13,071): Newly redesigned, the original minivans are back in peak form. Although not as peppy as the MPV, they offer somewhat more interior space and a greater range of options.

MODELS: CSABA CSERE, STEVE SPENCE, LARRY GRIFFIN, DON SCHROEDER, SUSAN MATHEWS, RICH CEPPOS, AND JOHN PHILLIPS.

MITSUBISHI ECLIPSE GSX

By Nicholas Bissoon-Dath

When fuel gets tight, sporty cars seem to suffer the most. Power is looked upon as an extravagance, and enthusiast cars become the villains of the road. So, not surprisingly, enthusiasts everywhere are now beginning to ask the same dire question: is it possible to combine a high fun factor with socially responsible fuel economy? The answer, of course, is "yes." Behold the ideal blend of economy and speed: the Mitsubishi Eclipse GSX. (The GSX's twin, the Eagle Talon TSi AWD, deserves praise, too, but we've chosen the Eclipse because it offers a more comprehensive warranty.)

The GSX's appeal begins with its body: a seductive blend of swoopy lines and an aggressive stance. Standard pieces include a body-color ground-effects kit and a prominent rear-deck spoiler; fog lamps are part of the package, too. Also included: handsome Mitsubishi 6.0-by-16-inch alloy wheels wearing fat Goodyear Eagle VR55 tires. One look tells you this car means business.

The cabin is equally appealing. A supportive multiadjustable cloth seat cradles your body. Fine controls lie within easy reach. Well-positioned pedals await serious heel-and-toe work. And the rear seats, though incapable of accommodating adults, fold down to add useful room to the luggage compartment. The GSX is a thoroughly practical coupe.

Turn the key and your ears are bathed in the refined hum of a four-cylinder engine equipped with twin counterrotating balance shafts. Blip the throttle and the smoothness is ruffled by the whir of the cam belt and a throaty exhaust growl.

Move away from rest and you immediately notice the silky clutch and the notchy but easy-to-use shifter. Press the accelerator to the floor and the 195-horsepower, turbocharged and intercooled 2.0-liter four builds boost rapidly. Launched properly, the GSX reaches 60 mph in just 6.3 seconds and flashes through the standing quarter-mile in 14.7

seconds at 92 mph. Top speed is 137 mph. Yet for all its speed, the GSX still extracts twenty miles from every gallon of premium unleaded on the EPA's city-cycle test.

Bend it hard into a corner and the GSX's four-wheel-drive platform remains stable and benign right up to its 0.84-g limit. Lift off the throttle suddenly or trail the brakes deep into a turn and the chassis rotates gently and communicatively—a definite aid to handling. And no matter what the road conditions, the four-wheel-drive system (which sports a viscous coupling in-unit with the center differential) assures that the power is always fed to the ground. That's the beauty of the GSX: you can make use of its abilities year-round.

A car as speedy as the GSX needs good brakes, and the Mitsu has them. The four standard discs haul it down from 70 mph in just 181 feet, though they suffer from moderate fade in hard use. An anti-lock package is now available as an option; we highly recommend it.

The bottom line for all this excitement and quality is a 1991 base price of $16,759. That sum includes tilt steering, cruise control, a rear wiper/washer and defroster, an AM/FM/cassette system with six speakers, and power steering and mirrors. Add in $680 for ABS and the base

price rises to just $17,439. Mitsubishi also offers several other options, including air conditioning, power windows and locks, and two sound-system upgrades.

The Eclipse GSX proves that you don't have to give up high performance, comfort, or practicality when the price of a gallon of gas increases.

Vehicle type: front-engine, four-wheel-drive, 2 + 2-passenger, 3-door coupe
Base price (with ABS): $17,439
Engine type: turbocharged and intercooled DOHC 16-valve 4-in-line, iron block and aluminum head, Mitsubishi electronic engine-control system with port fuel injection
Displacement . . . . 122 cu in, 1997cc
Power (SAE net) . . . . 195 bhp @ 6000 rpm
Transmission 5-speed
Wheelbase . . . . 97.2 in
Length . . . . 172.4 in
Curb weight . . . . 3100 lb
EPA fuel economy, city driving . . . . 20 mpg

1991 HONORABLE MENTIONS

Eagle Talon TSi AWD ($17,194 with ABS): All the goodness of the GSX—plus sportier wheels and all-season tires—for a tad less money. The warranty is marginally less complete, however.

Eagle Talon TSi/Mitsubishi Eclipse GS Turbo/Plymouth Laser RS Turbo $15,-534/$16,023/$14,879—all with ABS): These nearly identical front-drive triplets offer most of the features of the GSX and the Talon TSi AWD, but they produce five fewer horsepower and lack the stabilizing influence of four-wheel drive.

Honda CRX Si ($11,130): This pumped-up roller skate offers a rev-happy engine, terrific handling, and Honda quality at an impossibly low price.

Mazda MX-5 Miata ($13,800): Not the fastest car in the class, but this modern interpretation of the classic British roadster is a gas to drive and a hit no matter where it goes.

MODELS: JULI BURK, ARTHUR ST. ANTOINE, AND HOWARD THE GOOSE

HONDA ACCORD EX

By John Phillips III

If one of your children had been born the year that the first Honda Accord wandered into the U.S. market, that child would now be a fifteen-year-old adolescent deep into MTV, Clearasil, and 1-900 phone calls to sports stars. The Honda Accord, however, has galloped clean through childhood and adolescence and is now a full-fledged adult with clear skin and the impeccable manners of Clement Freud at Prince Rainier's polo club.

If you haven't driven an Accord lately, you may still think of it simply as a sedan that's small and Japanese. It's not exactly either. The Accord now rides atop a generous 107.1-inch wheelbase—an inch longer than the Taurus/Sable's—and has a back seat that will comfortably accommodate two and a half of those lumpy linebackers Tina Turner has mentioned in that *other* car company's commercials. What's more, if you warm to the idea of buying an American-built car, you should know that the Accord is assembled in Marysville, Ohio, with 73 percent of its parts produced domestically. When the figure hits 75 percent, the car technically becomes as all-American as a Chevy Caprice, at least in the eyes of our government.

For 1991, the Accord offered with an SOHC 2.2-liter four-cylinder engine, which produces 125 hp in the DX and LX models, 130 hp in the EX, and 140 hp in the top-of-the-line SE. Like all of Honda's four-cylinder engines, the 2.2-liter is fast to rev, quiet, and—thanks in part to twin balance shafts—about as smooth as a '76 Montrachet. From stand-still to 60 mph—a 9.7-second mission—the Accord EX is nearly a full second quicker than a V-6–powered Taurus L.

In their various trim levels, the Accord sedans for 1991 span a broad price range. You can sneak into a base five-speed 1991 DX for as little as $12,545. But you're better off starting with the LX ($15,095), if only because it includes the basic amenities that make life worth living: power windows, a good AM/FM/cassette system, cruise control, and air conditioning. The Accord dearest to our hearts, however, remains the option-loaded, manual-transmission, $16,795 EX. We're not so much drawn to the EX for its five extra horsepower (the upshot of a freer-flowing exhaust) as we are smitten by its gas-charged shocks, rear anti-roll bar, and fifteen-inch alloy wheels wrapped with Michelin MXV3 rubber. So equipped, the EX steers and handles superbly. Indeed, this sedan has a kind of European instinct for arrowing straight down the road. Drive one and you'll find your fellow carpool passengers asking why you keep nailing apexes and raising little tornadoes of dust on the way to the office.

If you insist on an automatic transmission, Honda will oblige with a fine four-speed, but the price of a '91 EX then soars to $17,545 and the car's EPA city fuel-economy rating drops by 2 mpg. We ad-

vise against it. You'll sacrifice some of this athletic car's versatility and miss out on a shifter that may be as slick and satisfying as the one in Mr. Senna's McLaren-Honda.

The top-of-the-line, automatic-only Accord SE adds standard anti-lock brakes, but its $19,545 base price puts it into competition with sedans that are both sportier and more luxurious. We think the EX is a better value.

If you need a dedicated family machine, Honda can respond to that, too. A wagon version of the Accord, built in Ohio, sells for about $18,000.

Mainstream America has clutched the Accord so snugly to its bosom that we're not sure we have to go on enumerating the car's virtues. The Accord used to be America's favorite import. Then it simply became America's favorite car, period.

Okay, okay. Not everything about this accomplished sedan sends us scrambling for the thesaurus. The Honda has motorized belts instead of a driver-side air bag (which is standard on the Ford Taurus L). And the Accord's styling is about as racy and carefree as Colin Powell's uniform.

Mechanically and dynamically, however, the Honda Accord remains the high-water mark by which other manufacturers judge whether their own family sedans run right or left of center. In no other family four-door that delivers EPA city/highway ratings of 24/30 mpg will you find as much driving pleasure, practicality, and poise.

On that there is widespread accord.

Vehicle type: front-engine, front-wheel-drive, 5-passenger, 4-door sedan
Base price: $16,795–17,545
Engine type: SOHC 16-valve 4-in-line, aluminum block and head, Honda electronic engine-control system with port fuel injection
Displacement . . . . 132 cu in, 2156cc
Power (SAE net) . . . . 130 bhp @ 5200 rpm
Transmissions . . . . 5-speed, 4-speed automatic with lockup torque converter
Wheelbase . . . . 107.1 in
Length . . . . 184.8 in
Curb weight . . . . 2950–3000 lb
EPA fuel economy, city driving . . . . 22–24 mpg

1991 HONORABLE MENTIONS

Volkswagen Passat GL/Passat GL Wagon ($14,990/$15,395): The manual-transmission Passats, both the sedan and the wagon, represent such a major miracle of interior packaging that both qualify as genuine crisis fighters. The back seats —with adjustable seat cushions, no less— offer far more leg and kneeroom than you'll find in either the Accord or the Taurus. VW's 134-hp 2.0-liter four-cylinder engine and the Passat's jellybean aerodynamics (the sedan's Cd is a low 0.31) contribute to 21/30-mpg EPA figures.

Ford Taurus L ($13,095): It just keeps winning. The Taurus landed on both our "Ten Best" and "Best Buys" lists in 1990 and remains a tremendous value, even if it does not encourage the spirited driving you'd undertake in the Accord or the Passat. With the 140-hp 3.0-liter Vulcan engine, the Taurus L is one of the few V-6–powered sedans with an EPA city rating meeting our minimum 20 mpg. Plus, of the three cars mentioned here, the Taurus is alone in offering a driver-side air bag.

GEO TRACKER

By Phil Berg

Seems like only yesterday there was a whole herd of these sport-utility vehicles—SUVs to you—that would have met our only rule to compete in this here crisis-fighter category: the thing has to score at least 20 miles to the gallon tooling around town.

Today you need only one foot to count the four-wheelers that get that kind of mileage. There's the Geo Tracker and its twin, the Suzuki Sidekick, both made in a joint-venture deal up in Canada, and there's the other Suzuki, the Samurai, and the Daihatsu Rocky, and that's it.

What happened to the Cherokees and Blazers and 4Runners is the boys at the factory fattened 'em up with electric this-'n-thats, they put doors in the roofs and mirrors on the doors, they dragged out the automatic transmissions and the chilled-air equipment. We suspect the reason for these upscale antics is the Suits in the marketing department found out most of 'em go off-road about as often as you'll come upon Ralph Lauren branding steers down on the edge of the Rio Grande. You get the picture.

All these middleweight V-6 four-wheelers are as popular as wearing the collar of your polo shirt up, but they get between 15 and 17 mpg around town. Each year about a million of these tony four-wheelers are going to be sold. Our four contenders' piece of that pie is about five percent. That's because they're modest little lightweights—they all have four-cylinder engines and the minimum fur factor—plus they don't have the words "Range Rover" stamped into the sheetmetal, which means it's Snub City at the valet shack of Spago on Sunset.

Right off the bat here, to break all this mounting tension, let us say the choice morsel in this class is the three-door hardtop version of the Geo Tracker, a whole ton lighter than the Eddie Bauer worldview café tourer. We like the steel-roof Tracker for its pep and its buttoned-lip noise level on the highway. Geo Trackers and Suzuki Sidekicks are propelled by 1.6-liter four-bangers that put out 80 horsepower. Sounds thin, true enough, but the Tracker can keep up with the middleweight SUVs. With a five-speed manual transmission, the Tracker feels lively, and it will deliver 25 mpg around town.

We also prefer the 1991 Tracker's price, which is $11,285. If that's too much, and you'd prefer to wear ear plugs when you're driving on the freeway, convertibles are available in two-wheel-drive form for $1010 less for the Tracker, and $1036 for the Sidekick. Suzuki sells only convertible two-door versions of the Sidekick, but a hard roof is available as a $1395 option. New for 1991 is a roomier, five-door Sidekick hardtop, which is sixteen inches longer than the Tracker and starts at $12,000.

The Tracker hardtop's base price includes rear anti-lock brakes. Air conditioning and power steering up the ante to $12,255, but we recommend those options. The uplevel LSi hardtop has a stereo and automatic-locking front hubs for another $1300, which also includes tinted glass, flashier steel wheels, and a cloth interior. But we'd stick with the base hardtop and forgo the auto-locking hubs. Why? We've found if you leave manual hubs engaged, you can shift the part-time transfer case to four-wheel drive at almost any speed. With auto hubs, you have to slow to a walk. An automatic is available in Trackers and Sidekicks, but we wouldn't spend the extra $565 for it.

How do the others in this class compare? The Rocky SE with a hard top is six inches and $660 longer than the base four-wheel drive Tracker hardtop. The

Rocky gets 23 mpg on the EPA city test, 2 mpg less than the five-speed Tracker. The five-door Suzuki Sidekick gets 23 mpg too, but its extra 450-pound weight penalty over the three-door makes it feel slow in acceleration. The cheapest of the pack is the Suzuki Samurai—a mere $8000—but it's not overloaded with fun in the driving department. Still, it gets 28 mpg. Ride is best described as bouncy, but we can live with the short Tracker and Sidekick. Both are highly maneuverable in town.

Most of the good dressers around here like the looks of the Tracker/Sidekick over the Daihatsu. The Geo/Suzuki machines look integrated—they don't have the "add-on" appearance of the Rocky with its large fender flares. The Daihatsu does have fourteen more horsepower than the Geo/Suzuki, but in this league the value in quickness is outweighed by the patience required with any of these little guys. Even the Rocky needs about fourteen seconds to reach 60 mph—bog slow. By

comparison, a six-cylinder Jeep Cherokee gets to 60 mph in 10.5 seconds.

If you really want to play in places where there's no asphalt, the Tracker hardtop is an SUV that is easy on the fuel tab and won't chew up the checkbook. So maybe the valet at Spago calls you "Hey!" instead of "Sir!"

Vehicle type: front-engine, rear/4-wheel-drive, 4-passenger, 3-door wagon
Base price: $11,285–11,850
Engine type: SOHC 4-in-line, aluminum block and head, Suzuki electronic engine-control system with 1x1-bbl throttle-body fuel injection
Displacement . . . . 97 cu in, 1590cc
Power (SAE net) . . . . 80 bhp @ 5400 rpm
Transmissions . . . . 5-speed, 3-speed automatic
Wheelbase . . . . 86.6 in
Length . . . . 142.5 in
Curb weight . . . . 2250–2300 lb
EPA fuel economy, city driving . . . . 23–25 mpg

1991 HONORABLE MENTIONS

Suzuki Sidekick JX ($11,999): This well-designed five-door wagon will give you the utility of larger SUVs, but it weighs 450 pounds more than the three-door Tracker—hampering acceleration.
Daihatsu Rocky SE ($11,697): An optional $372 gets you a hard targa rear roof, creating a convertible and a hardtop in one vehicle. For $685 more, there's a complete off-road package.

NISSAN SENTRA SE-R

By Larry Griffin

This Sentra SE-R's 2.0-liter engine pumps out 140 horsepower. It fires its 2500 pounds through America's asphalt arteries like gunpowder lit off by a Bunsen burner. The car boasts a 0-to-60-mph time of 7.3 seconds and a top speed of 126 mph—delivered in a shell both practical and comfortable. Yet it racks up 24 mpg on the EPA city-economy cycle—what a sneaky way to slip a quick one past our governmental exchequers of efficiency. Your exchequer of personal purchases will also find the SE-R's 1991 price of $11,670—including optional ABS—suitable for painless withdrawal from your travel-and-excitement allowance.

As you consider the car, consider the company. In the past three years, Nissan whipped up the Maxima SE family sports sedan. The zingy 240SX sports coupe. The rousing 300ZX sports car and its twin-turbo brother. And from the company's hoo-boy branch, the shockingly quick and capable Infiniti Q45 sports-luxury sedan. Each includes, at no charge beyond the one that unleashes adrenal ducts, a sporting nature that other car companies will invest millions to copy. Nissan switched

in 1989 and 1990 from pushing mechanical mediocrity to propagating meteoric performance. For that it ranks in the pantheon of automotive achievers.

The Sentra SE-R reaffirms that displays of speed need not confirm wasteful intentions. It arrives in time for fuel-conscious people. For now, drivers should celebrate any car able to produce speed as high at full throttle as its economy runs at part throttle.

Despite a swarm of competitors, the Sentra SE-R could become to the early 1990s what the BMW 2002 became to the early 1970s. That frisky sedanlet gained fame carving up beefy foes. The 2002tii, the most protein-packed baby Bimmer, made 125 horsepower from 2.0 liters, a single overhead cam, and two valves per cylinder. The hottest pocket rocket going, its keys could burn a hole in your pocket faster than flash powder. (Nearly two decades ago, a trio of 2002s, propelled by the brio of Bavarian energy, turned three current editors of this gazette into gleeful Bimmerites.) At the time skulking under its Datsun name, Nissan knocked out its first 510, a flyweight tearoff of a 2002. In

the SE-R, the idea at last hustles toward perfection. Compared with the tii, the SE-R's electronic fuel injection, double overhead cams, four valves per cylinder, and fifth forward gear provide its 2.0 liters with greater flexibility plus fifteen more horsepower. No stock 2002 could run gnashers-to-gnaw-bone with the SE-R. Neither can many of today's 3-series BMWs, at two to three times the Nissan's price.

The SE-R is based on Nissan's brand-new Sentra, and thus benefits from the space and weight advantages of front-wheel drive. Yet the SE-R does a fine job of standing in for rear-drive. A viscous limited-slip differential doles out the power per traction of each front tire. Nose-heaviness and the overall load have been minimized by designing an engine with an aluminum block, head, and oil pan. And, like the other new Sentras, the SE-R gets a separate front subframe to boost the stiffness of the suspension mounts, offset coil springs for ride comfort, a widened front track for stability, a lowered power-steering rack for better handling at high speeds and on rough roads, and reworked mounting of the rear suspension's parallel links.

With an independent strut-type suspension at each corner and anti-roll bars to keep it from strutting off line, the sporty Sentra handles well at the limit—though the tail, unexpectedly unsettled, can sidestep slightly. Seeking its own path, the SE-R occasionally follows its own lead rather than yours over surface imperfections. But big four-wheel disc brakes, which supplant the regular Sentra's smaller front discs and rear drums, buff down your speed easily.

The handsome cabin contains the most Recaro-like seats this side of Stuttgart, and the instruments and ergonomics give you as solid a feel for what's happening as the seats. Despite its high output and 9.5:1 compression ratio. Nissan's new engine runs on unleaded regular. A 13.2-gallon tank promises 400 miles per fill-up on the road. When the SE-R sits in your garage ready for an Italian tuneup—wherein your right foot takes care of everything—it's nice to know that not everything has changed since Germany's boxy little Bimmer showed what a fine-running sports sedan could do. Facing the 1990s, the Sentra SE-R gives you quicker results and fewer stops.

Vehicle type: front-engine, front-wheel-drive, 5-passenger, 2-door sedan
Base price (with ABS): $11,670
Engine type: DOHC 16-valve 4-in-line, aluminum block and head, Nissan ECCS electronic engine-control system with port fuel injection
Displacement . . . . 122 cu in, 1998cc
Power (SAE net) . . . . 140 bhp @ 6400 rpm
Transmission 5-speed
Wheelbase . . . . 95.7 in
Length . . . . 170.3 in
Curb weight . . . . 2500 lb
EPA fuel economy, city driving . . . . 24 mpg

1991 HONORABLE MENTION

Mercury Tracer LTS ($11,219): Mercury's sleek new four-door, which shares its platform with the new Ford Escort and Mazda's 323 and Protegé, houses a 127-hp 1.8-liter four-cylinder engine that delivers 8.3-second 0-to-60 mph sprints, a 121-mph top speed, *and* 26 mpg in the EPA's city test. The Tracer gets the nod over its siblings for being the handsomest member of the group.

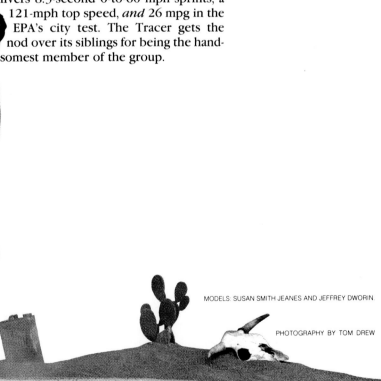

HONDA TODAY XTi

By Kevin Smith

Do you have any idea how little 650cc really is? It's a bit less than a pint and a half in volume—well short of the liquid content in most any wine bottle that doesn't have a screw-on cap. It was the displacement of the classic 1960s Triumph twin-cylinder motorcycle, the Bonneville. And it is roughly the swept volume of a single cylinder in a current Jaguar six or 327 Chevy V-8.

Is that enough engine displacement around which to build a decent family car? We hopped in a Japanese-market Honda Today to find out. The answer? A resounding "Well . . ."

The key issue here is context. In a dense, compact country like Japan, where road space is dear and so is a liter of gasoline, a tiny, frugal microcar works—and works well. It fits much less naturally into America's larger-scale automotive landscape. Our distances are vast and our fuel

(so far) is cheap. But even though the littlest Honda represents truly minimalist transportation, its charm and practicality suggest that if circumstances put a serious squeeze on America's energy supplies, the future needn't look unbearably bleak.

The Today's three diminutive pistons displace 657 cc. A single overhead cam operates four valves per cylinder. Fitted with a carburetor in the tame XL and XG models, this engine generates 41 horsepower at 6000 rpm. But the hotted-up XTi edition we drove uses electronic injection (and wilder cam timing) to produce a maximum of 51 horsepower at 7500 rpm. Peak torque is 40 pound-feet at 4500 rpm.

This compact engine, packaged with a five-speed manual gearbox, nestles way up in the nose of a conventional, if small, unit-construction steel body. The chassis uses familiar hardware, scaled down for

the lighter-duty task: an independent strut suspension in front, a solid axle in back, rack-and-pinion steering, disk brakes up front, and drums in the rear. The sporty XTi version wears racy 145/65R-13 Bridgestone Regno radials instead of the other models' 145/70R-12s.

The Today is meant to be simple and cheap, but it does not scrimp on style or quality. From the clean, chiseled nose to a hint of rear spoiler lip, the body is smooth, sleek, and assembled with typical care. It has a Honda-family look about the face, an unbelievably short hood, a steeply raked windshield, and a sharply cut-off tail. The wheels are pushed right out to the body corners; there is essentially no front or rear overhang. Our XTi was graciously equipped, with power mirrors, effective air conditioning, and a power sunroof (which slid rearward on the *outside*, CRX-style, so as not to rob headroom). In Japan, a Today XTi so equipped sells for about $7600.

When hustling the Today down the road, we detected no appreciable wind noise. Then again, the enthusiastic three-cylinder thrashes and wails enough that you can't hear much of anything else. It isn't bad below about 4500 rpm, but spin it closer to the 7500-rpm redline—as you

Vehicle type: front-engine, front-wheel-drive, 2 + 2-passenger, 3-door coupe
Estimated price (Japan): $7600
Engine type: 3-in-line, aluminum block and head, Honda PGM-FI electronic fuel injection
Displacement . . . . 40 cu in, 657cc
Power (SAE net) . . . . 51 bhp @ 7500 rpm
Transmission 5-speed
Wheelbase . . . . 91.7 in
Length . . . . 129.7 in
Curb weight . . . . 1550 lb
Fuel economy, Japanese city cycle . . . . 46 mpg
                        steady 37 mph . . . . 65 mpg

must to summon meaningful acceleration —and the din grows quickly. The five-speed shifter is happy to help you find revs when necessary, which is most of the time you aren't cruising gently on a level road. When you *are* cruising gently, the Today can deliver eye-popping fuel economy. In the Japanese-standard 37-mph steady-state test, the Today XTi—with air conditioning blasting—nets 65 miles per gallon.

Smooth steering gives the Today a friendly, maneuverable feel, though there isn't enough tire-taxing thrust to explore the limits of handling in the usual manner. Suffice it to say the car changes direction readily, maintains good balance, and rides as well as any 1550-pound car we've driven.

But here's the big question: is the cabin roomy enough to be useful? Yes. In fact, the cabin is shockingly spacious, considering the whole car measures only 129.7 inches long, 54.9 inches wide, and 52.4 inches high. (For comparison, a Daihatsu Charade is 144.9 inches long, a Geo Metro 146.1, and a Honda CRX 148.5.) And not only can a six-footer find a comfortable position behind the wheel (despite a marginally too short reach to the sloped floorboard/firewall in front), but he can even feel there's enough legroom in the back seat if the front seatback is adjusted just a tad more upright.

It's not an optical illusion: a huge interior has been crammed inside the Today's stubby body. The trick, of course, is that the interior extends nearly all the way to the exterior, that is, the "skin" around the passenger cell is exceedingly thin. Therein lies the rub. As it stands, the Today's crashworthiness could not begin to meet the U.S. government's requirements. And any effort to add the necessary impact absorption and intrusion resistance would only destroy a car like this—its usability would evaporate as the thickening safety skin compressed the cabin, and its performance (such as it is) would vanish under the burden of added weight.

Does that make the Today and its 650cc-class brethren irrelevant to the future of mobility in America? Not exactly. The 1620-pound Geo Metro (and its more powerful, 1716-pound Suzuki Swift sibling) may represent more realistic minimum levels of mass and size, given present crash standards, and tougher requirements in the future probably mean minimum necessary engine displacement will grow toward 1300cc rather than shrink to half that. But cars like the tiny and tidy Today demonstrate what is possible with clever engineering and a clear commitment to space efficiency and light weight. In that regard, the microcars can serve as valuable archetypes for the crisis-busting transportation of tomorrow.

TOP FIVE 1991 FUEL MISERS*

1. Geo Metro XFi, 53 mpg
2. Honda CRX HF, 49 mpg
3. Suzuki Swift, 46 mpg
4. Daihatsu Charade, 38 mpg
5. VW Jetta diesel, 37 mpg

* Based on 1990 EPA city fuel-economy ratings for cars sold in the U.S. To avoid multiple entries, each model is listed only in highest-economy form.

CHRIS ERVIN

SOLAR POWERED

By Steve Smith

For the most part, the network-TV new-sies approached this solar-car race as a kind of quirky comedy filler. News of GM's Sunrayce USA, with its promise of bizarre, cartoonlike cars, appeared toward the end of most broadcasts, in that parting segment when the anchorman chuckles and winks, as if to say, "After all this bad news, here's something perfectly silly."

Well, who could blame them? Who could suppress a snort on seeing a wheeled thingie called the "Safe Sex Machine" (two pilots on board, seated hammock-style, going in opposite directions), one of the entries in an improbable 1630-mile, eleven-day ordeal from Florida to Michigan, using the sun as a fuel source, running on all the horsepower of a hair dryer?

The cars in Sunrayce looked like an inventory of George Lucas's kinkier dreams: the shapely salmon, the wheeled surf-board, the soup bowl, the lunar lander, a car that looked as if someone had left a wet Shaker-style house in the dryer too long. A twin-hulled catamaran, the gratui-tous yellow submarine, a car with an extraordinarily sophisticated suspension, yet another steered by string. All of them light as kites, as airy as the imagination.

A source of boffo yuks to those ac-quainted with Fred Flintstone but unac-quainted with calculus equations, the cars were head gruel to the sliderules—the engineering students from 32 American universities and tech institutes who built and then trailered them to Orlando, Flor-ida, for the race. Very serious money was involved, too—one cost $800,000, an-other had a $6-million solar array—and some of the students had put in fifteen months' labor on the cars.

Also not laughing was the sponsor. The race was dreamed up by GM in part to capitalize on its smashingly successful solar car, the Sunraycer. Four years ago, this corporate sunshine car—purportedly worth $8 million for the hardware and $30 million in R&D fees—stomped the

Can the school that created Bo Schembechler do anything but win? No, and Michigan's big-bucks Sunrunner won hands down.

139

Popular underdog North Texas proved money wasn't everything.

competition in Australia's World Solar Challenge. Proving once again that money talks and the other stuff walks, GM was so far ahead at the finish line that it had to wait two and a half days for the second-place finisher. You can understand GM's sense of exhilaration when the number-two car arrived with Ford of Australia written all over it. At a time when GM's commercial victories are certainly less clear, the company went on a tub-thumping promotional tour and, deciding to retire undefeated—Honda is involved now —offered the Sunraycer to the Smithsonian Institute, which accepted.

Then the company announced plans for a solar race here. GM appealed to higher education to put forth its best and brightest, which is to say the world's biggest store offered $5000 to each college team and convinced the Department of Energy to kick in $2000. Finally, GM promised to send the top three finishers on an all-expenses-paid trip to the 1990 race in Australia.

As it turned out, the five grand amounted to pin money. Nevertheless, the entries poured in. The country's celebrated engineering schools—MIT, Cal Poly, Worcester Poly, Stanford—applied, and in April 1989, GM gave the nod to 32 teams and put the checks in the mail. It was fourteen months until race day.

The race would be decided on the open road, out there with the Bekins movers and the Winnebago set, an unnerving thought considering the paperweight cars —most weighed between 350 and 550 pounds—and their modest cruising speeds. The rulebook was considerable,

but it basically limited the cars to six meters (236.2 inches) long, two meters (78.7 inches) wide, and 1.6 meters (63.0 inches) high; on-board batteries could be used to store the sun's energy, and the vehicle's solar array, the device that looks like a huge windowpane and holds all the sun-sucking power cells, could not exceed four meters (157.5 inches) long by two meters (78.7 inches) wide and 1.6 meters (63.0 inches) high for single-seaters—an extra two meters of length was okayed for two-seaters.

The problem on the blackboard was how to get from point A to point B as efficiently as possible on a thimbleful of power. The equation possibilities seemed endless, which was, for example, the reason the safe-sex car had pilots positioned in both directions: when the angle of the sun shifted away from the car's tilted array, the car was turned around and the second pilot continued in the same direction.

There would be daily rankings, with the grand prize going to the best cumulative time on the final day, in Michigan.

There was no limit on what a team could spend.

On race day at Disney World, in a parking lot the size of Sudan and just as hot, the best and the brightest showed up with their 32 sunshine cars. Hundreds of college kids were making last-minute adjustments while GM engineers and official observers, who would police the race, circulated helpfully about. Meeting GM's rigid rules to qualify took three days, and some were better prepared than others.

Let us zoom in on a kid of about 19 who has a problem. Looking around anxiously for help, he spots a GM nameplate on the shirt of a gray-haired, bespectacled fellow in Sansabelt slacks and a Wunda-Weve golf shirt. The kid inquires, "Scuse me, you know anything about brakes?" The GM engineer kneels down, and they start talking shop.

A little later, this same gray-haired fellow is seen putting an arm around a crewman from his alma mater, Worcester Polytech. "Now don't forget your strategy," he admonishes. "Don't be out there burning up the batteries chasing for the lead." Coming closer, the nameplate identifies the fellow:

"Bob Stempel, GM."

Heavens to Betsy, it's the pope of General Motors, it's No. 1, out playing in this field of dreams!

All things of course being unequal, some teams, like the University of Michigan, had real dollars to spend, and others, like the University of North Texas, had dimes. For the latter, it was nice becoming the crowd's favorite underdog, but a truckful of pesetas would have been nicer.

Michigan's team captain, 27-year-old Susan Fancy, a mechanical-engineering major, could name all 120 members of her team. A year earlier, Michigan's Business School had sent out a fleet of finance majors to pound on the doors of 400 companies and astounded the sliderules by bringing $750,000 back to campus.

UM had so many engineering volunteers that they were divided into team committees to tackle specific assignments, like deciding on the car's design, its drivetrain, the body structure—there were even three meteorological gurus to feed weather forecasts into a computer operating aboard a chase car (GM provided two support vehicles for each team), which in turn was relayed to the pilot. Before race day, the UM team had been over the 1630-mile course *three times,* digitizing into the computer every stop sign, every railroad crossing, every unfriendly swerve on the course. The Wolverines arrived in Orlando with a team of 30, a racing trailer of Winston Cup size and quality, a mobile repair shop, even a portable generator to power the computers, and most prized, they all had hotel reservations. "A lot of people were jealous," says Fancy, "but it was by design—we came prepared, completely prepared." Bo Schembechler couldn't have said it better.

Michigan had money, and the team spent it. Take, for example, power cells. There are four kinds, from inexpensive amorphous silicone ones—"These would have cost us about five grand for the whole car," says Fancy—to exotic gallium-arsenide cells—"They're as scarce as one-of-a-kind Ferraris." Fancy points out that GM used up 40 percent *of the world's supply* of these cells to build Sunraycer.

Michigan opted for second-best cells—

Little-known Western Washington placed second, made the cover of Popular Science.

CHRIS ERVIN

that is, monocrystalline silicone—on its sun-sucking array, wrote a check for $187,000, and spent months installing them, one by one. The body, a Nomex and Kevlar combo, took seven months to complete.

Meanwhile, at North Texas, faculty adviser Dr. John Dobson recalls that "two or three students" did in fact venture out in the neighborhood of Denton to solicit contributions. "They came back with $500. That came from a nice guy at Safety Clean—they wash trucks—who was a graduate and interested in the subject." Dobson and a team of only six students designed and built the car on the cheap —$300 for a five-pack of low-tech lead/acid batteries ("We got them half-price, which was nice, and we got 50 percent off the bicycle rims, too"), there was plywood in the plug mold ("We did build our own electronics, which I was proud of"), and the university promised, within reason of course, to reimburse Dobson's personal checkbook ("and, uh, they still owe me a couple thousand"). Then, six months before the race, a GM official showed up and said they couldn't enter a car with the driver positioned headfirst. "That was a real setback—it cost us two months." On race day, they were ready— but only three of the six team members were on hand, because one student worked full-time and two others couldn't afford to cut classes. In the nights ahead, the North Texas team often slept in the weeds along the highway.

They finished 18th. "It was fun, a good experience," Dobson says, "but hard to sleep in the grass."

And then there was the team from fabled MIT. James Worden, a graduate student, is only 23, but he may have as much experience with serious solar cars—"I've been building cars since I was ten"—as most of GM's electric-car experts. Worden built and raced a car called the Solectria in the Australian race, finishing ninth. A graduate of MIT's class of '89 and now a grad student, he has recently formed a company that already is building real-world solar cars. Indeed, as many of the Sunrayce teams were rushing about to finish their cars in June, Worden—fresh from victory in a Massachusetts solar race the month before—was off in Switzerland driving another of his cars in the Tour de Sol, a 500-mile event.

Worden estimates that his team, which included six students, spent no more than two months in preparation, because Worden was already in the process of building the car at the time GM announced its race. Worden submitted a 60-page entry proposal and was accepted. MIT's car, like North Texas's, was more brainpower than bucks. It had a $6000 silver-zinc battery system, a $6000 "astro-power" array, and a total price tag of less than $30,000.

"The car was designed for land speed records," Worden says. "With a full sun on the salt flats, it's capable of 50 mph. We didn't have a lot of stuff—no computers, no radios, but we did almost as well

as the Michigan car." True enough, the tiny MIT car placed in the top five every day until an A-arm broke on day nine, and, according to Worden, an overly concerned GM official shut them down, unsatisfied that the car was safe to continue. "We finally made enough noise to get them to let us continue." The delay dropped them to 29th that day, and they finished sixth.

With his experience, Worden is a tad critical of the Sunrayce for reasons too lengthy to deal with here—suffice to say he believes "GM put it [the race] on with the idea that college kids do neat things, that kind of thinking. But really, it's not realistic. People should be trying to push the technology, not puttering along at 20 miles an hour. Why spend $800,000 to produce a car that averages 22 miles an hour when there are already solar cars that perform like combustion engines?"

Cal Poly/Pomona's team showed up with two solar arrays, one of them unnerving the Michigan team because it was chock-full of the exotic, superexpensive gallium-arsenide cells. (Dr. Dobson asked a gallium representative what eight square meters of the cells would cost, and after a calculator was employed, the man replied, "Six million dollars.") Ironically, the tiny cells, which require precise installation, didn't work properly, and the array was not a factor in the final standings. Cal Poly finished tenth. Sometimes money doesn't talk.

Little known Western Washington Uni-versity's Viking XX car was the surprise, knocking off the big-name schools with a second-place finish, just 1 hour and 19 minutes behind Michigan. Oddsmakers should have read the catalog more closely —the school's Vehicle Research Institute is well known in auto circles.

The University of Maryland's team finished in tenth place on day one but followed that with the most first-place days —four of them. A disastrous 29th-place day midway through the race cost them the grand prize. They finished third.

Michigan, as Captain Fancy noted, came prepared. The team never placed worse than sixth and twice won the dailies. The sleek maize and blue car rolled into the GM Tech Center first, 72 hours and 51 minutes after the start, the 575-pound car averaging 22 mph. It was the only car to complete every inch of the course. The others, at some point, had to be trailered and were penalized.

All 32 entries finished, and remarkably there was only one accident: the University of Waterloo's car, avoiding a pickup truck that appeared suddenly in its lane, wound up in a cornfield.

If nothing else, the event proved to GM that a solar-powered race can draw a crowd in the U.S. As the caravan of sunshine cars whispered along the blue highways through summer-green country, winding through hamlets like Petroleum in Kentucky and Skylight in Indiana, the curious came out in throngs to see. In

The boys from MIT were front-runners until an A-arm went south.

little Greenville, Ohio, a third of the town's 12,999 population lined the road: grizzled farmers in bib overalls, families in pickup trucks, teen-agers on bikes, old folks in lawn loungers, and everywhere the caravan passed, people hung off overpasses and waved from hayricks.

The corporate press releases said the race was held "to stimulate interest in technical education" and encourage all those sliderules who presumably may one day build these sci-fi cars, and so forth. But seriously—the TV newsies notwithstanding—GM has promised the world that electric cars are a certainty in the future. (As proof, it has built the Impact, an electric car it swears can go 0 to 60 in eight seconds and travel 120 miles on a single charge.) And California stands firm on its promise that all cars sold there in the year 2009—just 19 years down the road—will have zero exhaust emissions. And the only four-wheeled vehicles that can do that are donkey carts and electric cars.

Which is why, like the kid who needed help with his solar car's brakes, we grabbed Mr. Stempel's arm and inquired of GM's purpose with this show.

Mr. Stempel wrinkled his nose. "I'm going to need hundreds of engineers like this a year," he said, a reference to the idea that one day these cars will be a reality. "Where am I gonna get 'em?"

HOW OUR GUYS DID

An accounting was called for. The *Car and Driver*–sponsored car, Villanova University's sleek $270,000 Wildcat, came in dead last.

After all, we gave them some very nice baseball caps. (There's been some re-thinking, however, on the matter of the promised T-shirts.)

Wayne Pietrini, one of the sixteen crew members, tried to defer. "We really don't want to point the finger at anyone."

Say what, Pietrini? How could this possibly happen? Was not our Wildcat the third-fastest in qualifying, to the envy of those Cal Polynoids, those MITniks?

It was, he said.

And did not our Wildcat have the tony, airfoil profile? And the fine Kevlar-Nomex superfine skin? The absolutely dependable silver-zinc batteroonies—not to mention the four girls, *the four girl engineers* on board, Pietrini?

All true, sir.

Jesus, this is too much to take.

Turns out the thousands of little, sickeningly expensive "space-quality cells," as Pietrini calls them, were too close together on the blueprint to withstand the Florida sun, and somehow the manufacturer (who remains nameless, as they were a generous gift) approved this... this... *closeness.*

It was so hot in Florida that the plastic-like laminate and the cells heated up and began moving around, and shorting out, and the power output went from 1200 watts to 250, barely enough to tan a slice of bread in a toaster.

All right then, Pietrini, not your fault. Good show. Spot of bother, eh?

Must remind you our chaps did not quit. *Out of the question.* Simply not done. In it to the end. Reports have the lads producing the best set of original-design, custom-quality, homemade disc brakes ever seen on the planet. Left patches of duct tape all over the Disney asphalt. Damn good show, chaps!

Sense of the theatrical worth mentioning, too. Our fellows, made heartsick by these bloody expensive power cells, spent the entire day before the last leg of the race sucking every bit of power out of the sun and into the batteries. Still could get them only 75 percent charged for the final performance.

Starting from the last of 32 positions, with cars released at 30-second intervals, the Villanova Wildcats caught and flew past fifteen, I say *fifteen other race cars,* big-name universities still red-faced over that one, reportedly reaching 53 mph at one point. Nerves of steel. Hands of Ayrton. *Made Bo proud.*

We might, Pietrini, I say *might* come through with the T-shirts.

—*Steve Spence.*

RACING

THE BID TO QUALIFY

By Arthur St. Antoine

By October, the sun on the French Riviera has distanced itself from the beaches where just months earlier girls in the scantiest of outfits could be found in copious numbers. In October, the traffic has thinned out on the elegant Côte d'Azur, and at night there are fewer lights coming from the windows of the luxury hotels that line the beach.

In October, the Riviera can turn dark and drizzly and the mistral winds can lash in hard and cold from the mountains. Now the glassed-in cafés are almost empty and all the chic French leatherettes are back in Paris studying nude sculpture, so there's nobody to look at but crumbly old locals while sipping that five-dollar *café au lait* and trying to keep warm.

I am here on the French Riviera to raise worry blisters on my forehead, to attend the advanced race-driving class at *L'Ecole de Pilotage Renault-Elf Winfield.*

In the summer of 1990, I survived the Winfield School's four-day introductory course, as it's called, at Circuit Paul Ricard. In fact, I was one of five students in a class of eighteen to earn a Certificate of Merit and an invitation to return to France for round two, the autumn advanced class and student runoff, which is called the *Pilote Elf* competition. The winner—the *Pilote Elf*—is honored each year with a fully sponsored season of racing in the much-watched French Formula Renault series, courtesy of Elf Petroleum.

The Winfield School is best known as

the training grounds for more than twenty Formula 1 drivers, including The Man himself, Alain Prost. In short, the *Pilote Elf* title can be a launching pad to Formula 1.

Of about 120 Americans who train each year at Winfield's Paul Ricard facility (the school also operates a second branch at France's Magny-Cours racetrack), perhaps fifteen percent win Certificates of Merit and return in the fall. (The advanced course is open to all, but Merit winners receive a substantial discount.) So far, only one American has won the *Pilote Elf* title: Ron Emmick, who did it in 1985. Emmick, incredibly, abandoned his opportunity to climb the ladder after one tour and returned to race in the States. So the Winfield system has yet to produce an American F1 driver.

Admittedly, the odds are stacked against the Yanks. The Winfield School caters mostly to French and other European pupils—more than 200 flock to the Circuit Paul Ricard branch each year. And the generous Elf sponsorship program is set up primarily in hopes of obtaining talented young French drivers to carry the company's—and the country's—colors into Formula 1.

Also, because Grand Prix stars command front-page stature in Europe, there's no shortage of French youngsters seeking stardom at Winfield. The *Pilote Elf* competition may not warrant a line in your sports page, but in France it's a big, nationally televised deal—along the lines of winning the Heisman Trophy.

So here I am, back in France with 29 other American students (including nineteen Merit winners), all of us trying to keep our blood pumped up. And not just because it's cold. By the time we arrive, the year's top European pupils have already completed their advanced training and their qualifying runs. As the 30 of us assemble in our hotel for our first night's dinner, we learn that fifteen Frenchmen and three Swiss have earned spots in the *Pilote Elf* semifinals.

"Probably no more than five of you are going to join them," says a grim John Peterson, president of Franam Racing, Inc., the U.S. company that arranges Winfield trips for Americans. Peterson's grimness is warranted. Deeply committed to seeing Americans break into Formula 1, he has watched so many cocky hotshots blow it over the years that he now speaks with a cynical, at-times callous voice. "You people may think you've got these

French guys covered, but you have no idea how hard you're going to have to drive to make it," he says sternly. "French kids grow up dreaming of winning the *Pilote Elf.* They're motivated. They're hungry. They're willing to let it all hang out to win. If you want to beat them, you're going to have to drive like heroes."

Before we can drive like heroes, though, we first have to remember how to drive at all. It's been six months since some of us have been at the school. A day of review at the track is required—both to relearn the line on the school's portion of the Paul Ricard circuit and to recalibrate ourselves in Winfield's swift Formula Renault racers.

Peterson divides us into five groups of six, based on perceived ability. Each group will drive a twelve-lap session in the morning and another in the afternoon. Because all the racing will be done against the clock, the six cars will be spaced out on the track to allow each driver to run on a clear stretch of asphalt—unless he catches the guy ahead or is passed by the guy behind.

As I belt in with the rest of Group A, my adrenaline valve is on hair-trigger alert. None of our review laps will be timed, but the potential for failure is there nonetheless. Simon de Lautour, the French-speaking Englishman who presides over the Winfield School, gave us the good news earlier this morning: "Today is a day to refamiliarize yourselves

with the cars. Don't try to impress anyone with your speed, because all you'll do is get yourself noticed for your poor judgment. Along those lines, we don't want any of you being foolish and possibly hurting yourself or damaging one of our cars. So if you spin in the chicane or the sweepers, where you'll be carrying quite a bit of speed, you're out of the class. And that counts for the remainder of the course, too." Then he added with a smile: "So it's probably a good idea not to spin."

As we fire up the cars for the first session, de Lautour reminds us to use no more than 5000 rpm in each gear. "We'll be listening," he grins.

Oh, man. I'm rusty as hell. I forget to let the tires warm up before pushing the car and damn near lose it in the chicane. And, geez, the way my feet are getting clogged on the pedals you'd think they were webbed. But our group escapes without doing too badly. No serious mistakes in the other groups, either.

In the afternoon, at 5500 rpm, I find my rhythm and drive much better. In fact, my entire group gets good feedback after the session.

With one exception. Intoxicated by the red mist, an affliction that seizes racers who run a few good laps and then suddenly feel certain they're Alain Prost reincarnate, one student flies around the circuit at an outrageous pace. Chief instructor Roland Reiss notices and puts a watch on him. He's running brilliant times, but he's loose, all over the track, in danger of auguring into the Armco. As he pulls into the pits, brakes smoking, de Lautour all but yanks him from the car. "Very, very troubling, what I saw out there, old boy," de Lautour understates. "I'm really half of a mind to eject you from the course right here and now."

Somehow, though, Prost's ghost gains a stay of execution.

Day two marks the first of our timed

laps. Peterson has a word with us before we go out. "The performance of the cars varies slightly," he says, "so don't worry too much about how your times compare with those of the driver of another car. The key to doing well in the advanced course is to set the fastest times for *your* car every session. If you can't do that, don't expect to make the *Pilote Elf* semi-finals."

The morning session, at 5500 rpm, is a warmup—the times really only become relevant when you're shifting at the 6000-rpm redline. Still, one student succumbs to the pressure of lapping under the stopwatch and loops his car at the exit of the chicane. He returns to the pits, ashen-faced. His advanced course is over.

In the afternoon session, our first at 6000 rpm, another student overcooks the chicane and spins. He is uninjured and his car is undamaged, but he, too, is told to pack his bags. The rest of us now know that just finishing this advanced class will be an accomplishment.

If some students are revealing their

Winfield chief instructor Roland Reiss tells me, "You drive not bad for a boy so old."

weaknesses, others are displaying their skill. Two young Southern Californians, 19-year-old Rich Hearn and his buddy Waqar Mayer, 20, have come to Winfield with years of go-kart racing under their 26-inch belts. Hearn, in fact, is a seven-time national champion. Sporting brash black-and-neon driving suits and helmets, the two Merit winners strap into the Formula Renaults and attack the course with dazzling speed and control. After the session, de Lautour reminds them of the consequences of going too fast too soon. But as he turns away a smile creases his face.

That night, as we gather for dinner, I learn first-hand the ruthlessness of this game. Peterson posts everyone's lap times —grouped by car and also overall—on a chart near the restaurant door. "Read 'em and weep," he says as he steps back for us to look. We crowd in. Rich Hearn has clocked a few laps in the high-50-second range. Several others, including 26-year-old Matthias Nikolakopulos and 27-year-old autocross champ Jeff Altenburg (both members of my summer intro class), have run mid-to-low 51s. My face flushes when I see my times: no better than low 52s. And that's not the worst of it. At the bottom of the chart, I see that Peterson has dropped me back from Group A to Group B—presumably so I don't impede the fast guys. I take small consolation in the fact that I am fastest in my car for the day. I want to slink off to a café and down about fifteen Kronenburgs. Instead, I go to bed and stare at the ceiling.

The next morning at the circuit, I get some heartening news. The mechanics report that the car I drove yesterday, number 7, had a sick engine—it hadn't been running at full strength during my lapping sessions. I am only somewhat relieved.

Not that I can redeem myself today: it is pouring outside. Twenty-one-year-old Frank Ranum gazes at the somber sky and says, "Well, I guess two wasn't enough to appease the rain gods," a reference to the two students cut yesterday. We return to the hotel without driving.

The next day dawns clear and sunny. From the sidelines, I watch Group A run the morning session. They are impressive: smooth, confident, fast. Great. Just really freaking great.

When Group B's turn comes up, I jump for a car I haven't yet driven—number 5. Determined to never again suffer the humiliation of the evening lap-chart roast, I vow to go for it.

To turn a fast lap on the school circuit,

it's crucial to keep your right foot flat on the floor through the tricky fourth-gear sweepers that lead onto the long main straight. As I approach the sweepers on my first hot lap, though, I feel my nerve weakening and my right foot trying to feather the gas. No! I mash the pedal down as hard as I can. As the left-hander nears, I clench my buns together and deflect the wheel two inches. The car, aided by its sticky slicks and air-rending wings, hunkers down and hammers through the turn without a bobble. At the exit, with the outside tires nibbling the rub strips between the track surface and the dirt runoff, I shift into fifth. I've made it. Now there's nothing to do but sit back and survey the mirrors and the gauges as the Formula Renault blasts down the straight at 135 mph.

When Peterson posts the day's times that night, I grit my teeth and elbow in for a look. Yes! I've dropped my average to the low 51s and have set fastest time in my car for both sessions. Peterson moves me back into Group A for tomorrow's semifinal qualifying runs. I sleep just fine.

Qualifying day dawns cloudy and cool. But dry. Again, we will run one session in the morning and one in the afternoon. The instructors will pick the semifinalists based on each driver's best five-lap average from either session.

A little strategy is clearly in order. Knowing that the morning runs are invariably the best (because the track surface is cooler and the tires don't overheat as easily), I decide to go all-out in the a.m. and then, rather than risk a disqualifying spin, play it safe in the afternoon.

My car, number 1, is hampered by understeer—which prevents me from driving flat-out in the first part of the sweepers —but none of my carmates betters my times in the morning session. Sticking to my plan, I back off in the afternoon and cruise home safely.

It works. No one driving my car in the afternoon can beat my morning times. I am fastest in my car for the day.

But I'm not the fastest overall. Rich Hearn turns in a string of amazingly quick and consistent times both sessions, as does 26-year-old go-karter Kim Williams. Other standouts include Waqar Mayer and my summer classmates, Jeff Altenburg and Matthias Nikolakopulos. The lone woman in our group, 21-year-old Amy Rohan of Mountain View, California, drives quickly and cleanly and earns the respect of everyone.

Tom Cruise look-alike Rich Hearn set the pace from the first timed lap.

After Anne Delarue showed me my lap chart, above, I pondered how to go faster.

The day does not go without incident, however. One student who had clearly been a front-runner spins in the chicane on one of his last few laps—blowing his semifinal bid. He parks his car and quietly packs his helmet.

That night at the boisterous most-of-us-survived-and-lived-to-tell-about-it awards dinner, where we indulge in our first serious boozing of the week, Simon de Lautour delivers the news we've all been waiting for. Amid much tension, he recites the names of six Americans who have qualified: Hearn, Mayer, Altenburg, Nikolakopulos, Williams, and 20-year-old Chris Ridgley, who came to Winfield with absolutely no previous racing experience.

De Lautour informs me that I, too, have qualified for the semis, but at the geriatric age of 29 I'm too old to run in the competition. The cutoff age is now 27, and there are no exceptions—not even for writers from major magazines. Peterson had told me of the age barrier long ago, of course, so I knew going in that I wouldn't be able to run in the semis even if I earned a spot. Still, I feel a sadness. I have been left behind.

Two days later, I watch the semifinals. The members of Team America acquit themselves well. Driving freshly tuned cars on brand-new tires, every single American semifinalist drives faster than ever before. But the Europeans also look strong.

As expected, Rich Hearn sets the curve for the Americans, but he also turns out to be the pacesetter for all 24 semifinalists. Anne Delarue, Peterson's lovely French assistant, nods to me as Hearn flashes by the start line. "Roland and Simon are thinking Rich is very, very good," she says. "They say maybe he can do the whole thing."

Because comparing times from car to car would be unfair, the instructors select the five finalists based on how closely their times match those set by chief instructor Roland Reiss in their car. It's difficult to predict who's going to win.

That evening, as we dine in a small restaurant near our hotel in Bandol, John Peterson delivers the news. Three French and one Swiss have made the finals. And one American: Rich Hearn, who topped the semis by being just 0.112 second off Reiss's times in his car. Rich smiles modestly. "Well, I did feel pretty good about the second session," he says. The other five Americans keep their chins up. No quivering.

The finals, Peterson tells us, are set for Thanksgiving Day. The drivers will each run one timed ten-lap session alone on the track. The judges will then pick the *Pilote Elf* champion based on the average of each finalist's five best laps. *Five laps to determine a driver's entire future in racing.*

I had hoped I would return to Winfield sharing a race car with the next Alain Prost. As we toasted Rich Hearn's success that evening in Bandol, I was convinced that I had done just that.

Epilogue

On Thanksgiving Day 1990, driving on a rain-soaked track in front of a crowd of French journalists and Formula 1 drivers, American Rich Hearn won the Pilote Elf title. Although he had never before driven a race car in the rain, he crushed the opposition, turning in an average lap time almost one second faster than his nearest rival, Frenchman Vincent Talamandier.

THE ALCAN 5000 WINTER RALLY

By Phil Berg

"Always carry a can of dog food in your car," advised arctic rescuer Allan Errington. "If you have good food in your car, you'll eat it when you don't need it. But you probably won't eat the dog food unless you're really starving."

This was not the sort of briefing one expects to hear before beginning a road rally. Most road-rally driver meetings are endlessly boring and full of trivial details —such as what kind of watch is keeping time for the event, or what type of grease was on the rallymaster's speedometer cable when he measured the course. But the Alcan 5000 Winter Rally is no ordinary event. Far from it. Created by Jerry Hines, a longtime rallymaster best known for his course work on Brock Yates's One Lap of America rallies, the Alcan is a 6275-mile, twelve-day drive from Seattle to the Arctic Circle and back. In February.

I wasn't very troubled by Errington's warnings. Neither was my co-driver, Everett Smith—a survivor of the ill-fated *Car and Driver* One Lap of America entry a few years ago. Then again, neither of us had ever driven to the Arctic in winter.

"When the thermometer drops into moon temperatures," continued Errington, a veteran of more than 60 arctic rescues and a master on surviving in subzero weather, "it's said that human flesh will freeze in 30 seconds. But that's a myth. I've never seen any circumstance where the early stages of frostbite occur quicker than 45 seconds."

Errington then shared the story of a fellow arctic adventurer who spilled gasoline on his hand in −50-degree weather. Because the fuel stayed liquid, he foolishly surmised that it must have been at least 32 degrees—hardly harmful. But the

Left to right: Team members Everett Smith, the author, and Jack Christensen.

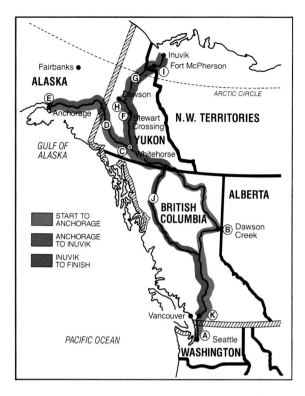

START TO ANCHORAGE

ANCHORAGE TO INUVIK

INUVIK TO FINISH

It was 40 degrees at the start in Seattle (A), but by Dawson Creek (B) the mercury had dropped below zero. Whitehorse (C) marked the start of an all-nighter through Beaver Creek (D), where we broke a spring. We got a day's rest in Anchorage (E). We found "the Subaru Valdez" in Stewart Crossing (F) before reaching Eagle Plains (G). Satch Carlson proposed a race to Dawson (H), but we forged on to Inuvik instead. Near Fort McPherson (I), birds felled a Suburban. The Cassiar Highway (J) held the last peril before the Harrison Hot Springs finish (K).

fuel was in fact at ambient temperature, −50 degrees, and it instantly stripped the top layer of flesh from the hand of the careless refueler. "Because you'll be filling your cars often," Errington continued, "you should keep that incident in mind."

Errington also informed us that the Arctic is as dry as a desert, and that the best way to keep warm in its "moon" temperatures—from −30 degrees Fahrenheit to −50, on average—is to keep your blood circulating. To keep your blood circulating, you need to drink more. "Don't worry about drinking *too* much," Errington concluded with a smile. "The body has an effective remedy for the overconsumption of liquids."

Right. And human flesh freezes in 45 seconds? We decided that if the situation came up, we'd opt for being a little chilly and thirsty, thank you.

"Bring leg gaiters," advised Chris Jensen. A Cleveland *Plain Dealer* writer and an Alcan veteran, Jensen was once a Vietnam War photographer which should explain his predilection for adventure. He and friend Bill Sadataki drove a Ford Ranger pickup in the 1988 Trans Amazon Rally—through nine South American countries and countless swarms of dangerous insects. Because Jensen has survived all of these escapades, we treated his advice with respect. And bought leg gaiters.

Jensen and Sadataki rounded out our in-

formal all-Jeep/Eagle team: one Cherokee Laredo and two Eagle Talon TSi AWDs. The Talons would, of course, be fun to drive, but Everett and I were confident that our Cherokee would be the hot setup. Why? Well, long rallies with complicated 30-mile timed sections following 600-mile transits the same day distill an inevitable, inescapable byproduct: exhaustion. To combat this, we would have a crew of three in our car—something not possible in a Talon loaded with blankets, sleeping bags, extra clothes, first-aid kits, fire extinguishers, spare parts, tools, and enough food to choke Roseanne Barr.

We enlisted Jack Christensen, inventor of the respected Timewise rally com-

Rally Rules and Savvy

The competitive sections of this 6200-mile rally totaled only about 300 miles, split into a dozen small segments ranging from two to 30 miles each. The remaining 5900 miles of the event were long-but-quick drives from one competitive segment to the next. Think of it as a baseball game with each inning played in a different city.

The competitive courses are measured to the one-hundredth of a mile. Teams are instructed to run at one-minute intervals from each other, and they are given a speed at which to travel. The distance of the course calculated by the speed of the car tells the teams when they should arrive at certain places on the course.

Cars are timed as they cross hidden checkpoints. Passing checkpoints early or late by one second gives you one penalty point. Ten seconds late, ten penalty points. Since the teams don't know where the checkpoints are they must try to drive at a calculated continuous speed.

Driving with this kind of accuracy on ice takes practice. Average speeds for the competitive segments ranged between 30 to 40 mph.

Every team that scored well did so with the help of a specialized computer connected to an odometer that could be adjusted to measure fractions of an inch. The computer calculates the exact speed to drive by means of its clock that teams set each day to the U.S. Bureau of Standards shortwave time broadcasts.

In two weeks of driving, the winning team was off the pace set by the rally organizers by only 24 seconds, which is remarkable considering the conditions. Remarkably, the next four cars varied from the winner's performance by no more than 22 seconds.

puter, to occupy the navigator's seat of our Cherokee. Jack is the sort of guy who can solve tangential equations in his head while the driver is pounding on the ABS and the rally car is sliding into a downhill, off-camber, ice-coated corner 20 mph too fast. He'd provide exactly the sort of edge we'd need if we figured to win the Alcan 5000.

We brought dried fruit and granola bars and candy bars and trail mix and microwave dinners. (Jensen advised us to bring microwave food because, in a pinch, you can heat it under hot running water.) We even bought those little candy bars sold in mountaineering stores that boast about 400 calories in every bite. A man could live off this stuff. No way were we going to buy dog food. Or need it. Or eat it.

Preparing for the worst, we also brought a host of spare parts for the Cherokee: a fuel pump, a fuel filter, a water pump, and plenty of hoses and belts—all supplied by Eastside Jeep/Eagle in Bellevue, Washington. "And you need a spare exhaust manifold," a mechanic told us.

"Why?" we asked. The 4.0-liter six in the Cherokee is a long engine, and its exhaust manifold is a two-foot piece of cast iron that must weigh about 75 pounds. We didn't exactly want another along for the ride.

"Look at that stack of manifolds," said the Jeep technician, pointing to a discard pile. "Every one of them is broken because the front exhaust-pipe hanger clamp breaks and the whole system pulls down on the manifold. Then you'll burn a valve and the car will stall. And you'll freeze to death."

After examining the clamp in question, we realized that we could bolt a second clamp on backward next to the original—doubling in strength. A neat fix, and one that not only saved us 75 pounds worth of cast iron but also made even more room for our dried peach pits and alfalfa-root snacks.

We also brought an engine-block heater and an electric battery blanket to keep the engine from freezing at night. The Jeep had been fitted with four huge Hella 2000 rally lights by Sadataki and Greg Lester (Jensen's co-driver) and also sported three inside map lights and a Timewise mileage computer. In addition, we had the latest K40 CB; all the truckers we talked to said that it sounded just like a real big-rig radio. ("What are them California cars with writing on 'em, race cars or what?" asked one confused eighteen-

wheeler.) We also installed a two-way Icom business-band radio that could transmit 70 miles in good conditions.

Our teammates' Eagle Talons were equally well outfitted. Michelin supplied tire designer Kevin Clemens to look after our studded snow tires and offer technical help, should we have problems. "Studs don't work very well at −30 degrees," Kevin explained. "But at that temperature the rubber can get an amazing amount of grip on ice."

The rally started in Seattle. From there, we would spend four days driving up the Alaska Highway before heading up the Klondike and Dempster highways through the Yukon and into the Northwest Territories. Finally, the route would turn back south toward Seattle with a swing west through the twisty Cassiar Highway in British Columbia.

As we made our final preparations, Jensen approached with a word of advice: "Watch for suicidal killer trucks on the Cassiar Highway." This sentiment was echoed by nearly every other experienced driver on the rally. "They should have closed that road to the public years ago," one fuel-station attendant in the Yukon later told us. "Sometimes the trucks crash into cars, the rest of the time they leave a snow cloud 100 yards long that blinds you."

We surveyed our competition. Looking hard to beat was longtime ace rally driver Gene Henderson, a veteran of the 1964 Monte Carlo rally and the Shell 4000 through Canada; he was the U.S. rally champion before such names as "Buffum" and "Millen" were recognizable. Henderson has been a "factory" Subaru driver for

Mid-morning at the Stewart Crossing. Gas was three dollars per gallon.

the past few years. He is sharp and by some measure one of the fastest drivers in the group. And he's very serious.

Henderson is a retired vice cop from Dearborn, Michigan. We had another lawman on the trip, too: Dan Goodwin, an active U.S. marshal. Goodwin spent twenty years with the Alaska State Troopers, so he was well prepared for the roads we'd be traveling on. He told us about the time he chased crooks headed from Anchorage to the Canadian border for 65 miles along the highway—until the fleeing felons crashed. "Chasing someone that far is not the frightening part," he said. "The scary part is when you catch them. You're completely alone. The nearest help is probably three hours away." Goodwin was as serious as Errington about the dangers we'd be facing: "If you go off the road at 70 mph in deep snow, you rise above it—like a skipping stone. You sail so far it takes two wreckers to get you out."

You don't need to be a cop to do well in an arctic rally, but you need to know your math and your computers. Art Issler and Fast Eddie Botwick planned to run the route without the expensive computers the rest of us had. Instead, Botwick armed himself only with a small programmable calculator. (The team posted remarkably good scores at the finish.)

Siegfried Lucka, a three-time German road-racing champion who now runs a construction company in Ontario, showed up in a Ford Ranger pickup supported in part by Ford of Canada. He planned to use the Alcan as a shakedown run before competing in the Australian Safari Rally and the Paris-Dakar raid in Africa's Sahara. Lucka and co-driver Michael Ruge entered the event specifically to

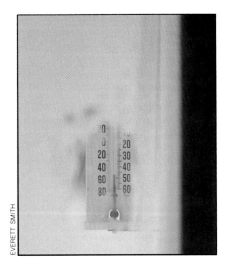

Stewart Crossing low: −54 degrees.

drive the untimed transit sections at high speeds.

Our entourage left Seattle and, after running two timed sections, headed for our first night's stop: Quesnel, British Columbia. There, the first scores were posted. We were only a second behind Henderson and co-driver Ralph Beckman. But, as the rally moved up the Alaska Highway toward Anchorage, that spot was going to be hard to keep.

The Alaska Highway, often called the Alcan Highway (for "Alaska-Canada Military Highway"), is a tough road, with spotty shoulders in places. But it is well marked on its 1500-mile length from Dawson Creek, British Columbia, to Fairbanks. Salt doesn't melt ice at the temperatures we were driving through, but on corners we found that the ice was coated with sand or shale chips.

As the rally progressed, the course called for a southern deviation toward Anchorage at a town called Tok. On our way to Tok, during an all-night drive from Whitehorse, the Cherokee developed a nasty and worsening tendency to bottom its rear suspension on what appeared to be small bumps. "It feels like there's nothing back there," Everett called out from his sleep in the back seat—the noise of the solid axle pounding into the Cherokee's frame rails no doubt influencing his dreams. The car felt as if it were being dropped by a helicopter each time it crossed a frost heave. And no wonder: when we hoisted the Cherokee into the air at Anchorage's Jeep/Eagle dealer, we found that the right-rear leaf spring had snapped off at its rear shackle. A new spring and four new shock absorbers later, the Cherokee was once again ready for the return ride on the tough highway —and for the trip north toward Inuvik, Northwest Territories.

Now we were worried. It was getting *cold* outside. As the temperatures dropped, we devised the official *Car and Driver* Arctic Temperature Test: you wrap a piece of duct tape around a can of Diet Coke and pinch the tape in one of the side windows with the can hanging outside. If the temperature is in the "moon" range, the soda will freeze completely solid in six minutes.

On the way to the Arctic Circle, in the wee hours of the morning, we stopped at Stewart Crossing, Yukon, and found Henderson and his Subaru Legacy in the only garage within a 50-mile radius. Henderson was busy barking orders into the phone. It turned out that an engine-oil seal had failed during a cold-morning start. Someone had noticed the pool of Mobil 1 on the ground and nicknamed the car "the Subaru Valdez."

Though we hadn't seen any scores from the timed legs after the Anchorage rest stop, we felt good about our performance. Following Henderson's misfortune, our most serious threat came from the second "factory" Subaru Legacy wagon of Ken Knight and Dave Harkcom, executives at the Subaru-Isuzu facility in Indiana. These two have quietly been running rallies for years. And Ken has driven up the Alcan Highway on engineering drives, so he knows the roads and conditions.

Because Knight and Harkcom were driving without a third teammate, we had made a team decision in Anchorage to keep them up all night—hoping their fatigue would give us an edge on the timed sections out of Anchorage. While Everett and Jack got needed sleep, I took the Subaru teammates to the bar for an extended "conversation."

My strategy backfired. As we drank our bottles of Kokanee beer, Ken and Dave told me their heart-wrenching story. Their car had been lovingly assembled by honest, hardworking Indiana folk, each of whom had signed the team's dark-blue Legacy. These people had stayed up nights away from their wives and children preparing the car. Dave intimated that these poor, honest, hard-working co-workers would suffer tremendous disgrace if the two were not victorious in the rally. Then, after several more bottles of beer, I think Ken began to tell me about how one of his daughters needed new shoes.

On the next timed section, Harkcom and Knight took only one penalty point. I, meanwhile, shaken by the tearful story of Dave and Ken, took five. When the scores were posted that night at the Eagle Plains Lodge near the Arctic Circle, we had fallen to third place.

Meanwhile, Henderson and Beckman showed in their rejuvenated Subaru—the car having been fixed with a hefty glop of gasket cement. That evening, Knight tried to tell us how a new seal had been air-freighted for Henderson's car from Subaru's Portland parts depot, and how mechanics were waiting on call in Whitehorse, and how the engineers at Fuji Heavy Industries told him over the phone that they would stay up 24 hours designing an improved oil seal for the Legacy,

Jack's magic box—the Timewise mileage computer. Mileage can be adjusted accurately to 1/100,000th of an inch.

and how they would soon fly in from Japan with a full rally crew and rebuild the Subarus, and how they were even going to install CD players and bring a team masseuse for Dave and Ken.

We didn't fall for Knight's routine a second time. But it was now clear that the competition from the Subaru effort was going to be fierce.

Some of the other teams posed less of a threat. Tim Paterson, the author of MS-DOS—the operating system on which IBM-class personal computers are based—was having problems in his Porsche 911 Carrera 4. His computer expertise had failed him: by feeding the wrong speed change into the team's computer, Paterson and co-driver Don Gibson dropped out of winning contention on a quick two-mile timed section in Whitehorse. Brian Davitt and Adrian Crane were driving a four-wheel-drive Talon and were frequently the first car to reach the end of each transit section—often by

Seventeen cars started the rally. One Suzuki broke before we hit really cold temperatures.

155

We'd been warned about killer trucks doing 85 mph and drifting 10 wheels through corners. No one told us we'd have to watch out for airplanes, too.

hours over the rest of the field—but a computing error also knocked them out of contention. Satch Carlson, still on "sabbatical" from *AutoWeek,* flipped a switch too soon in his Mazda 323GTX and racked up 85 seconds worth of penalty points in one swoop.

We left Eagle Plains and headed out in the dark pre-dawn hours to the Arctic Circle. Just past the Arctic Circle sign, at the Northwest Territories border before the town of Fort McPherson, we found a large sign proclaiming, "Radar Detector Use and Possession Illegal." A week ago, we would have expected to see a sign reading, "Go Back While You're Still Alive. Find Warmth. Buy More Thinsulate Polypropylene Garments."

By now, organizer Jerry Hines had decided that probably everyone was tired and most people wouldn't want to drive all the way north to Inuvik—about 114 miles one way from our Fort McPherson fuel stop. So he changed the course to make an Inuvik trip optional. We elected to go, summoning the spirit of the Yukon Mounties' Lost Patrol and the Mad Trapper of Rat River, but all but four other cars cruised down to Dawson City. We will forever consider our fellow competitors who went south for hot food and long sleep to be, in short, wimps.

The road to Inuvik is a broad two-lane highway, well graded and loaded with sweeping turns around rolling hills. We passed a few settlements of houses and a few locals in pickup trucks, but little else.

In the winter, Inuvik is quiet—as you'd expect in a place where the daytime tem-

perature hovers at −40 degrees. It is a clean, brightly painted town of 3000. For 57 days each summer, the sun is visible at midnight. Satellite dishes here are aimed straight across the ground.

Just as we were driving down the main street of town, a young woman dressed in bright clothes straight off the pages of *Vogue* and with coat open to the wind crossed the road in the sort of lightfooted gait you'd expect of a fashion model on a stage. Hmmmmm. Inuvik may be a desolate place, but it is clearly not a dangerous place.

Rounding a turn as we drove back toward the Arctic Circle and Eagle Plains, we came upon a group of suicidal ptarmigans on the road. These dim-witted birds look exactly like the snowballs left by a plow's blade, and they refuse to move when a car comes up on them. I stepped heavily into the ABS, but I collected a few before I stopped. Jack called back on the radio to warn the sweep Suburban following us of the hazard. Unfortunately, the birds spooked the Suburban anyway—it went off the road and into a ditch. We were ten miles ahead and entering a deep gorge when the sweep vehicle's plea for help came over the radio. Sixty seconds later, and we'd have never heard them.

The Cherokee couldn't budge the Suburban back onto the ice road, so we set off to find help. We found a road-maintenance camp twenty miles south and were assured by road workers Joe and Willie Snowshoe that a grader was on its way toward the Suburban to rescue it. While we were waiting, Joe served us fried cari-

Heading down the stretch, I stuffed the Cherokee into a snowbank.

bou heart—on Valentine's Day. In return we gave him all of our microwave lasagna.

I had computed our fuel range to be 320 miles exactly. But in the two hours we sat with the engine idling while we made sure help was coming to the Suburban (we left it running so it wouldn't freeze up), our fuel level dropped precariously low. For 60 miles south to the Arctic Circle, I used only enough throttle to keep us moving at 45 mph. The wind picked up as the sun went away, and it blew hard enough to send cold jets of air rushing in through the door handles of the Cherokee. The landscape looked colder than the moon. This is *the* wrong place on earth to run out of fuel. The Eagle Plains fuel stop was about 24 miles south of the Arctic Circle. At the circle sign, the Cherokee's fuel light came on. Two gallons of fuel remained, enough for 32 miles—if nothing went wrong. Fact: it is possible to sweat like a Finnish sauna attendant when you're running out of gas and the outside temperature is -45 degrees.

We made it to the fuel stop.

The Cassiar Highway heading south from Whitehorse through British Columbia gave rise to the famous Alcan 5000 saying: "The easiest part is behind you." Mindful of Jensen's earlier warning, we watched out for big rigs. We'd seen some logging trucks doing 85 mph behind Hines's Audi 5000CS Quattro, drifting ten wheels through the corners, but, luckily for us, a large bridge had collapsed at the southernmost tip of the Cassiar, and truck traffic was unseasonably light.

We had settled into a good routine on the timed sections, and after a breathtaking drive down the alpine Cassiar, only two timed legs were left before the rally's finish. Our calm and precise driving, I thought, had been honed to perfection in the past ten days. It was only bad luck that had us out of first place. This would be the stretch where we would collect the Subarus and wave the famous Jeep flag. This was, it turned out, where I stuffed the Cherokee into a snowbank with a *National Geographic* photographer in our fourth seat to record the incident. Fortunately, that leg of the rally was eliminated because of a bad route instruction.

When the final points were tallied at the finish in Harrison Hot Springs, British Columbia, we ended up in fourth place. After 300 miles of precisely timed sections during the twelve-day event, the difference in penalty points between Henderson's winning Subaru and Jensen's fifth-place Talon was only 22 seconds. We were only twelve seconds out of first, having lost third place by one second on the final timed section to teammates Sadataki and Dave Killian.

In 6200 miles, we had come close to getting stuck in the snow only once. In fact, we may have been overprepared: it is possible, we discovered, to take a normal vehicle, drive sensibly, and get halfway to the North Pole in the middle of winter. It isn't costly, and it isn't frightening. You can find an open gas station at least every 200 miles, and you can eat at a McDonald's any time of the day or night as far north as Whitehorse.

And, with luck, not once will you have to eat dog food.

ROBERT HARMEYER JR

IRONHEAD EARNHARDT

By Larry Griffin

I'm gaining on Earnhardt. This is no dream. He's the toughest son of Dixie to come pounding out of the South since Pickett charged, and I'm chasing this nightmare on wheels. Talladega. Watkins Glen. Michigan International. Hounding him race after race. I feel the draft he keeps breaking, snaking. You can't get a fender under him. The guy is sly, as much a will-o'-the wisp off the track as on.

But I am closing in. Slowly.

Weeks ago, running Alabama's I-way out of Birmingham, sniffing Earnhardt's trail to Talladega, I saw signs for the town of Irondale. Perfect: Irondale marks the way toward the triple-tough Carolinian who fans and foes call "Ironhead." You know the triathlon Ironman contest? In racing's case, no contest—Ironhead is one of a steely kind. Three times NASCAR champion, he runs true as the sport's infamous ass-kicker. And loves it. Though the man shows minor signs of mellowing, his name still stands for hard charging. Often lately, the name "Earnhardt" also suggests a racecrafter.

The Earnhardt name meant much the same twenty years ago: alone, Dale's dad kept his own lid on the NASCAR Sportsman Circuit. Ralph Earnhardt died in September 1973, but his teenager was already careering up through the ranks in the same singular way. Dale's mom, Martha, remembers when they tried to coax him back into the ninth grade with the lure of a showroom-new car. He turned it down to keep racing. Now—not that he races for the money—he's made millions.

No mama's boy, Dale is his daddy's son. Ask about his father and you sense a connection made, a knot of muscle tightened, still tied deep: "That's why I'm racing today. Grew up around my dad, so it just seemed natural that's what I did. He taught me good common-sense things. He didn't have a high-school education, but as far as I'm concerned he was pretty sharp. He knew race cars, knew what the ins and outs were and how to win, how to make the money count, how to take care of his equipment. He ran flathead Fords all the way up through overhead Fords and then the Chevrolets. He won so many races they hardly could count 'em all. Probably in the hundreds."

Young Dale learned from racers by the dozens.

"I sort of pattern myself after myself, but there's a lot of great drivers that I watched, my dad being the most dominant. If I get in jams, I think about things he did, and things work out. But I learned from so many—David Pearson, Bobby Isaac. When my dad passed away, Bobby Isaac helped me out. Pete Hamilton, Richard Petty. Donnie and Bobby Allison."

The day before Talladega, Earnhardt swivels around atop the Richard Childress Racing Enterprises transporter. His squint sweeps the racketing ARCA race. "I'm just watching what the draft is doing," he says, "but there are only about three or four good cars that aren't stringing out. Charlie Glotzbach's car has a lot of things on it we're trying."

"We" includes Richard Childress. The ARCA car, his test bed for Winston Cup ideas, wins its race. Its lineage traces to the same spit-and-sparkle Childress operation that severs fat from NASCAR's larder. Earnhardt's $11 million in prize payouts add up to more than anyone else's winnings in any kind of racing. Big-time bucks for two small-town bucks.

Childress put his team in the Carolina burg of Welcome because technical leaks and personnel changes are anything but welcome. The RCR cadre holds the fort far from the technical incestuousness common in Charlotte. Aiding team morale deep in the social boondocks, Childress's 35,000-square-foot shop and neighboring welcome center overlook Welcome's community swimming pool.

Childress goes that extra mile for his 25 car crafters. The pit crew, the "Flying Aces," has been NASCAR's fastest four years running.

"It feels awful good," says Earnhardt, "to come down the pit road and know them guys are standing down there waiting to change tires. I've been offered a lot more money to go somewhere else, but that opportunity is not such a bargain if you can't take the whole team with you. And I would be foolish to go drive for somebody else for maybe 500,000 or a million dollars more than I make driving for Richard if I couldn't win races. When I come in with a problem on the chassis, Kirk and I will get right in there and make adjustments."

Crew chief Kirk Shelmerdine makes the parts and the pit-crew choreography work together. Observers say one of the team's biggest advantages is that Earnhardt is the best at getting in and out of the pits fast. His eyesight, backside, inner ear, and right foot take the full measure of time, speed, and distance. They allow him to run in harder and to brake later and more accurately coming in, then make the most of it smoking the hell out again. Meshed with the Aces' winged feet, that gains irreducible seconds.

Shelmerdine says Dale's part amounts to still more: "He's a lot more sensitive to the car than people think. He's got a reputation for being hard on equipment, just wide-open sideways every lap, and he does drive like that. But he also is real sensitive and can feel a lot of things chassiswise that help us to set it up. That's the

key—getting the car so the guy can do what he's capable of doing.

"But he doesn't like testing—there's nobody out there to race with."

Who does Earnhardt like to race with besides his own kind? Al Unser, Jr., for one. Dale told Little Al he's one of the few guys who could run two NASCAR races a year and win at least one. Told him he was glad he's sticking to Indy cars.

Better those than Dale's bumper.

Once upon a time, Earnhardt raced his team owner. Childress gave up driving when Junior Johnson convinced him the NASCAR of the future needed another full-time owner more than the journeyman driver he'd been. Childress hitched up his pants and buckled up a deal with Wrangler (the blue-jeans company) and Earnhardt. His hair suitably outlawish and the handlebars of his mustache flared to Harley-Davidson dimensions, Dale gained fame his father never knew by sporting around in denims and scowling off blue-and-yellow billboards as "One Tough Customer."

Racing fortunes changed again for the better. The tough customer got a better deal from Mr. Goodwrench. A deal so good that RCR builds its brilliant Chevrolet Luminas from the ground up, not short-shrifting with chassis tacked together on the lines in Charlotte. Childress doles out stout bonuses, profit-sharing, and a retirement plan. Expanding into outside businesses, he aims to provide his guys with jobs for the years after—when they no longer want to go busting off to races 30 times per season.

Disruptions split families. Earnhardt, now 38, sowed his oats early; a teen marriage fell apart. Two divorces and his abbreviated schooling left a man bent on higher educations for daughter, Kelley,

Richard Childress's 35,000-square-foot shop is tucked away in Welcome, North Carolina. That's Earnhardt's black paint and Number 3.

called 'Semi-Modified,' little six-cylinder cars, wasn't much to them. But you could see there was a lot of ability there. There's people drove for years and Dale run with them. He used to get his nose in places he ought not to, but now he's just as aggressive but under control. Ralph was a good teacher. He taught Dale patience. When the car's not the best, he will make something of it. You can miss a setup and he'll come home with something. You could read it in his face that the next day never came fast enough.

"Anything you'd put under him," recalls David, "Dale could tell what the car was doing and relate it back. But then he went for his first day at Charlotte, and he really wasn't going anywhere. He come down to the house that night a little puzzled. He says, 'Man, I really don't know if I ought to be there.'"

David Oliver said, "Dale, just go on back over there, you'll be all right, just run your race. Do what you born to do."

He made the race and ran 600 miles.

"He looked like a whupped puppy—little old arms and no power steering—but he pumped that big Dodge all day. I think then you could see it—'Nothing I can't do . . .' Next time you could see a big difference, more an aggressive driver."

Eventually, owner Rod Osterlund needed such a driver. A handshake deal, at first for a Sportsman race, then to Atlanta to go onto the high banks with the big boys.

David Oliver stares off.

"He like to wore them out down there."

David's eyes hint at a smile.

"You've seen it's just been a steady climb, and I don't know if it's peaked yet. He just keeps amazing you."

Bob Tomlinson manages Cale Yarborough Motorsports. Bob and David got swinging-doored in the Earnhardt betrothal brood and found themselves brothers-in-law.

David says you can't sucker Dale into a wreck, and Bob nods. "His daddy was like that. He would always be there to where the other guy made a mistake. He'd tell Dale—and I heard him say it time and again—'You get paid for the last lap.'

"I don't know if Ralph ever really encouraged Dale to be a racer. But when he started, Ralph said, 'Well, the boy's going to do it—I'd better help.' He used to draw little racetracks on the floor and use welding rods as race cars, and show us how to work the traffic. Seemed like some people had to go out and practice, but Dale never

18, and sons Kerry, 20, and Dale, Jr., 15. Eight years ago, Dale's third wife, Teresa, brought in fresh brains and beauty. Last year, she delivered baby Taylor Nicole into the lime-lit racing life. Teresa came complete with a degree in interior design. Says Dale: "She's always been a good friend, but when we got married she became instrumental in helping me work out contracts and tax and insurance stuff. She does a little interior decorating on the side. Sells a little property. Models for an agency out of Charlotte. Raises a family, runs Dale Earnhardt, Incorporated, helps run Dale Earnhardt Chevrolet in Newton. And keeps Dale Earnhardt straight."

Dale's always-racing father supported mom Earnhardt, Dale, and four more brothers and sisters. The era was the 1960s, and the flavor, like Coke, "the real thing." (Dale's mother remains an eager Elvis fan whose famous son picks up Presley mementos in his travels.) Like rock-and-roll, car lore heated Dale's head and bearing grease packed his pores. The Kannapolis kids grew up in an area called "Car Town," among streets named for cars and engines. While Dale gauged how to turn piles of parts into race cars, a soap-operatic entanglement of sisters, brothers, kissing cousins, next-door neighbors, and happeners-by started piling up a heap of marriage licenses, birth certificates, and divorce decrees.

Neighbor David Oliver raced, but found one of Dale's sisters made his heart go faster, so he sped her down the aisle. Divorced now, David works on Ken Schrader's Kodiak Chevys. He helped Dale get into racing: "First time I saw him race, he drove a car for us. What they had to. It was just there. He knows what's around him. He's race-aware. He knows who's in the lead lap. He knows what he's got to do to take care of a tire, whatever he's got to do. And I don't know if you can teach that."

It is Dale Earnhardt's gift.

"He's probably the only driver I been around," Bob says, "that whether he's behind you or in front, he can do things to find out what the second-place guy's got. And before long he can dictate, can make a man use up his race car, and this is just ability that's God-given."

David says, "The first time Dale went to Daytona, he just loved that big track, and the love has got to be there—the 'wanting-to-do-the-race fever,' if you want to call it—and he's got it."

Tomlinson describes early Earnhardt as a happy-go-lucky guy who worked at the Great Dane Trailer Company and earned everything he got. But that "fever" was what first put him into the Olivers' 1955 Ford. Bob says, "David's daddy built the car, and then Dale got permission from his daddy to drive it. We took it to Concord, and about the seventh lap a caution come up. I think he was running sixth or seventh, and he came in and asked, 'Well, you think Mr. Oliver would mind if I went ahead and passed a few people now?' And so we cleaned the mud off, and I asked Mr. Oliver for Dale, and he said, 'Well, yeah, it's his butt—whatever he wants to do.' "

What he wanted was a win. What he did was put together a string of twenty.

The first win came outside Charlotte at Metrolina Speedway. (Closed but still standing, it nests five miles from the spectacular Charlotte Motor Speedway, which pulls NASCAR's largest crowds, due in part to Earnhardt.) Dale tore into the car so early the next morning that he woke up the whole family. Once, at 14, wanting to help his exhausted dad (who'd been off racing for the family), Dale built him an engine overnight. Ralph came down at sunrise and found it in the middle of the living-room floor, ready to run. To this day, Dale hits the floor running at redline when the sun reddens the horizon.

It gives him a head start on the things he does more quietly. A young friend, checking to be sure Dale isn't nearby, relates a special memory. The fondest hope of a dying child was for a real ride with the great stock-car racer Dale Earnhardt. Earnhardt made it happen, and fast, but demanded the closest thing to privacy.

When the car flew past with two pairs of eyes shining out, few onlookers but the family knew the true heart of the mission: a mutual commitment, with everything to gain, to the ride of a fleeting lifetime.

Relative secrecy also surrounds Hickory Speedway early one summer evening. At 18, daughter Kelley will take her first try at a race car. Go-kartist Dale, Jr., a declared candidate for a racing career, is three years wetter behind the gears. He'll suit up next time. Earnhardt is elsewhere. Like his dad, he's putting the sprouts out to seek their own patch of sun. He also helps young drivers not blessed with the big name. He had help, and he wants the next bunch coming up to get the same; that's the way it's done. Racing's more chauvinistic elders would never expend such wisdom on "just a girl..." Yet Kelley's father has already given her a gift of wisdom, because "just" means something else entirely to an Earnhardt.

Wisdom is nowhere when Dale gets out on the same body of water as racer and bass-boat buddy Neil Bonnett (involved in a devasting NASCAR crash last year). They fish and hunt together without holing anything critical, but their 100-mph, big-motor boats side-by-side produce Wilkesboro on water.

Dangers do not escape Mr. Earnhardt's attention: "Sometimes I do a lot more dangerous things at the farm than I ever do in a race car. Running a bulldozer on the side of a bank. Cutting big trees. Standing beside a 2000-pound bull to give him a medicine shot and he don't want one."

Hardly anybody disbelieves the boast

The banner says it. Earnhardt merchandise outsells other driver keepsakes five to one.

on black-and-silver tee-shirts: "Real men wear black and silver." Mr. Goodwrench's public-relations pipeline claims Earnhardt souvenirs outsell other driver keepsakes almost five to one. Moral: hanging tough puts your trinkets over the top.

Earnhardt dominated the 1990 Daytona 500. He led three-quarters of the race. A cut tire two bends from the finish popped him back to fifth. Stunned, Earnhardt and his gang blasted back. They won twice in a row, at Atlanta and Darlington, got shut out thrice running by misfortune, took the first of two wins at Talladega. Earnhardt also won the second of two IROC victories, plus the series championship.

In a rush, Earnhardt knocks off a 400-miler at Michigan International Speedway; puts his number-three Chevy on the pole for the first time in 96 races and wins going away at Talladega's second race of the season; and qualifies quickest ("I drive like somebody's chasing me") on upstate New York's Watkins Glen circuit.

Miles rip past in crisscrossing flight paths to autograph sessions, match races, and Sundays' blasts of serious racing. Reporters and hangers-on reduce pursuit to low comedy. Hoping to pick Earnhardt's brain and pin his hide to a board like a science project, multiple media crawl out from under their pincushions to take a stab at him.

Racing's buzzword mavens call Earnhardt "The Dominator" and "The Intimidator." These days, the guy who skipped school for racing could be "The Educator." His racing style has matured, could even be called instructive. He seems all-seeing, possessed of 360-degree vision even in ravels of drafting race traffic. One Goodyear engineer says he's "got insect eyes, 'cause he's the only guy out there who can see past his own ears."

His intensity at everything he does fires him off like .357 hollowpoint on a .22-caliber mission. During marathon autograph sessions, "Dale Earnhardt" unscrolls in longhand thousands of times at a sitting. Though his time grows shorter due to increasing commitments, he tries to make himself more accessible. Sort of.

Keep studying and you'll feel as if you're pulling closer. Maybe to something discomfitingly like a holographic representation of the real Dale Earnhardt. Beset by commitments, he drives the rest of his life any way the whim blows.

In 1989, Hurricane Hugo almost blew Earnhardt's 300-acre farm off North Carolina. The tract hunkers outside Moores-

Childress is known to dote on his team.

ville, 200 miles inland from the Atlantic, but suffered disruptions to its woods, fences, power lines, and the five dozen head of Angus and tens of thousands of cooped-up chickens, whose biorhythms blew out. Modern shops housing two Busch Grand National V-6 Luminas fared better. The Earnhardts' main residence, a house on nearby Lake Norman, suffered least. It bulges with racing and hunting trophies and a herdlet of hobbyhorses wrangled by Taylor Nicole. Her parents intended to hide a new home in the farm's pastures and woods, but they're caught in a stink over a toxic-waste dump. Needing support from his fellow drivers and NASCAR fans, Earnhardt barnstorms the state's media—a rare instance when he's out to chase the press rather than the other way around.

Thus he materializes right beside me.

Finally I've got him where I want him. Sure, he's dragooned me into chauffeuring him to a toxic-dump press conference. On the road, unlike most racers, Dale may cede the wheel for the boring part of driving. Here and now, Earnhardt's quit fidgeting for the first time since I've been pestering him. Outside a race car he's almost always antsy, jittering for something better to do.

We buzz off to Statesville Airport. Earnhardt meets his family, pilot and twin-engine King Air F90 for a flight to Michigan. They're going where I'm going, but that's it, I've lost him again.

Ask me who Dale Earnhardt is and I'll tell you he's a North Carolina hard case with a corporate-trim mustache who wins come what may.

He did let a little slip in Alabama.

"The fun time," he said building up to his winning race-day tingle at Talladega, "is when I sit down in that car and crank her up and she rolls off the line—and there's not anybody around but me. And we go out there and do our business."

Just like Ralph taught him.

MINI-PICKUP RACERS

By Csaba Csere

So, you want to be a professional racer. You dream of driving—or wrenching, or team managing—in NASCAR, CART, or Formula 1. But you just don't know how to convince Rick Hendrick, Roger Penske, or Ron Dennis to give you a ride. How do you break in?

Paying your dues would be a good way to start. Pro football, basketball, and baseball players serve apprenticeships in college or the minor leagues before they're considered ready for the big time, and racers need to do the same. One of the most attractive such racing minor leagues is the SCCA's Truck Guard/Shellzone Challenge.

The notion of the Sports Car Club of America sanctioning a racing series for compact pickups may seem strange, but upon close examination it makes good sense. For starters, there's strong manufacturer involvement. Last year, more than one million mini-pickups were sold in America, many of them to first-time vehicle buyers who chose them instead of cars. Manufacturers, rather than ignore sales volumes and demographics like those, aggressively promote their products in every way possible—including racing. The truck market also includes the accessory and maintenance industries, and in turn, these marketers are attracted to the fray. That translates into a rich pool of potential sponsors for the racers, as well as a $15,000 purse for each race, a $25,000 points fund for the drivers' championship, and tempting chunks of contingency money.

The Truck Guard/Shellzone Challenge also provides plenty of exposure—particularly when the pickup race is used to support another event. Just such a supporting race came to Detroit in 1990, the day before the CART/Valvoline Detroit Grand Prix. John Torok, head of Mazda-equipped Team GRR, told us the race is "our Indianapolis 500—our show." Not only does the pre-CART race provide plenty of media spillover for the trucks, but Detroit is also the home of Ford and Jeep, two of the major supporters of the series. And winning in Detroit tends to have a salutary effect on a team's budget for the following year.

The actual expenditures in the Challenge are a couple of zeros shy of NASCAR or CART levels—mostly because a fully prepared racing truck can be built for about $25,000. But finding the money to field a competitive effort is as challenging as it is in any form of professional racing. The first-class teams—such as the Spencer Low Nissans, the Saleen Auto Express Ford Rangers, or the Archer Brothers Craftsmen Jeep Comanches—spend big bucks. Each of them entered three trucks and three drivers for Detroit, and each team arrived on the scene with spare trucks, spare parts, transporters, and platoons of crewmen. Maintaining this level of commitment—even running only two

trucks in the other nine series races—costs somewhere between $300,000 and $500,000. For a real professional racing series, of course, that's cheap.

Most of the expenses are for travel and logistics, because the rules are designed to keep the price of the machinery within reasonable bounds. Only short-wheelbase, rear-drive, four-cylinder, manual-transmission mini-trucks are eligible. The rules state that engines can be modified only by internal balancing and by adding an open exhaust downstream of the manifold. The driveline must be stock. Suspension modifications are allowed, but all pieces must bolt up to the original mounting points. All trucks must run on seven-

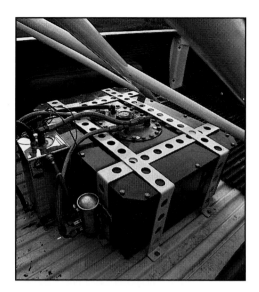

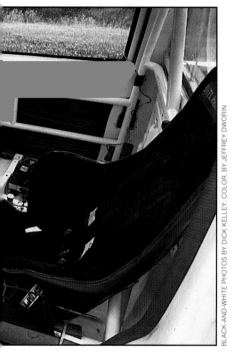

ing more than a framework for loopholes —loopholes to be exploited by canny racers at every opportunity.

For example, when examining how the fat tires filled the wheel wells of the normally skinny-legged Nissan pickups raced by the Spencer Low team, we noticed the obvious negative camber in the front tires. And despite the solid rear axle suspension, the rear wheels hardly seemed more upright than the fronts. Indeed, we observed a similar condition on most of the race trucks. Adding camber to rigid-axle suspensions is an old trick in both Trans-Am and NASCAR racing, so these truck racers were obviously learning their lessons well.

Under the Nissan's hood, we found an engine that, well, *stretches* the rules a bit. Current Nissan pickups come with three-valve-per-cylinder, single-plug 2.4-liter four-bangers, but the racer uses an older two-valve, twin-plug engine of the same displacement. It sports a new camshaft, a heavy-duty radiator, a cylinder head that was never sold in this model of truck, baffles in its oil pan, full blueprinting, and specially programmed chips in its engine-control system.

Other trucks use similarly modified powerplants. The quick Jeeps are apparently running much stouter camshafts than stock, and all the Ford Rangers have a bored-out version of the 2.3-liter overhead-cam four that actually displaces 2.5 liters. Moreover, the race engine sports the same cylinder head used on the turbocharged engine in the old Thunderbird.

How do the racers get away with such seemingly blatant cheating? Amazingly, the SCCA actually sanctions it. Certain manufacturers demand liberal engine modifications in order to make their trucks competitive. Such situations invariably escalate, especially as the SCCA struggles to keep the competition even. So to give the privateers an even break, the SCCA requires that the special factory engines be available to non-factory racers for no more than $3000.

The SCCA uses two other tools to try to equalize the racing: a minimum height and a minimum weight for each machine. Because weight is so easy to add and subtract, the SCCA alters the minimum frequently. At the Detroit race, the three Jeeps from the Archer Brothers team went a bit too quickly in qualifying, so the SCCA slapped them with an additional 100 pounds of ballast before the race.

Such rule bending quickly educates the

Minimum modifications to stock trucks are permitted, including the additions of a roll cage and racing seat (bottom right), standard safety equipment, and (top right) a fifteen-gallon fuel cell.

inch-wide, fifteen-inch diameter wheels fitted with 225/60R-15 street tires. Although race compounds are permitted, competitors must start the race on the same tires used for qualifying—eliminating supersticky, short-lived rubber. Bodywork changes are limited to adding an approved front spoiler and replacing the rear bumper with an approved variation. Full roll cages, a racing seat, and the usual safety equipment are mandatory, as is a fifteen-gallon fuel cell mounted in the bed.

All of this seems relatively straightforward, but therein lies another valuable lesson for the apprentice pro racer. In professional competition, rules are noth-

truck racer about the importance of politics and craftiness in racing. Maintain good relationships with manufacturers and sponsors and you can enlist them as allies when the sanctioning body tries to slow you down. This is particularly effective if you've been crafty enough to hide your true speed until it becomes absolutely necessary to reveal it.

Old pros Bobby and Tommy Archer know both of these lessons well, so they weren't fazed by the SCCA's eleventh-hour weight penalty. After all, ballast can take the form of lead bolted to the front of the bed, or it can be accommodated more creatively—say as a rear bumper made from thick steel plate that might place the additional weight where it would help lessen the truck's inherently front-heavy weight bias.

Sure enough, Tommy Archer, with eight victories the winningest driver in the 1990 race-truck series, added a ninth by eking out a victory in the closely fought twenty-lap event. In the process, he beat such luminaries as Trans-Am drivers Max Jones and Dorsey Schroeder.

Which left us with but one question: how well does a race truck perform? Before he left to prepare for the next race at Laguna Seca, team manager Spencer Low agreed to bring one of his race Nissans to our test track. There, we used our test gear to compare it with a stock Nissan Hardbody.

The racer's myriad suspension modifications paid off with a huge improvement in grip. While the stock truck could only manage 0.71 g around the skidpad, the racer pulled 0.93 g—with excellent stability. Not bad for a tall vehicle with 54.1 percent of its weight in front.

We expected to see similarly impressive gains in straight-line performance but were quickly disappointed. Top speed of the race truck turned out to be just 108 mph, only 2 mph quicker than the stocker. Because the racer is lowered two inches—enough to improve top-speed performance all by itself—we'd guess that the racer's highly modified engine makes about the same power as the 134-hp stocker.

We didn't bother with any other straight-line tests. Because Low could easily have improved the engine's performance simply by swapping a chip in the engine-control computer, we weren't going to learn any more about his truck's prowess than he wanted us to. Moreover, going fast for our test would only have led to potential handicaps from the SCCA, and Low is keen to repeat the team's manufacturers' and drivers' championships. Obviously, the Truck Guard/Shellzone Challenge has taught Spencer Low plenty about being a real professional racer.

Clockwise from above left: Bobby Archer, Team GRR's John Torok, and Nissan ace Spencer Low. Below: the stock Nissan Hardbody and Spencer Low's modified Nissan.

PEOPLE AND ISSUES

Always be certain.
—Frederick Henry Royce

AMERICA'S ROLLS-ROYCE AYATOLLAH

By John Phillips III

If there lives a man who is certain, he is Hermann G. Albers, founder of Albers Rolls-Royce. Of the thousands of Rolls-Royces he has sold or serviced, Hermann remembers every one. Remembers every serial number, in fact.

As he talks, a chocolate-brown Silver Shadow glides silently into a service bay. Before Hermann can get within twenty feet of the car, we ask if he remembers it.

"Let me see the door handles and wheel covers," he says, putting on his spectacles. As soon as his milky-blue eyes focus, he responds: "Oh, sure, I delivered this car new on this day in 1974. It had 900 miles on the odometer. Looks like LRC16748."

We walk to the windshield and peer at the vehicle identification number: LRC16748.

Two minutes later, Hermann pulls out the original bill of sale. But there is a frown on his face. The receipt shows he is wrong. Hermann G. Albers actually sold the car eight days later than he remembered.

"Must be getting old," he says.

In America, there are only three dealerships devoted exclusively to the Rolls-Royce marque. One, as you might imagine, is in Beverly Hills. Another is in Manhattan. And if you had to guess the third, you'd say, what, Dallas? Miami? Maybe Newport Beach?

Nope. Try Zionsville, Indiana, population 3948.

That particular Rolls franchise is right next to the Dairy Queen, partly hidden by

169

the Three Tuns Liquor Store, and just down the street from the Sow's Ear Antiques. State Route 334 takes a nasty jog through Zionsville. If you screwed up the turn on a rainy day, you'd crash right into Hermann Albers's showroom.

It would be an expensive crash. Inside the dull, gray display area are a Bentley Eight, a Bentley Turbo R, and a Rolls-Royce Silver Spirit. There is not room for a fourth car. Because "How much?" is the first thing people always ask, Hermann posts a sign in the corner:

Silver Spirit Standard: $143,200
Silver Spur LWB: $157,700
Corniche Convertible: $218,800
Bentley Eight: $117,100
Bentley S: $136,200
Bentley Turbo R: $170,400

Albers doesn't want you to crash into his showroom, but neither can you just walk in. A discreet notice in the window warns passers-by: "Sales by appointment only. Arrangements to view the motor cars by the sincere, interested purchaser can be made in the office or by calling 873-2360."

Zionsville is not Beverly Hills, yet underestimating the jet-set wallop of Albers Rolls-Royce would be a big mistake. In 1988, this tiny Indiana dealership was the largest seller of Rolls-Royce and Bentley parts in the world. In the *world.* Since then, the dealership has remained the largest parts dispenser in North America. And it will always be America's oldest exclusive Rolls-Royce franchise.

The accolades aren't so hard to understand once you realize that the only place to find an engine-gasket set for a 1925 Phantom I is in Zionsville—on the second floor, above Hermann Albers's service bays.

We walk up there—to the place he calls "the treehouse"—and 50-year-old Albers paces between row after row of obscure, neatly stacked parts. He knows them all by number. At the end of one row, he spies a discarded rag on the surgically clean floor. As he stoops to pick it up, a flash of anger contorts his face. He immediately sets about locating whoever dropped it there.

When we stroll through the service bays and the used-car storage area, we see Rolls-Royces and Bentleys jammed cheek-by-jowl—sixteen on the day of our visit. Their license plates reveal far-flung homes: Florida, Ohio, Kentucky, Missouri, Michigan, Illinois, Pennsylvania, and, of course, Indiana—but none from Zionsville. "I have customers all over the country," says Hermann, "but usually they only come from a 750-mile radius."

In the corner rests a forlorn-looking Rolls with Oregon plates. It is painted metal-flake blue with pearlescent white stripes down the sides. "That was one of the Bhagwan's cars," says Hermann, who is jarred by the sight. "Like taking a marking pen to a Picasso."

The Zionsville dealership employs thirteen people. Two of them—28-year-old Greg and 25-year-old Mark, who jointly share the parts and service operations—are Albers's only sons. Hermann is proud that the business will continue with the Albers name on the sign after he retires. His is the only dealership in America permitted to use both the words "Rolls-Royce" and a family name in its title.

If Steven Spielberg ever requires a ready-made set for Indiana Jones's home town, Zionsville is his place. The main street is brick, bordered by wrought-iron fences and maple trees. American flags hang from the light standards. That the village is at the geographic center of the state makes the whole place almost too perfect to bear.

Talk to the earthy citizens of Zionsville and you'll hear a lot about the price of corn but little about Rolls-Royces or Hermann G. Albers.

"You'll laugh at me," says a waitress at the Friendly Tavern, "but for years I thought Hermann's sign said something

Hermann Albers's showroom in Zionsville, Indiana. Albers has one of only three American dealerships devoted exclusively to the Rolls-Royce marque.

about 'Roy's Real Estate.' " (She later adds, "I may have been born yesterday, but I got up early and stayed up late.") A worker at Metzger's lumber is a little more attentive: "I once helped Mr. Albers unload an engine," he recalls. "He didn't tell me how much it was worth until we got it on the ground. A guy I know, he says he saw Elvis Presley's Rolls-Royce over there. Also, I saw Liberace."

Although he may cater to celebrities, Hermann is definitely no celebrity in Zionsville, and he intends to keep it that way. "You can introduce him as 'Hermann,' " says office/sales manager Mike Long, "but don't ever introduce him as 'Hermann Albers, owner of the Rolls-Royce store.' " On the day we interview him, Hermann has driven to work in a gray Plymouth station wagon.

Albers's father was a German immigrant who worked as a painting contractor. Right out of high school, Hermann got a job as a mechanic in a Rolls-Royce agency in Indianapolis, then quickly became the service and parts director. When the agency failed in 1963, Albers opened his own shop. Six years later, he moved the business to Zionsville, where he was rewarded with the only exclusive Rolls-Royce franchise in Indiana.

Now in his fourth decade of working on Rolls-Royces, Hermann Albers's whole existence is dedicated to the Flying Lady, the Spirit of Ecstasy. He has no hobbies. His favorite movie is *The Yellow Rolls-Royce*.

What is his favorite car from Crewe? "Don't have one," he says without hesitation. "Color, styling, that doesn't mean a lot to me. What I like is the car's mechanical condition. If it's perfect mechanically, then that's my favorite Rolls-Royce."

He gestures toward the corner of the showroom: "Look at that nine-year-old [Silver] Spirit. Forty-eight thousand, one hundred miles, but it's so perfect that it's indistinguishable from a new car. To me, that's rare. That's collectible. I sold that car new. Serial-number SCAZS42AO-BCX03637. When it was purchased in '81, it was sitting in precisely the same location it's sitting in now. Precisely. And it looked just the same."

Hermann will not talk about his personal cars, but it was easy to figure there is a twenty-car garage behind his house. In a newspaper photo on his office wall, Hermann poses with two automobiles from his private reserve: a '59 Silver Cloud I and a '69 Silver Shadow.

Inside the dealership, you'll spy a peculiar manifestation of Hermann's obsessive attention to detail. Every screw head in every electrical outlet, every junction box, every overhead light switch is carefully turned so that its center ridge points perfectly up and down. Every one. Hermann insists.

Saying that the place is clean is like saying that George Steinbrenner is short on charm. You could drop your DQ Dilly Bar next to the drain in the service area, pick it up, and never have to worry about tasting a molecule of dust, oil, or grease. There are no tire tracks on the shining red floors. How the cars get in the service bays is a mystery.

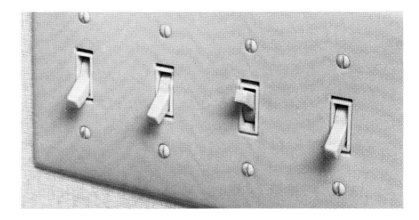

Every screw in every light switch is turned so its slot is precisely vertical.

On every wall hangs a Dustbuster. At any site in the service bays where a mechanic might scrub a part, he must pull down a white plastic blind, from ceiling to floor, so that the dust or solvent cannot sully a car. When Mike Long opens the door of a Silver Spirit, he first folds a handkerchief into his palm. "Fingerprints," he whispers conspiratorially, as if he is about to commit a crime. In obvious places around the dealership are signs bearing the same legend: "Your mother doesn't work here. Please clean up your own mess."

"Yes, very finicky about his cars is our Hermanh," says Rolls-Royce spokesman Reg Abbiss. "I call him 'the ayatollah of Rolls experts.' "

The ayatollah's fastidiousness extends to the dealership's voluminous records. Hermann meticulously maintains files on hundreds of Rolls-Royces and Bentleys—every car that he has sold, serviced, or touched. The files are arranged by vehicle serial number. Many are two or three inches thick.

The dealership has one brand-new computer, used to record part numbers,

but even it is redundant. "I am the computer," says Hermann, tapping the side of his head. "And I don't have any power outages. Some people say I have a photographic memory." Albers remembers the license-plate numbers of every car that his father ever owned.

Warned of Hermann's legendary memory, we arrive ready to test it. We know of a Rolls-Royce from Columbus, Ohio, that Hermann serviced in the early sixties. It belonged to a gentleman named Fitzgerald, who hasn't set foot in Zionsville for a quarter of a century.

When the question comes, Albers isn't even momentarily caught off guard. "Fitzgerald?" he says. "Of course. First name Edward, a lawyer. A Silver Cloud II, sand in color, 1962. He lived in Upper Arlington, not Columbus. Moved to Florida. The car's serial number was LSWC618."

Later, we phone the Ohio Department of Motor Vehicles. Hermann is correct.

Moreover, Hermann can always prove he is correct. His files contain, in chronological order, not only sales receipts and work orders but also handwritten notes from the cars' owners. "See, here," he says, waving a blue piece of stationery. "This is a note from a man who typed out nine things wrong with his car nineteen years ago. I sold that car to him. It cost $22,000." On the top of the stationery, in Hermann's handwriting, are the date and the car's odometer reading. (Later, when I hand him my business card, he methodically writes the date on the corner.)

Hermann is peeved by anyone whose memory isn't as sharp as his. "I had to give my son a lecture the other day," he says with a furrowed brow. "A car came in here, and I said, 'My God, Mark, you didn't recognize it? Get with it. When you were born, you rode home from the hospital in that car.' "

On top of Hermann's two-by-four-foot wooden desk rests a new touch-tone telephone. "See this?" he says, pointing with disgust at the automatic-dialing button. "Sheer laziness. This will cause you to forget important numbers."

Given Hermann's intimate knowledge of North American Rolls-Royces—a knowledge perhaps broader than any other human being's—it is no surprise that nervous folks from around the country call to ask for buying advice. "Unless I know the car they're considering, I won't advise them on anything," he says. "Fact is, there are no so-called good deals out there. No sleepers in barns. You want a good Rolls-Royce, it's going to be real expensive. You find a cheap car, something's wrong with it."

For entertainment, Hermann circles errors in classified ads. "I find them all the time," he says. "You know, the seller claims 'Thirty-three thousand actual miles, original paint.' Then I'll see the VIN and say to myself, 'Hell, I know that car. Last time I saw it was six years ago when it showed 78,000 miles and had a brand-new fender.' Some of these guys honestly don't know the real story. Some are just plain liars."

"Cars aren't serviced anymore," observes Hermann, annoyed. "They're simply repaired—you know, somebody just fixes a water pump. Our cars are serviced. When they leave here, somebody has poked and probed that thing, given it a physical exam like a doctor." Albers often puts in sixteen-hour days. About 25 to 30 Rolls-Royces and Bentleys move through his shop each week.

His customers are fiercely loyal, and they're also patient. Appointments are booked 60 to 90 days in advance, and that's only if you originally bought the car from Hermann. If it was purchased elsewhere, the wait could be longer.

When a car appears for which Albers has no file—no documented service history—he calls it a "stranger." As in, "Hey, that black Corniche over there in the second row, next to Doc Peterson's Spur—it's a stranger."

Hermann will work on "strangers" but prefers to work on the old friends he sold twenty years ago—cars whose pedigrees he knows. "A woman called the other day for service," he recalls. "I asked her the VIN. When she told me the number, well, it was a car I hadn't seen in a long time." Hermann scheduled the car immediately. He wanted to get his hands on it again.

In August 1990, the flat rate at Albers Rolls-Royce was $36 an hour, cheap by today's standards. "The difference," explains Hermann, "is that we'll charge for the real time we spend on a car."

Some people complain about the expense of maintaining Rolls-Royces. It makes Hermann mad. "Let me tell you something," he says as his fist thumps the desk. "The real Rolls-Royce buyer has three qualifications. He can afford to buy the car with cash. He can afford to service it even when nothing is wrong. And he takes a personal interest in the car. A guy like that, usually he got his money by stacking one dime on top of another. When I started selling, Rolls buyers were doctors in their seventies. Now they're kids and stockbrokers in their forties."

Sellers of vintage Rolls-Royces know that one of Hermann's three-inch-thick files can add a three-inch stack of dollar bills to a car's selling price. But the files are not for sale. "The previous owners' names, that's confidential," he explains solemnly.

Hermann updates his files continually, noting changes of ownership, deaths, and customers' personal preferences. He often reads the files for fun, just to see where his cars have gone. If there's no activity in a file for two years, he tries to find out where the car went, what happened to it. The implication is that such cars have fallen from grace, are not part of the Zionsville congregation anymore. Hermann Albers takes it personally. You can watch him calculate whether there's a way he can get the car back before the thing is polluted by an aftermarket radio or disfigured by scarred wheel insignias. Or even worse, a car inactive too long could become a "stranger."

After lunch, Hermann cleans up the crumbs surrounding his plate, and then—oblivious to the look I give him—leans over and cleans up the crumbs surrounding my plate.

If he couldn't sell and service Rolls-Royces, Albers confesses there would be only one other marque that could command his attention: Ferraris. "They're just like Rolls-Royces," he says. "They may change hands, but they don't go away. I'm interested in cars that stay alive."

In the breezeway of Albers's service area hangs a large metal plaque. On it are etched these words: "Our cars will outlast us. We don't completely own them; we have a sort of life tenancy. It follows that we have an ethical obligation to preserve them."

A more tangible sign of Hermann's ethical obligation rests in a locked glass case behind his desk. Inside are six scorched chunks of metal, each roughly two inches tall and five inches long. Each has been torched from the frame of a Rolls or Bentley that was crashed or burned so badly that it was headed for the crusher. Each has the car's serial number stamped in the metal. "You see, for these unfortunate cars," says Hermann G. Albers, speaking now with the reverence of a Methodist preacher, "I can't update their files anymore. So I keep their chassis plates. I don't want to forget the numbers."

Albers torches the serial numbers from cars headed for the crusher and keeps them in a locked case.

SAFETY'S GENERAL CURRY

By Patrick Bedard

Here's a quote from a speech to a group of auto engineers:

"Drastic increases in CAFE standards [laws ordering automakers to produce cars with greater fuel economy] are highly impractical since they radically curtail consumer choices. Forcing products on the public against consumer wishes is what the Soviets call 'centralized economic planning.' Mr. Gorbachev says it doesn't work in Russia. Can we expect it to work here?"

If I told you that quote came from Ronald Reagan, you wouldn't be surprised. If I said it came from the president of General Motors, you'd say, 'Hmmm, a bit too vivid for a corporate type, but right in line with the industry position." And if I attributed it to the head of the National Highway Traffic Safety Administration, our national watchdog over the CAFE num-

bers and the government's leading regulator of the automobile, you'd say, "Get outta here."

In fact, the speaker was Jerry Ralph Curry, NHTSA boss since the Bush Administration took over in 1989.

NHTSA bosses have ranged from the discreet Washington pro, such as Diane Steed in the Reagan years, to the car-hating inquisitor exemplified by Joan Claybrook of the Carter era. Curry, by those standards, is completely off the charts.

The quote above came from his "Aral Sea Agenda" speech that warned of the risks inherent in government regulation. He used the example of the huge, inland Aral Sea in the Soviet Union that three decades ago covered 26,000 square miles (slightly larger than the state of West Virginia). Now the water area is 40 percent smaller and so salty that marine life has been pickled into extinction. Worse yet, the surrounding parched sea bed gives off a saline dust that's poisoning fertile lands for miles around. This ecological disaster was the inadvertent result of a well-intentioned government project to grow cotton by diverting entire rivers to irrigate new fields. The planners reasoned that it was worth sacrificing the sea to gain the cotton, and in their enthusiasm for a result they valued so highly, they overlooked the salt problem.

"An example to all the world of a well-meaning, well-intentioned effort that went awry," said Curry, who then went on to warn of the potential side effects of the proposed 40-mpg CAFE standard.

Who is this guy Jerry Ralph Curry anyway, and how did such an astute observer of man's follies end up running the office that says yes or no to a large chunk of proposed automobile regulations?

As Bush draft choices go, the Curry selection would appear to be fully as imaginative as Dan Quayle. The man has no regulatory experience whatsoever. He's 58, retired from the army as a major-general after a 34-year career. He has a master's degree in international relations from Boston University and a doctorate from Luther Rice Seminary. And he's black, which raises the suspicion of an administration seeking to achieve a politically correct color mix.

According to the *Wall Street Journal,* the safety advocates "groaned" when they learned Curry was to fill the NHTSA job. His only political experience amounted to an unsuccessful 1988 campaign for a Congressional seat from Virginia as a Republican, a campaign highlighted by Curry describing Jesse Jackson as a "pygmy" and in turn being labeled a "so-called black" by a prominent black. The safety lobby figured him to be yet another conservative, anti-regulation, Reaganaut of the sort that had controlled the NHTSA during the previous administration.

Instead, they got a guy who has jolted the agency into a frenzy of rulemaking. Side-impact standards were finally issued last autumn after being bounced up in the agency's internal bureaucracy for thirteen years. The safety performance long required of cars is now mandated in pickups and vans, too. There are new school bus standards, and rollover protection is hot on the burner.

Yet despite all of this, no one is accusing Curry of being a stooge of the safety crusaders. In fact, he's been openly criti-

cal of them, most recently after the NHTSA reopened a costly investigation into Jeep CJ rollovers, its fourth such inquiry. The usual safety spokesmen claimed in voices loudly amplified as usual by the media that they had significant new information. They didn't. When the case was closed once again, Curry lambasted the special-interest safety lobby in *Automotive News:* "I would be much less willing to give credence to allegations or petitions filed by the groups. You still have to look at them, but I am not going through another one of these. The American people don't deserve this."

A little background: the NHTSA was established by the National Traffic and Motor Vehicle Safety Act of 1966. In its quarter-century of existence, the agency has for the most part viewed the car as a source of public harm that needs to be regulated. Conversely, we enthusiasts see the car as a source of joy and fascination, so there's never been much common ground between us and the NHTSA.

Still, Curry's public pronouncements suggest that he's an independent thinker who could explain to us the motives and the mission of the agency.

So we picked up the phone and asked for time in the man's office.

National Highway Traffic Safety Administration boss Jerry Ralph Curry is a retired Army major general. He's a critic of the kind of central planning that limits consumer choices.

The first surprise on arrival? Model cars: a scarlet Ferrari F40 and a silver M–B Gullwing the size of footballs pose in the sunlight slanting through his window. His walls are office-building-modular steel panels covered with the same sort of simulated wood-grain that wasn't very convincing on the dashboard of a 1976 Caprice. With the requisite conference table to one side and a living-room ar-

rangement to the other, the ambiance is very executive, yet not so lavish that we taxpayers need be alarmed.

We started at the conference table. Curry is a substantial presence. His shoulders are thick, his arms heavy, his mind alert. He pounces on ideas. I said my Sony would keep him from being inadvertently misquoted. He caught the quip in midair.

"The job of NHTSA [he says 'nitsuh'] is to save lives, and my job is leadership, to lead the agency and to take the blame."

This distinction between the agency's role and his role caught me by surprise— I'll bet Claybrook thought she *was* saving lives. Curry definitely sees himself as a manager.

"The first thing I asked when I arrived," he continued, "was 'Let me see your priority plan.' There wasn't one. Every department had these wonderful things it was working on. But all the departments weren't working on the same things. I forced them to make a priority plan.

"The second thing, if we know what we want to get done over the next three or four years—how do we measure it? So we had to come up with a measurement device so we all know where we are."

When asked what's the most significant thing he wants to have accomplished when he leaves the job, Curry unhesitatingly points to this new and demonstrably more productive organization.

Curry is a military man who believes in clear commands. He's posted a bronze plaque outside his office, for all to see, stating the "Mission of the NHTSA":

• Raise the national highway safety consciousness with the goal of increasing safety belt usage to 70 percent by 1992.
• Decrease number and percent of alcohol and drug-related highway accidents

and fatalities by reducing the probability of crashes.
• Decrease the highway fatality rate to 2.2 deaths per 100 million miles of travel by 1992, by reducing crash injuries and increasing crash survival rates.

Because the 2.2 death rate was achieved early (in 1989), I asked why he didn't save the taxpayers some money by closing shop for a few years?

"I'm not comfortable with walking away from it. Why not drive it from 2.2 down to 2.0? I think it's worth the effort."

Was he saying, I asked, that it's an endless grind, this driving the rate down without regard to cost-effectiveness?

"I don't think so. My guess is, for the next year or two, we may see significant improvements. After that, unless there's a breakthrough nobody can predict, we may be just fine-tuning. At that time we'll have to evaluate what's worth doing."

How will that be decided? What's a reasonable cost per life saved?

"I don't think anyone would dare go on record on that."

Instead, he would rely on the "common-sense test." For example, he said the NHTSA was petitioned to require seatbelts in all school buses. Studies were done. On the average, fifteen deaths occur each year in school buses (he said more children are run over by buses than are killed *inside* them). If belts were installed, the best estimate predicted they would save about a half a life per year.

Curry asked out loud: "Is that something we should force on America for half a life a year? My judgment is no.

"Another example, this Jeep CJ rollover business. This is a question of lifestyle. Do Americans have the right to drive narrow-track, short-wheelbase, high-center-of-gravity vehicles? My answer is 'absolutely.' They need to know, though, that you can roll over and kill yourself.

"Motorcycles are the single riskiest means of transportation. Do Americans have the right to drive them? Yes.

"I have trouble with the folks who want all cars to get 50 miles per gallon. We have those vehicles today and they don't sell. What these folks don't say is, they believe the federal government has the right to determine the size, the class, of the car you and I drive. But they never say that to the public. They don't tell the public that if you follow their logic you'll end up driving a Geo.

"That's wrong. Americans have the right to drive any kind of car they have the money to buy, provided it's safe and for sale in America.

"Every week I get suggestions [about what] the agency ought to do. You don't have to send them to an engineer to see they don't make sense. They make sense only to someone who believes the government ought to do centralized economic planning. My job is to filter out a lot of that stuff, protect the consumer from people who would 'help' us."

I asked if part of that protection was to avoid creating regulations that raise the price of cars to the point that many people can't afford them.

"Absolutely," he said. "I decided two years ago not to mandate anti-lock brakes, and we're not going to mandate traction control even though I think they're good ideas. Because the market is going to take care of that. I could see they [the automakers] were working toward that themselves."

This awareness of cost puts Curry at odds with the safety advocates. Around NHTSA headquarters, the loudest three are collectively known as the Terrible Trio: Clarence Ditlow, the executive director of the Center for Auto Safety; Joan Claybrook, now the president of Public Citizen; and Ben Kelley, president of the Institute for Injury Reduction. They are invariably characterized by the media as "consumerists." Does Curry believe they represent consumers?

"No, they're special-interest groups. They represent their own interests. The notion that these self-righteous folks should be setting the people's agenda, spending the people's money, doesn't make any sense at all."

These groups have often used guerrilla tactics that wind up irritating the bureaucracy.

"The Terrible Trio gives me very few petitions [official requests for rulemaking]. Their technique is to announce it [an alleged safety problem] in a press conference and send me a letter at the same time. When I first got here I asked, 'If you people really care, why don't I hear from you in the beginning, when we could do something preventive, instead of waiting until there's a serious problem?' But they don't work that way.

"And they manipulate Congress. They tried to get Congress to write into law that any time we reject a petition, we could be sued. Anybody could write me a stupid letter, I say it's dumb and denied, and they sue. We'd always be in court. Fortunately, we were able to get that thing defeated."

That's Curry, the manager, speaking. He wants the agency to produce results. He says bureaucracies avoid risk, and his people wouldn't put their necks on the line if they thought they'd get sued. Along the same lines, he says, "The perfect is the enemy of the good." The side-impact standards were held up for thirteen years because they weren't quite perfect. GM has what is possibly a better test dummy, but it needs a few years more work. Should they wait for the perfect? He pushed the agency to go with what it had, which he calls good.

"At some point, you make the judgment," he says. "If it turns out to be wrong, you adjust."

Barry Felrice, the NHTSA's associate administrator of rulemaking, said of Curry in the *Wall Street Journal:* "He isn't your typical bureaucrat. He likes making decisions."

The NHTSA's heavy lifting is about done now, Curry said. Apart from the rollover standards that are still in process, the next three or four years will be devoted mostly to adjusting past regulations rather than adding major new ones. Seatbelts that attach to the door—and therefore allow the occupant to be ejected if the door opens—is one example of a regulation that needs revising. Who can argue with that?

For the most part, Curry provokes few arguments because his positions are so logical. He has often said the NHTSA should be the "honest broker," listening to all sides on an issue, then making "practical choices."

Again, who can argue?

"Americans have the right to drive any kind of car they have the money to buy, provided it's safe and for sale in America."

Our 'Idiotproof' Speed Limits

Speed limits and driver skills are two issues of special interest to enthusiasts. What does the head of the NHTSA think about them?

I read to him this quote from the Tignor and Warren report, *Driver Speed Behavior on U.S. Streets and Highways,* recently prepared for the 60th annual meeting of the Institute for Transportation Engineers: "Our studies show that most speed zones are posted 8 to 12 mph below the prevailing travel speed and 15 mph or more below the maximum safe speed."

"That's probably right," he said.

Shouldn't we get our speed limits coincident with real, practical speeds, I asked?

"That has two parts," he said. "I drive a lot of country roads and there's nothing more annoying than to come into a curve, it's posted at 35, I hit it at 45, and know I could have hit it at 50. There's a dishonesty in that. It says you can't trust the posted sign.

"What we're doing is setting a speed limit so low it's idiotproof. I don't like that. I probably can't affect it. Federal Highways does that, states do it, cities."

Could NHTSA support an effort elsewhere in the Department of Transportation to raise speed limits to a credible level?

"If you ask what do I support, publicly I have to support the lower limit. But from a personal standpoint, I don't like it."

Would he oppose an effort to raise the limit?

"No. The administrator after [me] might, but I wouldn't."

Idiotproofing, whether it's the speed limits or the cars, seems to be the government's only answer to safety. Elsewhere in the world, drivers must show real skills before they can be licensed. Why not here, I asked.

"Part of the problem, we're states' rights people, the DMVs are states' [jurisdictions], and the states aren't interested in bumping up the training. When I joined this agency, our position said there was no benefit (to driver training). That's the dumbest thing I've ever heard. Give it the common-sense test. If training doesn't make sense, why do we train pilots and truck drivers?

"I did the undemocratic thing, wrote out the paragraph myself that said the official position of the agency until I leave is, 'We're going to do our very best to train people.'"

When I volunteered *Car and Driver*'s help, he replied, "Thank you, we may end up coming to you, because I'm not getting any support from the consumer groups."

"When I joined this agency, our position said there was no benefit [to driver training]. That's the dumbest thing I've ever heard. Give it the common-sense test. If training doesn't make sense, why do we train pilots and truck drivers?"

SPEED LIMITS

By the Editors

If you regularly drive ten to fifteen miles an hour over the speed limit on freeways and surface streets, don't feel guilty —according to an engineering study, everyone does it.

A scientific survey by two Federal Highway Administration engineers supports what auto enthusiasts have been hollering about for decades: that American speed limits have been set artificially low.

The survey, *Driver Speed Behavior on U.S. Streets and Highways,* is the work of Samuel C. Tignor and Davey Warren, both traffic research engineers with the FHA in McLean, Virginia. The FHA is not known for espousing the sort of radical findings

that the two engineers ultimately set forth in their report.

The study was undertaken, they said, because of "concern about widespread [speeding] violations and the seemingly arbitrary level of many posted speeds." In short, the researchers wanted to know if speed limits were realistic, or if the nation's drivers had turned outlaw.

Two tests were conducted. The first recorded the speeds of motorists on "moderate speed" streets in "urban, small-urban and rural built-up areas," a description that seems to fit the old view of Middle America. The engineers set up measuring devices on 52 streets in four states—Delaware, North Carolina, Colorado, and Arizona—and monitored speeds for 24 hours. They also obtained data on accidents in those areas during three prior years in an attempt to learn if there was a relationship between accident risk and travel speed.

A second study measured the speeds of drivers on 102 streets and highways in 23 states where speed limits had been changed. Speeds were measured in these areas a year before the changes, and then a year afterward. At the same time, speeds on similar roads were checked at another 102 sites where posted speeds had remained unchanged.

"The sites represent a full range of speed limits and road types, including a few 65-mph freeways," the engineers said.

And guess what the study discovered? Almost everyone speeds, and apparently without creating havoc anywhere.

"Only about 1 in 10 speed zones has better than 50-percent compliance," they reported. In other words, the vast majority of drivers in this country do not accept these speed limits and are breaking the law.

Worse, "the posted speeds make technical violators out of motorists driving at reasonable and safe speeds."

And that, Tignor and Warren conclude, "could lead to a loss of respect for all

speed limits and create the impression that traffic law enforcement and the judicial system are unfair."

So why, then, have all these speed limits been set too low, and how did it happen?

Tignor and Warren venture an explanation. Officials in all states and most localities, in deciding speed limits, have simply gone out and clocked the speeds of motorists traveling on the roads in question. They then determine what the "85th-percentile speed" is—the speed at or below which 85 percent of the traffic is moving—as the basic number in determining what the speed limit should be. What could be more democratic? It is the indicator of what the driving public considers the correct speed.

And then the monkey wrench is tossed into the formula. "The posted speed is often set up to 10 miles an hour lower than the prevailing speed based on a subjective consideration of other factors, such as roadside development."

The report doesn't mention the great array of "subjective considerations" that get tossed into this formula. They are also known in some circles as "social engineering"—the embracing of a well-intentioned popular belief, a notion that appears to serve the public good by being the right thing to do, but whose real-life

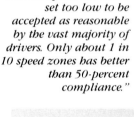

"Current speed limits are set too low to be accepted as reasonable by the vast majority of drivers. Only about 1 in 10 speed zones has better than 50-percent compliance."

benefits cannot, in most cases, be proved scientifically. For example, as Mr. Brimley declares on television, eating oatmeal is "the right thing to do" (which also seems to somehow imply that your alternative choice will be akin to eating hog jowls).

The findings got scant attention in the national press. Here are its highlights:

• Speed limits are intended to inform drivers of the maximum reasonable and safe travel speed. However, there is little agreement on what constitutes a safe speed.

• Even though a great deal has been written and said about speed limits, there is almost no scientific research on the precise effects on the number of accidents of altering speed limits.

• Driver compliance with speed limits is poor. On average, 7 out of 10 motorists exceeded the posted speed in urban areas.

• Compliance tended to be worse on low-speed roads, better on roads with prima facie limits, or where the speed limit was based on an engineering study. Better does not mean good compliance; less than 10 percent of the sites had more than 50-percent obedience with the posted speed.

• The accident involvement rate on streets and highways in urban areas was highest for the slowest 5 percent of traffic, lowest for traffic in the 30-to-95-percentile range, and increased for the fastest 5 percent of traffic.

• The risk of involvement in accidents is minimum near the average speed of traffic and increases dramatically for vehicles traveling much slower or faster than average.

• Speed limits should be set in the 70-to-90-percentile range or roughly 5 to 10 mph above the average speed to correctly reflect maximum safe speed.

• If speed limits were raised to more realistic levels, would drivers automatically drive 5 to 10 mph over the new limit as is commonly believed? The answer is no. Raising the speed limit by various amounts up to 15 miles per hour has little or no effect on speeds over a broad range of road types and speed levels.

• Conversely, lowering the speed limit will not slow down traffic.

• There is no evidence in our studies that raising the speed limit to 65 on rural interstate freeways led to an increase in speeds off the freeway.

The researchers, who prepared this study for the 60th annual meeting of the Institute of Transportation Engineers, ended by saying:

It would be premature to draw any firm conclusions since the research is still underway. However, the findings to date suggest that, on the average, current speed limits are set too low to be accepted as reasonable by the vast majority of drivers. Only about 1 in 10 speed zones has better than 50-percent compliance. The posted speeds make technical violators out of motorists driving at reasonable and safe speeds.

For the traffic law system to minimize accident risk, then speed limits need to be properly set to define maximum safe speeds. Our studies show that most speed zones are posted 8 to 12 mph below the prevailing travel speed and 15 mph or more below the maximum safe speed.

Increasing speed limits to more realistic levels will not result in higher speeds, but would increase voluntary compliance and target enforcement at the occasional violator and high-risk driver.

One way for restoring the informational value of speed limits requires that we do a better job of engineering speed limits. Hopefully, the results of this research will provide engineers with the knowledge and tools needed to set maximum safe speed limits that are defensible and accepted by the public and the courts.

"Increasing speed limits to more realistic levels will not result in higher speeds, but would increase voluntary compliance and target enforcement at the occasional violator and high-risk driver."

PHOTOGRAPHY BY CINDY LEWIS

STEALTH CORVETTE

By Phil Berg

Most people drive naked. But out in the barren Nevada desert, near Tonopah Test Range—home of the stealth fighter—we found one man who drives under a shield of electronic armor. This protective cloak—made of one part black paint and ten parts moving electrons—surrounds his 1986 Corvette, making it nearly invisible to his enemies. And his enemies are traffic police.

We met Bob (not his real name) on a deserted Nevada road near a tiny ghost town. There, while a cold wind blew tumbleweeds and dust across the weather-beaten pavement, we were allowed to examine his "stealth" Corvette.

Bob's Corvette can tell him the proximity of the nearest police cars. It can speak assertively to police radar guns in their own electronic language. It can eavesdrop on a remarkable variety of audio and video broadcasts from military, business, or private sources—and record those broadcasts on tape. It can transmit video signals, change its nighttime lighting signature, and reach a top speed of about 180 mph. And, Bob says, it can do all this without anybody else in the world knowing what's going on.

Which brings us to the obvious question: why?

There is but one simple, obvious, unquestionable answer: to speed.

After following a complicated series of instructions guaranteed to confuse our sense of direction, we visited Bob's home in Nevada. We never did determine exactly what business takes place in Bob's house, but we did see a large room with enough radio and computer equipment to run a nuclear submarine. Several machines whirred away, printing messages —including faxes and computer memos —transmitted over radio waves from around the globe. None of the messages we saw were addressed to Bob, so clearly none of the parties involved knew what he was up to. (This type of eavesdropping is legal as long as it is not done for profit. In fact, it's a growing hobby.)

Bob's Corvette is an extension of his electronic headquarters, and inside its cockpit lies more gear for keeping tabs on the world than exists at, say, the *Akron*

Beacon Journal. Included in his electronic arsenal are no fewer than four voice radios, not one of which is a high-fidelity cassette or CD player.

Nestled where you'd normally find the Corvette's AM/FM/cassette system is a Kenwood RZ-1 receiver. This wide-band radio is a smaller and cheaper version of the Kenwood R-5000 used by network news stations to eavesdrop on world events. The RZ-1 can pull in a wide range of broadcasts: everything from low-frequency AM transmissions to FM stereo, public service, police, and amateur-radio bands, 24-hour time and weather reports, television audio and video signals, and even—way up the frequency spectrum—cellular-phone transmissions. The legality of listening to car phones is still a gray zone, according to the Federal Communications Commission. Bob just says, "It's illegal, but not *illegal* illegal."

Under the steering wheel hangs a CHiPs Detector warning scanner made by Gray Electronics. This radio is designed to pick up the low-power repeaters that many state-patrol cars use to rebroadcast messages to an officer's hand-held walkie-talkie. If the CHiP's Detector comes within three miles of a patrol car using a repeater, it sounds a warning beeper.

"Because we have not evaluated the CHiPs Detector," states California Highway Patrol commissioner Maury Hannigan, "I cannot comment on how effectively the device works. But it appears that anyone who would purchase such a device does so with ill intent—to circumvent the law. Nor does the device seem to have any direct application that would enhance traffic safety. I would discourage your readers from purchasing it."

Also inside the Corvette are a standard CB radio and a two-band ham (amateur) transceiver that Bob has modified to transmit on a wider range of frequencies. (Bob has a license for many of the frequencies he uses, but not for all of them.)

Mind you, the stealth gear in Bob's Corvette is not limited to radios. A video camera is permanently mounted behind and between the two seats; next to it rests a rear-aimed Colt radar detector. And hanging from the Corvette's padded roll cage, along the trailing edge of the car's windshield, is a radar-jamming antenna wired through an Escort radar detector. The jammer—which is most certainly *illegal* illegal—is designed to confuse police radar guns for about twenty seconds after the Escort's signal strength reaches a pre-

determined level. Bob's unit operates at an output level four times greater than those of state-of-the-art jammers from just a few years ago. "It's overkill," says a spokesman for Remote Systems, the company that designed the jammer and also sells remote-mounting kits for Escort detectors. Remote Systems sells the circuitry for the jammer in kit form only—which is legal—but because kits start near $2000, few are sold.

In the center-console space that normally contains the Corvette's ashtray sit four LEDs arranged in the same pattern as the car's taillights. Two corresponding switches allow Bob to illuminate the taillights as he sees fit.

Bob's Corvette is also far from ordinary under the hood. The car's 5.7-liter V-8 sports a host of power-increasing alterations by ace tuner John Lingenfelter. Bob claims the engine produces 400 hp. And the transmission is a highly modified four-speed automatic. There are no mufflers on the car, but thanks to careful tuning of the exhaust-pipe lengths, Bob's stealth Corvette runs acceptably quiet at 2000 rpm —good for about 50 mph in third gear, 65 mph in fourth. At other speeds, and during full-throttle acceleration, the Corvette is notably noisier. But by keeping the revs near 2000 rpm, Bob can keep his Corvette —or at least its exhaust noise—virtually undetected.

Surprisingly, Bob rarely takes advantage of his car's potential. During the time we rode shotgun, Bob drove no faster than the speed any one of us normally drives to work. He says he once saw 160 mph on a closed course, and on an abandoned de-

Completing the radio array: (A) the ChiPs Detector, which warns of patrol-car proximity; (B) the Kenwood RZ-1 wide-band receiver; (C) the Orion equalizer, which tunes out shortwave static; (D) a Remote Systems radar jammer control unit; (E) a Kenwood TM-731A ham transceiver; and (F) a Cold CB.

sert road he reached an indicated 169 mph. But Bob drives the speed limit through school zones. Despite his car's 180-mph top speed and plethora of ticket-prevention gear, Bob seems bent simply on beating the system for the sake of beating the system. He doesn't appear to have any ulterior, antisocial motives.

At least, we hope he doesn't. Bob's eavesdropping equipment enables him to reach out and hear almost anyone. He can listen to baby-sitter monitors in neighborhood households, tune in to cordless-telephone conversations, monitor television-crew remote links, and—with the exception of low-frequency submarine-radio waves and radio telescopes mapping Andromeda—listen in on just about anything else broadcast on this planet. Preparing for a ride in the stealth Corvette, we sat in Bob's driveway enjoying "The Voice of the Andes" from Quito, Ecuador.

Bob's neighbors are unaware of his peculiar preoccupations. Bob affixed the "STEALTH" Nevada license plate you see on the car for our photos only; he normally drives with standard-issue plates. Well, almost standard issue. The license-plate frame on Bob's Corvette is embossed with bogus radio call letters similar to those assigned to police departments. Bob says it's a growing trend for law-enforcement officers to identify their personal cars this way—a sort of secret handshake that allows professional courtesy without personal contact.

The only exterior clues to the Corvette's clandestine capabilities are the two small antennae mounted at the front edge of the glass hatchback. And many people mistake these thin wires for cellular-phone antennae anyway, Bob says. The Corvette also sports a small black rubber air dam, a removable dark shade under the rear hatchback glass, and specially painted, low-gloss wheels. In other words, it looks like a lot of other late-model Corvettes on the road.

Despite the car's low profile and stealth equipment, Bob has occasionally been stopped by the police. After a peek in the cabin, they invariably ask, "What's all this stuff for?"

"I tell them I'm a ham operator," Bob says. "Usually, they don't want to know more than that. They know I'm not a problem, because only one person in a million has all this stuff in his car.

"The secret is to not let anybody know you're there," Bob says. The more you know, the less you advertise, the easier it is for you to hide in your car, he adds.

Bob's desire for speed and invisibility have cost him dearly in time and money. The engine work added $15,000 to his Vette's $32,000 price. The transmission beef-up cost him about $7000. Suspension upgrades added $2000, and the roll cage cost $1000. Combined, the electronics inside are worth about $4700. Installation and wiring added an easy $1500 to that. Total outlay for the stealth Corvette: $63,200.

Why this expensive obsession with anonymity? Bob is not a scofflaw by nature. He pays his taxes, supports his family and community, and by all outward appearances is an upstanding citizen. Why does he choose to dodge traffic cops and phone bills, to test eavesdropping laws and noise regulations, and to bend a few of the FCC's rules?

Bob is a tinkerer. His enthusiasm for cars is matched by his fascination with radios and the world that exists in the airwaves. Bob's record is not criminal but extrasocial, an enthusiast gone mad with the possibilities of what kind of mobile information headquarters can be made with readily available electronics. Asked why he built the stealth Corvette, Bob replies with a smile: "I noticed the country had a stealth bomber and a stealth fighter, and I thought we might need a stealth car. I could donate it to the war on drugs as a surveillance vehicle."

There is another possible explanation: Bob would like to listen for extraterrestrial perpetrators, streaking across space with their CHiPs Detectors blinking, watching for space cops enforcing the laws of light speed.

That's not a pipe dream—not for Bob. "Nobody's been able to get into Groom Lake," a supersecret military base in Nevada also known as Area 51, Site S4, Bob says. "They have nine UFOs kept up there." He believes that. Thus the video camera in Bob's stealth Corvette: one day, he hopes to film the UFOs allegedly stored in Area 51.

That filming, Bob admits, would have to be done from outside the boundaries of the secret base, while the UFOs were on test flights over southern Nevada. Why off the base? Rumor has it that trespassers in top-secret military bases actually *do* become invisible.

Two push-button switches control the pattern of the nighttime taillight signature.

DRIVING

ITALY BY AUDI

By Jeffrey Dworin

When I set out to tour Italy by car, little did I know I would be entering a fiercely competitive motoring event. The course turned out to be anything that resembled a street. Everything you've ever heard about Italian drivers is true, even the stuff that isn't. All the stories warning motorized visitors to avoid eye contact with Italian drivers at intersections, and about how every stoplight is in fact the equivalent of a drag-racing Christmas tree . . . well, it's all true. I don't mean to suggest that Italians drive poorly. They don't. Let's just say they take driving quite seriously.

On a Sunday afternoon outside Linate airport in Milan, I got the green flag. Easing the Audi 80 out of the lot, I was overwhelmed by a whirling swarm of Fiat 500s, three-wheeled Piaggio scooters, and a host of nondescript microcars that made the Audi seem enormous by comparison. As I attempted to merge into the swarm, I was reminded of the first time I went roller skating, except this time there was nothing to grab on to but the steering wheel. Well, when in Rome, et cetera: I mashed the throttle, groped for second gear, and was in the thick of it, blasting around pesky little cars, threading my way through clogged streets, tapping my mirrors with the mirrors of parked cars. Soon, it was quite fun.

As it turned out, the Audi was good at this kind of fender-to-fender competition. But after a couple of hours catching glimpses of the city at racing speeds, we were ready to ditch the car and search for our hotel on foot.

The first thing the desk clerk wanted to know was did we have a car with a radio? Turns out they have a radio-theft problem in Italy, but trying to tell the room clerk that our radio wasn't worth stealing, that it was a truly lousy aftermarket unit that didn't even work, was not going over well. The clerk was trying to be helpful, and I was being a jerk, repeating how cheap the radio was. Finally, I agreed to park the car in the hotel lot.

The next day we were back in the race, aimed for Venice. The Audi was right at home on the autostrada, humming along in the right lane at 140 kliks an hour. I was able to con my companion into believing we were daredeviling along at 140 miles an hour. Actually, 140 kliks (87 mph) did seem a tad hairy—until the occasional Benz or Bimmer blasted by on the left.

After two days in Venice I was itching for a road. May I never experience another wacky water-taxi ride. On the way south to Florence, we abandoned the main highway just north of Bologna for a narrow mountain pass through some charming villages that met all my preconceived expectations of old-world Italy. For a brief time it seemed the race was over. As it turned out, we were under a yellow. We motored leisurely through the mountains, taking in the view, lingering over fields of brilliant wildflowers.

Sooner than we would have liked we were back on the highway to Florence, and the race resumed. Once again our Audi battled for position against minis and scooters. As we neared the city, the narrow width of the streets made it clear that our competitors would enjoy a considerable advantage over us. Many of the brick and stone streets were barely wide enough for one car—and parking was somehow permitted on both sides (this is done halfway on the walkway and halfway in the street). A Fiat Panda suddenly made great sense. We parked the giant Audi, which had taken on, at least in our minds, the girth of a GMC Suburban. Happily, we walked the city for two glorious days.

From Florence we headed west toward the sea, stopping in Pisa to see the tower. (Going to Italy and not seeing the leaning tower is like stopping off at a 7-Eleven and not getting a Slurpee.) We followed the coastline to Livorno and then to Genoa for the night, where we parked our car inside without a fuss.

The next morning we joined the furious swarm of cars. Because they were in a hurry, so were we. After all, this was a race. We arrived in the south of France in time for a Nice dinner, having spent much of the day zooming around San Remo and Monaco and behaving like tourists.

Our last day arrived. We headed north back to Italy along the strada, zipping through more tunnels than in a day's worth of rides in an amusement park. Arriving at Linate Airport, we returned our car, radio still intact, and boarded a plane

for home. We never did find out why everyone behind a wheel in Italy is in such a hurry, or who won the race. We did find, however, that we like Italians, and we especially like their food—of which we consumed great quantities. Like most travelers, what we learned was how to do it right the next time. Which is to bring helmets.

The drive from Venice (top) on the Adriatic sea across to Italy's west coast port of Genoa (middle, bottom) took us through Bologna, Florence, and Pisa.

THE HILLS OF OHIO

By Steve Spence

The boys here at the magazine were going to exercise some sedans in the "hills of southern Ohio." Did I want to come?

I did not. Largely because my tribe is from the West, which is, as the TV reminds us nightly, Where It Is At. In that world's view, the Midwest is an enormous kind of beanfield trip, you drive through its repetitive landscape fast and late at night behind extraloud Bob Seger, wrapped tightly by infusions of caffeine, a heat-seeking missile roaring toward the East, land of the tall buildings, which is Where It Used to Be At. The tribes on the two coasts believe the Midwest to be Where Wonder Bread Is At.

The *hills* of Ohio? I had to see this. We headed south from Michigan on a cold pitiless day, the nearness of winter like a threat. It started to rain, then hail. We took a two-lane road. We followed fields of dead-yellow cornstalks backdropped by faraway stands of trees turned a cold blue. I felt like Dr. Zhivago in this silent,

PHOTOS BY STEVE SPENCE

serene land. We passed a Civil War cemetery, its weathered markers leaning every which way, like the hair of a kid just out of bed, the names of the dead obscured by all the years. In California, someone would put up a restaurant nearby and name it "The Graveyard."

We stopped at a restaurant in a nondescript town and for some reason I had two with onions, I don't know why. It was mid-afternoon, and people were eating pie. (Where's the torte cart with the kiwi quiche?) There were a lot of girls not old enough to vote, with babies, driving around in their husbands' Camaros with their girlfriends, who had babies too. The Midwest: pretty girls, babies, Camaros, pie in the afternoon.

The edges of Columbus are as forgettable as the edges of Sacramento: cluster malls and reflecting-glass offices and never any place to sit.

At Logan, the countryside made me sit up and look. Hills, like roller coasters. Beaten-up, leaning barns somehow bringing to mind my long-gone ladylike grandmother. I can see her on that porch in a thin flowered dress, shelling peas, shaking her head in shock at Eddie Fisher's bold love songs on "Coke Time."

We come around a corner and I am startled by a town so tidy, so remarkable in its extraordinary, pristine plainness. So calm. Clapboard wood houses in sensible white. There's the State Farm office, there's the sundry store, Buck's Tavern, a filling station. A dog walks blissfully free on the streets, which have names like Ash and Maple instead of Pasta Primavera Circle. Not a single ostentatious home with sweeping two-lane driveway and *porte cochère* and signs impaled in lawns warning of burglar systems. No gates or garage doors are moved by electronic devices. Not one professional gardener in sight, not one private tennis court, not one theme restaurant, not one exotic dog with a goofy hairdo drooling on the window of a Bimmer, not one Spandexed jogger with a silk headband and lip gloss, not one tourist in Birkenstocks sucking on a three-dollar waffle cone of gelato. *Nothing in sight to make you think of money and how to get it.*

It's 1957 again, I Like Ike. I wish to stay here forever, get a cord of wood, a large happy dog, yank the cable TV, learn how to put down high-octane apple cider and make biscuits with sausage gravy.

John Phillips has booked us into a lodge at Burr Oak. It's after dark, and we are drawn to the bar, which, like everything in the Midwest, has a name: The Wren's Nest, open only on Wednesdays and weekends. A sign admonishes drinkers to leave their guns elsewhere. (Various egg combinations on the breakfast menu have names: the Cardinal, the Robin, so forth.)

We have the bar to ourselves, but even in our privacy we are so addiction-conscious in the enlightened nineties that we limit ourselves to light beer. We swill the stuff till boredom sets in. A place in California calls its bartenders dispensing agents, and our D.A. is a thirtyish woman whose brown hair is secured with an ordinary plastic barrette, unlike the breathless bims on "Entertainment Tonight," whose moussed-out electric tentacles suggest that each has just arrived flush-cheeked from her invigorating sex life. She has a directness of eye; she could just as well be selling us worms for fish hooks instead of beer.

"I've never been to California," she says, "but I hope to go some day." Doesn't everybody. As though something there will change their lives. Something like money.

The next day, I see a clothesline of vividly colored sheets, reds and blues, beside an old, peeling two-room house set down in a gully. I want to photograph the white Dodge with the clothesline in the background. I park and head down a gully to the old house, but am stopped by a security-minded dog. A light is on inside, so I just yell: "Hello, anybody home?" Nothing. But I can hear a television set. Finally, the dog hunkers off. I go to the porch and knock, causing the house to tremble. Somebody inside hears this, and responds *by turning up the TV.* I've always wanted to do that when the save-the-whale guy comes looking for donations. I left.

Our test cars have been exercised. We are photographing them in front of some old barns when a huge guy bounds on to the property in a pickup. Ceppos, who is from New York, says it all: "Uh-oh." Big guy parks, gets out (is that a gun rack?), and walks over, not smiling.

"Want to see a real ol' tractor?" he says.

He shows us. He smiles and nods. He never asks, but we tell him who we are and what we're doing on his property. We could have pitched tents for all he cared. He's dealing in a commodity you can't sell: trust.

All this information I'll take back to my tribe in the West. Along with the news that the Hoover Country Kitchen in Laurelville makes the best cream puff on Earth, and that includes Paris. France.

"I wish to stay here forever, get a cord of wood, a large happy dog, yank the cable TV, learn how to put down high-octane apple cider and make biscuits with sausage gravy."

189

"Hello, Rewrite? Make that 1500 feet and move the sign."
Richard Bagg, Rochester, New York

And up next: Idaho!
Joe Ellerston, Vancouver, Washington

ROAD SIGNS

Thanks. We have 236 pounds of semi-hysterical road-sign photos to lighten our considerable load here at Hogback Road. Two readers took a you-know-what on Pee Road in Hawaii, a girlfriend catching the goofy awkwardness of the way men stare vacantly, open-mouthed, into space while accomplishing this task. A road sign cautioned: "Changed Priorities Ahead." (Are yours in order, or is it too late?) There's a town in Germany called Bras, and a reader sent a shot of his wife showing off her substantial one in front of the sign. Dorothy, we are here to testify that there is indeed a Home on the Range, and right next to the sign announcing Lake Surprise is another that reads, "Crocodile Crossing."

Here are our winners.

The Proust Turnoff
Randy Riggs, Middleville, New Jersey

Use a porta-potty; go to jail!
George Garcia, Henderson, Nevada

Well, what the hell, you weren't going anywhere anyway . . .
Mark Swigart, Shalimar, Florida

Irregularity's Last Stand
Mark Nekic,
Eastlake, Ohio

"Hi, is that your prostate
or are you just happy to see me?"
Richard Shunkey, Whittier, California

In a world of uncertainties,
something you can count on.
Brian Dix, Mentor, Ohio

Well, they spelled 'shopping' right.
David Murawski, London, Ontario

Around midnight, the Yugos start looking good.
Mark Dagitz, Des Moines, Iowa